Ready for Change?

READY FOR CHANGE?

TRANSITION THROUGH TURBULENCE TO REFORMATION AND TRANSFORMATION

EDITED BY

CORA LYNN HEIMER RATHBONE
Director of Executive Education, Aston Business School, UK

First published 2012 by
PALGRAVE MACMILLAN

Palgrave Macmillan in the UK is an imprint of Macmillan Publishers Limited,
registered in England, company number 785998, of Houndmills, Basingstoke,
Hampshire RG21 6XS.

Palgrave Macmillan in the US is a division of St Martin's Press LLC,
175 Fifth Avenue, New York, NY 10010.

Palgrave Macmillan is the global academic imprint of the above companies
and has companies and representatives throughout the world.

Palgrave® and Macmillan® are registered trademarks in the United States,
the United Kingdom, Europe and other countries.

ISBN 978–0–230–34269–9

This book is printed on paper suitable for recycling and made from fully
managed and sustained forest sources. Logging, pulping and manufacturing
processes are expected to conform to the environmental regulations of
the country of origin.

A catalogue record for this book is available from the British Library.

A catalog record for this book is available from the Library of Congress.

10   9   8   7   6   5   4   3   2   1
21 20 19 18 17 16 15 14 13 12

Printed and bound in Great Britain by
CPI Antony Rowe, Chippenham and Eastbourne

Contents

LIST OF TABLES AND FIGURES

Tables

Figures

FOREWORD

Change. Ironically enough, change is the one constant feature of running organizations in modern times, and it is happening at an ever-increasing rate. At least, that's what twenty-first century people, especially managers, seem to think. However, try telling that – if we only could – to a nineteenth century entrepreneur facing the arrival of steam power. They might not easily be convinced. One thing is relatively certain – people do not seem to be very good at learning lessons from history (the past) about how to manage organizations (in the future), whether those lessons are about change or something else. Part of the reason for this is that people are not very good at predicting the future.

Two common mistakes are that: (a) they assume that the future will be too much like the present; or (b) they assume that the future will turn out to be the way they would like it to be.

So, let's take stock and try a little bit of future prediction ourselves. We can be confident that change will continue, and it really does not matter whether that will be at a faster or slower rate; we still need to cope with it. We can also be fairly confident that some of the changes will take almost everybody by surprise. For example, no one foresaw mobiles/cellphones as an essential teenage possession, let alone a fashion accessory, until the breakthrough into that market was already starting to happen.

What we need then in being ready for change **is to be ready to engage in a process of change rather than ready for specific changes**. We need organizations – and people in them at all levels – that are agile, flexible and adaptable. We also need to try to make sure that the changes we can influence go the way that we would prefer them to. Again, much of this is therefore about the process of change and readiness for change, not the content of that change. And fortunately, lessons from history about process are lessons that are a little bit easier to learn.

Academics and business researchers have been working on some of these lessons for many years. As a result, a manager can now find plenty of sources of help. Business schools are often simultaneously criticized for being out of touch with reality and blamed for the failings of modern organizations, but there is plenty of sound thinking available to those who realize that other people's work can only ever provide part of the answer – some principles that the individual manager has to apply themselves in their organization in a way that works for the people in it and the circumstances it faces at the time.

Aston University and its predecessors have been involved in business education for many years. Back in 1947 we were the second institution in the UK to set up a department to help people run organizations and manage change effectively – the Department of Industrial Administration (now Aston Business School). At that time all the students were studying part-time in addition to their normal work, so practical relevance was essential.

We are proud of the continuing practical relevance of our teaching and research. This book is intended to communicate some of the practical messages from the various specialisms within the School that we can offer to those running organizations in the twenty-first century.

Prof. John Edwards

PREFACE

Change is exciting for leaders and daunting when you feel that you have no control. Change is both a critical and an inevitable feature in business.

One of the global challenges that is going to change all aspects of the way we live and do business over the next 20 years is that of climate change. The consistent conclusion from the work of the world's leading climate scientists is that we have to drastically reduce our greenhouse gas (GHG, predominantly CO_2) emissions if we are to avoid seriously damaging effects of increasing global temperatures on crop yields, water resources, many species of animal, biodiversity more widely and the habitability of our planet for future generations. The best estimates indicate that we need to achieve at least a 50 percent reduction in GHG emissions globally, and 80–95 percent in developed countries, if we are to provide a reasonable level of confidence that average temperature rise by the end of the century will be limited to no more than 2.5°.

This rapidly decarbonizing world is where the next generation will live. New graduates in the UK today have the challenge of delivering the decarbonization of industry, business, agriculture, transport, health and other services, and indeed of their personal lives, over the 40 years or so of their working careers. It will require a lot of change – new technologies, new products, new processes, new ways of working and new behaviors. There will be a lot of challenges. It will also be a time of enormous opportunity for innovative and fast-moving businesses and entrepreneurial people.

In 2007 I was appointed by the Chancellor of the Exchequer (at that time Gordon Brown) to examine the vehicle and fuel technologies, which could help to decarbonize road transport over the next 25 years. In the *King Review* we made a number of recommendations for a range of short- and medium-term actions that would both enable the UK to reduce CO_2 emissions from transport by at least 80 percent by 2050 and to play a leading role in low-CO_2 automotive developments. Being a leader in reducing emissions will help ensure that our existing businesses and future entrepreneurs can seize the international market opportunities that lower-emission road transport offers. Delivering this vision of the future requires a readiness and an appetite for change among policymakers, business leaders and customers, to position the UK as a location for high-technology companies in the field, encouraging inward investment, collaborating with developing and emerging economies to enable them to introduce affordable low-emissions technology at the earliest opportunity, leading in key areas of science and engineering for future low-CO_2 vehicles, and being an influential international voice in promoting global solutions.

To meet these critical challenges, it would be great to be able to base our decision-making as leaders on a full portfolio of evidence, covering 100 percent of the issues, combined with tried and tested rules, strong analytical thinking, logic and fairness. But life for a leader in business and industry isn't very often like that. Decisions have to be taken with incomplete evidence, and sometimes the best argued case isn't the best route for the company. It isn't always fair.

Leadership is about judgment and being capable of making decisions quickly, and often without access to all the information; it's about learning to take well-judged risks and having the courage to make decisions in the face of ambiguity. Of course, we need to take risks in a rational way, using the principles of risk management, but as leaders we must avoid the temptation to always err on the side of caution. We need to consider the value of taking the next step and make courageous judgments to move forward, and at the same time communicate the vision in a positive and empowering way. Of course, this means that we will sometimes be wrong, and being decisive means being on the look-out for mistakes, admitting them promptly, and having the courage to stop or change course.

The challenge of developing the business leaders of the future is to move people out of their comfort zones, to inspire analytical individuals familiar with rules and certainty to move into the realms of uncertainty with confidence and courage, and to help them learn when to trust their intuition in making decisions. We need them to move beyond the management of risk into the management of risk-taking. We need them to become willing to make judgments with only partial information, to have the courage to stop if the wrong decision is made, and to reassess and change direction. We need our new leaders to recognize the importance of communication – to understand that change can be exciting at the top of an organization, but frightening on the frontline if you feel that you don't know what is happening and you have no control. Leaders must have the ability to read how people are responding.

The cult of personality can be overplayed. But leaders have to remain optimistic in challenging and changing times. Combining a degree of charisma with a feeling of empathy is necessary to stand up and present a vision for innovation and therefore change that people will follow.

Prof. Julia King

Acknowledgments

A compendium such as this, which aims to showcase world-leading research that Aston Business School faculty can offer the business community, bears the fruit of many individual minds working collaboratively toward a common purpose. We wish firstly to thank the Aston Business School faculty who contributed elements of their research in chapter form for the purposes of this publication. Without their participation and partnership, this project would not have been possible. First and foremost our grateful thanks therefore go to our contributing authors Professor Michael West, Professor Duncan Shaw, Dr Helen Shipton, Dr Michael Butler, Professor Nigel Driffield, Dr John Rudd, Professor Mark Hart, Professor Paula Jarzabkowski, Professor Pawan Budhwar, Dr Prasanta Dey, Professor Robin Martin and Dr Christopher Brewster. We also wish to thank Professor Julia King, Vice-Chancellor of Aston University and Professor John Edwards, Executive Dean of Aston Business School for their invaluable support and encouragement, as well as for their individual contributions to this compendium.

Additional thanks go to two further faculty members who joined those named previously in contributing their research expertise at an early stage in the project when we built the series of "Sixty Second Nuggets", which is at the heart of our Aston Thought Leadership campaign "Readiness for Change": Dr Patrick Tissington and Dr Omneya Abdelsalam. To view our "Sixty Second Nuggets" thought leadership slidecasts please visit our website at www.aston.ac.uk/ced.

We also wish to thank the Aston University Marketing Department for their advice and expertise, in particular David Farrow for his strategic input and Andrew Blake for his graphic design skills.

Special thanks go to our publisher, Palgrave Macmillan, and in particular we wish to thank Eleanor Davey Corrigan for her encouragement to us when the idea was still in embryonic stage and for her subsequent patience and advice, and to Hannah Fox for her administrative support during the latter stages of publication.

Last but not least, we would like to thank all of the members of the Centre for Executive Development at Aston Business School, in particular Steven

Joesbury for his consistent eye for detail in preparing the final drafts for publication.

The graphics at the head of each main chapter have been produced using the web application available at www.wordle.net.

Richard Terry – Associate Editor

Introduction

Cora Lynn Heimer Rathbone

How ready are you as an organization for today's pace of change? How prepared is your organization to transition through turbulence in order to reform and transform itself for the future? How able is your organization to do this again and again? One thing for most of us is certain: the competencies that brought us to the present are unlikely to be those that take us to future success. Indeed, studies in the field of strategy strongly suggest that organizations that survive – much more those that excel – are constantly refreshing themselves to address and create new markets and new customer needs. Several go so far as to make their products and services redundant before the market does that for them. Think Apple.

Introduction

Change has from time immemorial presented challenge and opportunity. Whether big or small, evolutionary or revolutionary, change ushers in new reality to which all that remains relatively unchanged in the "status quo" must reorientate.

The management of change has therefore naturally preoccupied many, not least those who have much to lose from alterations to the present reality.

Google the phrase "change management" and you get more than 100 million results. Popular subject!

Wikipedia defines change management as "a structured approach to shifting/transitioning individuals, teams, and organizations from a current state to a desired future state. It is an organizational process aimed at helping employees to accept and embrace changes in their current business environment." But why limit it to business?

Take a military context and a quote that exemplifies how depersonalized organizational change can be as pointless as the rearrangement of chairs on the Titanic: "Every time we were beginning to form up into teams, we would be disbanded. I was to learn later in life that we tend to meet any new situation by reorganizing; and a wonderful method it can be for giving the illusion of progress, while producing confusion, inefficiency and utter demoralisation" (Attributed by many to Gaius Petronius (210BC), Rome's greatest satirist). Could it actually be that while change is our greatest constant, "plus ça change, plus c'est la même chose"?

Not necessarily. For Mahatma Gandhi (1869–1948), "change" required embodiment, was personal and led to transformation. "We must become the change we want to see," became his rallying cry. With this he singlehandedly stirred a peaceful revolution that not only reshaped the boundaries of what has become the world's largest democracy but also set an unparalleled global example that most cannot help but admire and none has replicated.

John F. Kennedy observed that when written in Chinese, the word "crisis" is composed of two characters. One represents danger, the other opportunity. Not that all change arises from or creates crisis, but there are hues of potential crisis, as well as opportunity, in most change scenarios. And it is perhaps in order to avoid "crisis" that those who understand chose to engage in the structured management of change.

Returning to Petronius' quote, if change has been around for so long and has posed similar challenges of adjustment and assimilation, why is it still a subject of study? What is so special about change today? After all, factually, to not change is more unusual than to change, and should therefore be more demanding of management than the constancy of change. Some suggest the continuing interest is due to a new order of magnitude and pace. There are two examples, the first on which many books have already been written, the second of which might inspire entire new libraries.

On the economic front, the magnitude and speed of the financial crisis of 2008–10 was a consequence, at least in large part, of the globally interconnected nature of our banking and insurance systems. So-called subprime loans created bad debts that once parceled and sold off through a multiplicity of derivatives eroded, like a cancer, the equity base of virtually every global bank, irrespective of where those were nationally headquartered. Beyond this, within days of the demise of Lehman Brothers in 2008 – at that time the fourth largest investment bank in the USA – AIG, once the 18th largest corporation in the world, teetered on the brink of collapse. Rescue reluctantly came from the US government, which purchased 80 percent of AIG's greatly devalued stock.

Just two years on, and of a political nature, in early January of 2011, we watched the pace with which Tunisians then Egyptians and then Libyans led a grassroots, social network-enabled revolution. In only a matter of days, sparked by the suicide of Mohamed Bouazizi, a Tunisian fruit and vegetable vendor, youth galvanized to threaten and overthrow long-standing and previously thought impervious regimes across the MENA region. The "Arab Spring" began. It was as if all the strong men of the region were given yellow, and some red, cards. This time, arguably, it was speed that shocked most, enabled by the previously unimaginable ability of dispersed people to communicate and coordinate action through Facebook and Twitter. Together with 24-hour media coverage and shared, internationally available real-time information, coalitions formed into one voice to demand change. That this occurred outside of the media savvy, digitally comfortable developed world makes it even more amazing.

In this context it is not surprising that the challenge of managing change is a regularly identified issue within major corporates. How do we manage change that we envisage? Even more taxing, how do we manage change that emerges unexpectedly? How will we manage the as yet unfathomable changes driven by social media that at the very least mean personal privacy can never again be assured? How will corporates guard their most precious asset, their reputation, in an era where a singular complaint, however unsubstantiated, will drive many to boycott major brands? How do we create organizational flexibility to embrace both envisaged and emergent change so that we can leverage our strategy to gain competitive advantage above and beyond that which our competitors might manage to achieve from the same changing times?

We have to rewrite the texts on change, particularly those that look upon the management of change purely as a programmed series of steps. While that remains vitally important for those organizations that lead and create new markets, and can still forge the change that others surf, change of an emergent nature is far more taxing, demanding different competencies than that of the planned, even strategic variety.

It is to that kind of change, of the emergent variety, that this compendium speaks. How ready are you as an organization to change – is the question it poses. With each chapter we aim to unpack a collection of topics that enhance that capability, that help you understand both how able you are to change and how ready you are to drive and respond to change in your market.

First, though, it must be recognized that to address the issue of plant change, of the management of change, theories, guidelines and checklists abound. To name but seven iconic favorites:

1. K. Lewin (1947) outlined **three phases of change**: unfreeze, transition and refreeze. Consider an ice cube. What starts as a *cube* needs to melt before it can *flow* to *reform* and refreeze. This third stage needs to remain more fluid (forgive the pun) in the twenty-first century. Many talk of the need for "stability" so that change is "embedded", yet today's organizations have to remain relatively "agile", comfortable in ambiguity, without boundaries and able to embrace new change.

2. Beckhard and Gleicher (1969) conceptual equation, popularized by Michael Tushman, simply states: **DxVxP>C**. That is to say dissatisfaction (D) with the status quo times the vision (V) for change times the process (P) for change must be greater than the cost (C) of change if change is going to happen. If any of these three factors is missing, change will not happen. This reminds us that a compelling case must be created for change if change is to be accepted and followed through to completion and normality.

3. John Kotter in 1996 (*Leading Change*) specified **eight steps for effective change management**. Starting with the need to establish urgency, this theoretical progression moves to the creation of a coalition, the development of a vision and strategy, communication of that vision, empowerment of action, generation of short-term wins, consolidation of gains to conclude with the anchoring of new approaches. Kotter's approach is a blueprint for organizing a group to accept, embrace and drive change.

4. John Fisher's 1999 model of personal transition through change, itself an extension of the work done by J. Adams, J. Hayes and B. Hopson in 1976 and popularly known as the "**transition curve**", depicts the emotional stages that individuals go through when transitioning through change. The journey maps performance against time. The challenge is one of managing an uncomfortable yet normal cadence of first declining then re-emerging ability and confidence.

5. Otto Scharmer's **U Theory** has since 2000 capitalized on the fact that ambiguity and uncertainty abound. More than ever, unexpected change is coming from unexpected quarters. Notwithstanding, Scharmer presents a meditative seven-step approach (suspend, redirect, let go, just be, let come, enact and embody) to open yourself to be authentically receptive to emerging change. Even from such unexpected quarters a plan peeks through.

6. Veronica Hope-Hailey and Julie Balogun through their **Change Kaleidoscope** (2002) recognize the fact that change is not homogenous and should not be managed in a single manner. There are a variety of approaches, paths, starting points, styles and roles that must be selected as appropriate to the context of the change. Each proposed change needs to be analyzed to identify the best combination of these factors to achieve the desired result.

7. A latter-day model for change management, **AITA** works from the premise that people need to be persuaded for change to succeed. It proposes that people must be *aware* of the need for change before they are likely to be *interested* enough to *trial* it, after which point they might

accept it. AITA plays particularly well into the Gen Y mentality that asks, "What's in it for me?"

Synthesizing the aforementioned and from the perspective of programmatic practice, five steps emerge for the mindful management of change, of a pro-active (planned) or reactive (emergent) variety. Though the order of the first two steps is interchangeable depending on the culture of the organization and the nature of the change itself, a preferred strategic order for what I call the "Strategic Scroll" is as follows:

Step 1: define the vision and mission – the value that you aspire the change to deliver and what the quantifiable end result of the change will be (the "to be" state).

Step 2: diagnose the current reality to understand the starting point for change (the "as is" state). Between step 1 and step 2 lies the gap into which the management of change should focus.

Step 3: strategize how best to get to the "to be" from the "as is", identifying strategic interdependencies and assumptions, ensuring that communication features as a strategy in its own right.

Step 4: produce a project plan that specifies project team and full communication Implementation.

Step 5: embed the new reality into "business as usual", streamlining and standardizing operations to the new business model while retaining the flexibility and capability for ongoing and emergent change.

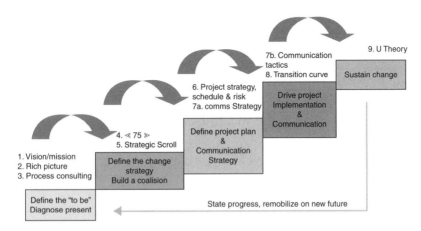

Figure I.1   Strategic change management: a methodology

For each of the previous steps there is a collection of business school tools and frameworks, as depicted in **Figure I.1** for a customized program for a global brand leader. These facilitate the thinking of operational teams tasked with the management of change – big or small. At the risk of being prescriptive, this toolkit can include as few as nine "tools", borrowed from various academics, practitioners and consultancies. Though we could debate one tool's value over another equally attractive option, by using this methodology a route map for logically mapping the process for change can be agreed and applied in almost any setting.

What new wisdom then can a business school add to the aforesaid, to the subject of the management of change? Fresh thoughts! Quite simply, this book is a collection of short synopses that together present a storyline for change. It is the result of independent lines of research pursued by some of the faculty at Aston Business School with whom I have had the pleasure of working between 2010 and 2011. This book brings fresh perspectives on change as a strategic, holistic and whole-of-business reality.

Each chapter presents an aspect of the management of change. Each aspect can be applied in isolation, to analyze or improve performance at an individual or organizational level. Each can also be taken as part of a wider, more systematic approach to change to build organizational resilience in the face of constant turbulence.

From a loose collection of previously unrelated yet rigorously pursued research, *a "red thread" emerges on readiness for change*. Thus what we present in this book is a high-impact practitioner-orientated collection of "short pieces" that fuel effective change. We postulate through this compendium that there needs to be, at an organizational level, a heart (a desire for), a mind-set (a way of thinking about) and a capability (a way of acting upon) inclined toward change if change is to happen effectively. Our research suggests that all three aspects can be developed to prepare individuals, groups and organizations for change, to render organizations more perceptive, more agile, more resilient and more responsive to change that they envisage as possible and that they see approaching.

With that in mind, we offer you the following storyline for our work:

Apropos **matters of the heart**, fostering a desire for change:

1. *Two HRM capabilities that drive change from the inside out*
2. *Five factors for responding to change that comes from the outside in*
3. *Two forces that fuel entrepreneurial growth and sustainable change*

Apropos **matters of the head**, framing the thinking around change:

4. *Six actions for collating collective intelligence to inform and accelerate change*
5. *Seven steps to collaborative decision-making for robust, innovative, broadly owned change*

Apropos **matters of the body** – enabling action toward change:

6. *Eight characteristics that drive high performance and team-delivered change*
7. *Seven enablers of* leader-follower relationships *that sustain impetus for change*
8. *Five principles for accommodating cultural nuances to accelerate envisaged change*
9. *Four strategies toward key external relationships to effectively implement strategic change*
10. *Five questions for conducting marketing as a profession that ushers in strategic change*
11. *Two rationales for attracting inward investment that affects structured regional change*
12. *Eight steps for projectizing continuous improvement to deliver desired change*

So, are you ready for change? Are you ready to develop your organization's capacity for change? We are!

Further reading

Adams, J., Hayes, J. and Hopson, B. (1976) *Transition, Understanding and Managing Personal Change*, London: Martin Robinson.

Beckhard, R. and Gleicher, D. (1969) *Organization Development: Strategies and Models*, Reading, MA: Addison-Wesley.

Lewin, K. (1947) "Frontiers in Group Dynamics: Concept, Method and Reality in Social Science; Social Equilibria and Social Change", *Human Relations*, 1(1), pp. 5–41.

CHAPTER 1

Spurring Innovation through Strong HRM Systems

Helen Shipton

Two HRM capabilities that drive change from the inside out

Introduction

With increasing worldwide competition and ever more pressing environmental turbulence, an organization's ability to innovate is increasingly seen as a key factor to ensure success.[1] The logic is that by introducing new products and new technology, organizations are able to diversify, adapt and reinvent themselves. While researchers have accumulated a lot of knowledge about the relationship between human resource management (HRM) activity and an organization's financial performance, our knowledge of the extent to which HRM practice promotes organizational innovation is still relatively scarce. This is

{ *... extent to which HRM practice promotes organizational innovation* }

therefore the subject of this chapter and my life's research.

Innovation is defined as "the intentional introduction and application within an organization of ideas, processes, products or procedures, new to the unit of adoption, designed to significantly benefit the organization or wider society". Innovation is a continuous, evolutionary process, involving the application and reapplication of existing as well as new scientific knowledge.

Perhaps not surprisingly, companies find it difficult to innovate on a sustained basis. Some scholars suggest that innovation can be achieved by ensuring that all members of the organizations are receptive to – and have the necessary skills and motivation to support – change. The argument is that change and innovation frequently fall outside the remit of technical specialists such as R&D professionals, that successful implementation of change and innovation involves those who have most knowledge of the task and the technology required to ensure such change and innovation reaches effective completion. Thus employees at all levels of the business play an important role in either putting forward suggestions for improvements or in supporting others as they do so.

My interest in researching this subject arose from an increasing awareness that HRM practitioners are faced with the challenge of developing and implementing the practices necessary to facilitate this process. Quite simply, there is a research imperative to identify which specific HRM practices, or combination of practices, are associated with encouraging relatively high innovation at an organizational level.

{ ... which specific HRM practices, or combination of practices, encourage high innovation }

Research investigating relationships between HRM and the financial aspects of performance provides a useful reference point. Two themes are relevant. The first suggests that some specific HRM practices, collectively comprising an HRM system, promote performance – that is, human resource planning, profit sharing and results-oriented appraisals, selectivity in staffing, training and incentive compensation. The second holds that the combined effect of interrelated practices, such as those named previously, has more of an effect on performance than any one single variable on its own. While there is as yet no commonly agreed frame of reference about exactly what constitutes an HRM "system", many agree that a typical system encompasses training, appraisal and performance management, sophisticated selection and socialization of employees as well as practices designed to promote participation and involvement, such as teamwork and reward systems.

Studies investigating the relationship between HRM and innovation have pursued a similar line. A longitudinal study of 30 manufacturing organizations showed that a combination of sophisticated HRM practices predicted organizational innovation to the extent that they influenced each stage of the organizational learning cycle (defined as the creation, sharing and implementation of knowledge). Studies by Laursen & Foss, for example, concluded that organizations should adopt "high performance" HRM practices, such as those that elicit decentralization, arguing that these facilitate problem solving at local level, thereby enabling organizations to draw upon the latent "tacit" knowledge of those closest to the task in hand. They further suggested that knowledge dissemination is enhanced where organizations implement team-based working and where they are committed to practices such as job rotation and project work.

Building on this argument, we suggest that innovation is a two-stage process: the first stage involves the generation of a creative idea, the second focuses on implementation. The first stage signifies "exploration" – employees taking risks, experimenting and being flexible in their quest to discover new and different phenomena of interest. The second stage reinforces "exploitation", where employees work within an environment that values consistency, where they are encouraged to follow prescribed rules to enhance efficiency.

In this study, we consider the role that HRM can play in managing these two competing agendas. According to our argument, HRM practitioners have two main responsibilities. Firstly, they establish the framework that allows for exploitation

{ HRM practitioners have two main responsibilities ... }

{ ... to establish framework for exploitation of existing knowledge }

of existing knowledge, such that employees are clear about their tasks and have the basic skills necessary to perform them effectively. A number of HRM practices are important in this regard. Appraisal and performance management systems, for example, clarify where responsibilities lie and offer support to individuals as they acquire the skills necessary to work effectively. Secondly, HRM practitioners instigate the mechanisms necessary to promote exploratory learning. Through project work, job rotation and visits to parties

{ ... to promote exploratory learning }

external to the organization, employees can achieve the attitudinal change required to question and challenge existing ways of operating. Broadly speaking, the first approach involves the "exploitation" of existing knowledge, while the second represents a concern with "exploration" of new and different opportunities for the future.

There is one proviso attached to this theoretical position. Although there are conceptual differences between approaches designed to promote an exploratory focus and those intended to exploit existing knowledge, in practice it is problematic to delineate precisely where the boundaries lie. Our argument holds that each set of practices will directly promote organizational innovation, and that the effect will be amplified where mechanisms designed to promote exploratory focus are used in conjunction with those intended to exploit existing knowledge.

> { ... effect amplified where mechanisms for exploratory focus are used with those to exploit existing knowledge. }

To understand the relative contribution made by different elements of a holistic HRM system to both exploratory learning and exploitation of knowledge in the context of performance and more importantly innovation within a corporate, we identified a set of hypotheses and pursued a very focused piece of research as follows.

HRM practices that promote exploratory learning

Exploratory learning involves the generation of new ideas by actively searching for alternative viewpoints and perspectives. This happens in part as employees engage with parties external to the organization, and in part as knowledge is exchanged within the organization. Exposure to different experiences and points of view makes individuals more willing to examine their own mental models and to make any necessary adjustments, thereby avoiding the tendency to become locked into limited perceptual frameworks. For example, engagement with customers and suppliers can lead employees to question the perceptual model that they hold and to embrace opportunities for change. Similarly, intra-organizational secondments (to fulfill a project or complete a placement in a different part of the organization for a fixed duration of time) may facilitate the internal transfer of knowledge and enrich individual's perceptions of the challenges faced by other organizational members.

Contentiously, "on the job" development may be a more effective strategy for this type of learning than external training events. Through experiential learning, employees gain knowledge that is relevant for the tasks for which they are responsible. They are also likely to anticipate knowledge transfer issues, so the learning acquired has the potential to be applied. This process is facilitated where organizations have developed systems for managing the transfer of knowledge. Such systems formally legitimize the value of learning from others within the organization and, where operated effectively, encourage disparate groups to share their learning.

Hypothesis 1: HRM practices that promote exploratory learning will predict organizational innovation.

HRM practices designed to exploit existing knowledge

HR practitioners should establish a framework to facilitate the "exploitation" of existing knowledge, a framework that ensures employees are clear about their tasks and have the basic skills required to perform effectively. This would include guidance and support to employees about what behaviors are valued, recognized and rewarded. Such HRM "systems" typically encompass training, appraisal/performance management and sophisticated socialization as well as practices such as teamwork and reward designed to promote participation and involvement. We narrowed our focus in this study on these factors to understand their impact on organizational innovation.

Induction

There is some debate surrounding the extent to which induction activities (initiating people into the organization and providing them with knowledge about goals, processes and norms) promote organizational innovation. Herbert Simon (1991), for example, argued that early socialization inhibits creativity and develops a mindset of compliance that may be detrimental. Such perspectives are in line with the "Attraction, Selection and Attrition" model proposed by Benjamin Schneider, Harold W. Goldstein and D. Brent Smith (1995). They suggested that organizations recruit and retain only individuals who exhibit characteristics similar to those already employed, holding that new employees in particular are under pressure to conform rather than to challenge, thereby promoting "exploitation" to the detriment of exploration.

On the other hand, induction enables people to operate effectively in the organization and to recognize performance gaps. This in turn is likely to enable innovation since people will try to close the gaps between current and desired performance, often innovating in order to achieve this closure. Furthermore, by being aware of performance gaps, individuals may look for opportunities to acquire the skills necessary to contribute to organizational innovation. They may, for example, need to improve their capacity to articulate ideas and to work constructively with others, thereby facilitating knowledge dissemination. An effective induction process should put in place a developmental plan to support the acquisition of such skills.

Hypothesis 2: Sophisticated and extensive induction procedures will predict organizational innovation.

Appraisal

Arguably the relationship between appraisal and organizational innovation is likely to be positive, although little research addresses this point. A meta-analysis conducted by Richard A. Guzzo and Jeffrey S. Bondy (1983) found that appraisal promotes productivity, quality and cost-saving initiatives. Some studies suggest that feedback given during the appraisal process leads to a recognition of the gaps between performance and targets (R.A. Guzzo, R.D. Jette & R.A. Katzell, 1985), thereby motivating employees to work innovatively. Through appraisals, employees gain a clearer view of how their tasks "fit" with the organizational agenda (S.D. Bach, 2000). Furthermore, appraisals conducted in a way likely to foster learning and growth, may help employees to acquire the confidence necessary to take advantage of opportunities for higher-level learning (L. Gratton, 1997).

Hypothesis 3: Organizations that have in place an appraisal scheme will exhibit relatively high organizational innovation.

Training

Formal, structured training is no longer regarded as a universal panacea, in part because two streams of research (the situated learning school and the "experiential" learning school) have highlighted a number of deficiencies.

1. Training may be implemented by people who do not fully appreciate the challenges faced by individuals as they conduct their day-to-day work
2. The problems of transferring learning to the workplace are endemic
3. Training designed to achieve specific organizational objectives is unlikely to promote the creativity associated with exploratory learning

Training is nonetheless associated with better organizational performance. Training facilitates the development of employees' capabilities and ensures that individuals have the basic skills to perform their roles effectively. These attributes are important for fostering innovation, as individuals are unlikely to assess their tasks critically and make constructive proposals for change where they are preoccupied with day-to-day survival at work. Highly planned and organized training is therefore important to promote employee skills, and should be backed up by appropriate investment.

Hypothesis 4: Extensive training will predict organizational innovation.

Contingent reward

Contingent pay represents that proportion of total remuneration paid when specific performance stipulations have been fulfilled. The term encompasses "pay for performance" schemes at individual and team level, and organization-wide schemes designed to enable the workforce to share in the success of the enterprise. Some scholars argue that "pay for performance" schemes fail to enhance creativity because they undermine intrinsic motivation. Another related argument suggests that where people feel controlled by another party (by whichever person or group is responsible for determining how contingent pay is apportioned), they will be relatively less likely to look for new and creative solutions to problems, preferring instead to stick to tried and trusted methods of working.

However, emerging research evidence suggests that it is possible to design reward systems that do not displace attention from the tasks and that external rewards can encourage both creativity and innovation implementation. In a series of studies, Amabile and colleagues showed that reward perceived as a bonus, a confirmation of one's competence or a means of enabling one to do better and more interesting work in the future can stimulate creativity. There is also a body of work examining "gain sharing" (systems used to involve staff in developing new and more effective means of production) that supports this as a device for stimulating productivity and innovation. Evaluations of "gain sharing" programs suggest they are effective in increasing innovation, productivity and employee involvement (J.L. Cotton, 1996).

Hypothesis 5: Contingent reward will predict organizational innovation.

Teamwork

Teamwork will promote organizational performance and innovation to the extent that members are engaged in tasks that are intrinsically motivating within a supportive organizational context. We argue that organizations committed to teamwork will achieve innovation to a greater extent than those adopting alternative structural arrangements. Effectively operating teams present a framework of support for individuals as they deal with the emotionally challenging aspects of change. Teams also enable individuals to share the tacit knowledge exhibited by more experienced members. For example, through close working with others, uninitiated individuals are encouraged to observe, ask questions, receive feedback and thus achieve optimum performance. Furthermore, teams offer opportunities to draw upon diverse knowledge and skills. Where such diversity can be effectively focused and channeled, there is scope for higher levels of creativity and innovation than would be the case where individuals operate independently.

Hypothesis 6: The extent of teamwork will predict organizational innovation.

To reiterate, in our view there is conceptually a distinction between mechanisms designed to promote exploratory learning and those intended to exploit existing skills. We argue that while traditional training, for example, can lead to the effective deployment of existing knowledge, it does not necessarily promote the exposure to new and different experiences to which we refer in our depiction of "exploratory learning". Training interventions, teamwork and the other HRM practices that we consider in this study will impact upon organizational innovation to a greater extent when they are implemented in conjunction with practices designed to promote exploratory learning.

Hypothesis 7: There will be an interaction between HRM practices designed to promote exploratory learning and those intended to exploit existing knowledge, such that combinations of these practices will promote innovation above and beyond the direct effects of these practices in isolation.

With the previous hypothesis in mind, and in order to understand which combinations of HRM practices best promote organizational innovation, we conducted the following research across 111 individual companies, narrowing our focus down to 22 for deeper analysis we undertook as follows:

We started this particular research by asking managers to describe the practices they employed to promote exploratory learning, using the following eight binary questions:

1. Are visits arranged to external suppliers or customers for employees who would not normally have such contact as part of their normal job responsibilities?

2. Are employees working on the shop floor in one department ever seconded to another department so that they can learn more about the processes and procedures in that area?

3. Are employees working in management in one department ever seconded to another department so that they can learn more about the processes and procedures in that area?

4. Does the company support learning/training that is not work related (e.g. basic skills, hobbies, such as through TEC-supported Employee Development Schemes or Employee Led Development, or other such employee development skills)?

5. Is training available to management that is work related, but not directly necessary for the individuals' current job (e.g. learning about processes that occur in other parts of the factory, courses to increase computer skills)?

6. Is training available to shop floor employee that is work related, but not directly necessary for the individuals' current job (e.g. learning about processes that occur in other parts of the factory, courses to increase computer skills)?

7. Do you have any procedures for recording solutions to problems or best practice?

8. Do you have any mechanisms by which this knowledge (problem solutions or best practice) is transferred to other areas of the business?

Additionally, to understand the HRM practices used to exploit existing knowledge, managers were asked about approaches to induction, training, appraisal, contingent reward and teamwork.

Separately, we gathered information about product and technological innovation via a postal questionnaire sent to senior managers in each participating organization. This measured the extent and quality of product innovation on a 1–7 scale. Respondents gave estimates of the (a) number of entirely new and adapted products developed in the last two years; (b) percentage of production workers involved in making the new products; (c) current sales turnover accounted for by the new products; (d) extent to which the new products were new and different for the organization concerned.

We also measured the extent to which organizations were committed to innovating across the range of technical (as opposed to administrative) aspects of the business. The measure encompassed product innovation as well as innovation in production technology and production processes. Account was taken of responses to questions surrounding the introduction of new machines or systems such as single cycle automatics, CNC and robots. Respondents were also asked about changes in production techniques/procedures, such as the introduction of scheduling and planning systems (e.g. MRP II), Just-In-Time management (JIT) or Total Quality

Management (TQM). Respondents listed the three most significant changes in these categories introduced over the previous two years. They also gave estimates of the magnitude and novelty of the changes for their organization on a 5-point scale, ranging from "very small" (1), to "moderate" (3) and "very big" (5). Further questions were asked (e.g. "what percentage of your production workforce had to be retrained to use this different technology?") and responses were captured on a 7-point scale, from 1 "not at all innovative" to 7 "very innovative". These were based on the types of changes introduced, their magnitude and novelty and the impact on the workforce and the manufacturing process. An overall innovation rating was given to each company and to each company's technical systems, as described earlier.

The innovation questionnaire was first piloted in six companies. Following minor changes to terminology, it was sent out to the managing director and the head of production of each of the 111 companies. Eighty-one out of 111 companies of similar size, productivity, profitability and HRM practices returned completed questionnaires.

Results

There were statistically significant interaction effects between:

- Exploratory learning and appraisal when predicting product innovation but not when predicting innovation in technical systems
- Exploratory learning and both training and induction when predicting innovation in technical systems

These results provide partial support for hypothesis 7 that there is positive effect on product and technical systems innovation:

1. When approaches to exploratory learning are combined with mechanisms designed to promote existing knowledge (training, induction and appraisal)
2. To the extent that teamwork is evident
3. When high exploratory learning is combined with formal appraisal

This supports the interpretation that **a combination** of exploratory learning and skill development may be a potent cocktail for encouraging innovation.

{ ... exploratory learning and skill development – a potent cocktail for innovation }

High exploratory learning in organizations strongly relates to sophistication and extensiveness of training in organizations. This again supports the interpretation that a combination of exploratory learning and skill development may be potent in encouraging innovation. In fact, it is apparent upon scrutiny that high exploratory learning combined with weak approaches to training seems a worse combination (in terms of innovation in technical systems) than low exploratory learning and weak approaches to training.

High exploratory learning together with sophistication and extensiveness of induction practices also leads to stronger product innovation than when exploratory learning is low. Counterintuitively, high exploratory learning with poor induction is associated with *lower* levels of product innovation than when there are few mechanisms designed to promote exploratory learning and induction is poor. Finally, there is a significant positive effect on innovation in technical systems when we combine contingent reward with HRM practices promoting exploratory learning. This significant relationship was not observed for product innovation. Thus we present some, but not complete, support for our seventh hypothesis.

Discussion

Scholars have for many years been preoccupied with identifying which HRM practices are associated with various dimensions of organizational performance. Empirical studies suggest that certain specific HRM practices are associated with effectiveness. Our research additionally suggests that HRM "systems" which combine a number of practices may have a stronger collective effect on organizational innovation than any one practice in isolation. Few studies before have explored the relationship between HRM and organizational innovation, although this theme is important for organizations seeking to respond proactively to the challenges presented by the external environment.

Results (See Table 1.1) from this study suggest that two groups of HRM mechanisms are likely to enhance innovation in products and technical systems: those designed to promote exploratory learning (i.e. project work and placements) and those intended to exploit existing knowledge (i.e. training, induction, appraisal, contingent pay and teamwork). Contingent reward has no direct effect upon either type of innovation, but does have a significant effect when combined with exploratory learning. Similarly, training, induction and appraisal, combined with exploratory learning, have a more powerful effect in combination than where they are applied separately. This applies for appraisal combined with exploratory learning where we focus upon product innovation. The effect is apparent for innovation in technical systems where

Table 1.1   HRM Practices that promote innovation

Hypothesis	Supported
1. HRM practices that promote exploratory learning will predict organizational innovation.	Yes – for product innovation and innovation in technical systems
2. Sophisticated and extensive induction procedures will predict organizational innovation.	
3. Organizations that have in place an appraisal scheme will exhibit relatively high organizational innovation.	
4. Extensive training will predict organizational innovation.	
5. Contingent reward will predict organizational innovation.	No – no significant results for either type of innovation
6. Extent of teamwork will predict organizational innovation.	Yes – for product innovation and innovation in technical systems
7. There will be an interaction between HRM practices designed to promote exploratory learning and those intended to exploit existing knowledge, such that combinations of these practices will predict innovation above and beyond the direct effects of these practices individually.	Supported in part – Where our measures of induction, training, appraisal and contingent reward were combined with "exploratory learning", the positive effect variable was significant. There was no significant effect for teamwork combined with exploratory learning on either type of innovation.

training is combined with exploratory learning, and for induction combined with exploratory learning. Furthermore, our measure of contingent reward, while not significant when entered separately for either type of innovation, was significantly and positively related to innovation in technical systems when combined with our measure of exploratory learning focus. There was, however, no significant effect when combining teamwork and exploratory learning for either type of innovation.

Why does the combined effect of exploratory learning and other HRM practices considered in the study not apply to both types of innovation? We suggested in the introduction that change and innovation frequently fall outside

$$\left\{ \begin{array}{l} \text{... change and innovation frequently fall} \\ \text{outside the remit of technical specialists} \end{array} \right\}$$

the remit of technical specialists because successful management of change and innovation requires the involvement of those who have most knowledge of the tasks and technology necessary for successful completion. There is thus an imperative to take steps to ensure that all members of the organization have the necessary skills and

$$\left\{ \begin{array}{c} \text{... imperative that all members of the} \\ \text{organization have the skills and motivation} \\ \text{to support change} \end{array} \right\}$$

moti-vation to support change.

Our results suggest that employees may exert a stronger influence upon innovation in technical systems than upon product innovation. This may be because workers have a deeper knowledge of the work systems and the technology that they use than about potential new products. Thus, the interaction effects that we observe in this study apply by and large to technical system innovation. In other words, both induction and training focus on the process of doing the job and the means of achieving organizational objectives rather than on product innovation specifically. Contingent reward similarly tends to promote focus upon goals perceived to be readily achievable and encourage innovation within a domain familiar to the employees.

Appraisal, on the other hand, combined with exploratory learning, appears to impact significantly upon product innovation. Given that many manufacturing organizations are likely to invest responsibility for product innovation in R&D departments or specialist functions, this represents an important new perspective. Perhaps, as literature suggests, appraisals exert a more powerful influence upon employees' motives, learning orientation and understanding of organizational goals than many other HRM practices. Deeper understanding of their performance combined with a willingness to consider the new and different alternatives gained through exploratory learning may lead employees to make constructive suggestions for new products, either independently or in combination with specialist functions.

There has been much debate about the role of contingent reward in promoting performance. In line with research suggesting that where people feel controlled by another party they are unlikely to look for new and creative solutions to problems, we found no direct relationship between contingent reward and either types of innovation considered in this study. The exception was where contingent pay worked in conjunction with practices designed to promote exploratory learning. This indeed presented as a constructive strategy for promoting innovation in technical systems With low exploratory learning, the relationship between contingent pay and innovation is negative, but with high exploratory learning the relationship is positive. We would suggest that by applying these mechanisms in combination, individuals acquire a breadth of knowledge and are simultaneously encouraged to look for opportunities to apply the knowledge that they have gained. By emphasizing exploratory learning, organizations may overcome the limitations associated with pay for performance schemes that closely prescribe behavior.

To promote exploratory learning and encourage both types of innovation, our study strongly supports secondment visits to customers and suppliers, training

> { ... to promote exploratory learning and encourage innovation }

beyond job requirements and knowledge management practices (such as the recording of best practice solutions to problems). On balance, organizations that engage in exploratory learning by adopting the combination of experiential and knowledge management practices are more likely to be innovative than those which exhibit no such commitment. This is, in part, because people generally learn better through the work process itself than by engag-

> { ... people generally learn better through the work process itself }

ing in classroom-based activity and in part because individuals are more inclined to think creatively where they are exposed to new and different experiences.

> { ... more inclined to think creatively where exposed to new and different experiences }

They may, for example, make connections between divergent stimuli, and envisage possibilities that may not have occurred to them otherwise.

The literature highlights the importance of balance: of engaging in exploratory learning while simultaneously supporting individuals as they exploit the knowledge that they

> { ... importance of balance: exploratory learning while supporting exploitation of knowledge }

have acquired in this way. We argue that the HRM practices most considered in this study (training, appraisal, induction and contingent reward) are designed to promote learning toward the "exploitation" end of the exploration/exploitation continuum. Research suggests that these practices tend as a general rule to promote the achievement of specific organizational objectives, thereby promoting compliance rather than creativity. This may explain why appraisal, induction, training and contingent reward account for more of the variance for innovation in technical systems when they are applied in conjunction with measures designed to promote exploratory learning.

Interestingly, teamwork, even as a singular practice, is significantly associated with both product and technical system innovation, accounting for 32

> … teamwork, even as a singular practice, is significantly associated with innovation

percent and 48 percent respectively of the increase in innovation. Not surprisingly, this endorses many scholars' views of the importance of teamwork as a practice on its own as a mechanism for achieving innovation. Indeed teams (where they operate effectively) create an environment in which individuals are enabled to deal with the emotional and cognitive challenges associated with change and innovation. Perhaps teamwork more than any other practice presents opportunities for exploratory learning while simultaneously facilitating the exploitation of existing knowledge.

It is important to reiterate that, most intriguingly, the results of our research suggest that high exploratory learning in combination with weak approaches to training or to induction is a worse combination for promoting innovation in technical systems than low exploratory learning and weak approaches to training. We speculate that a failure to train or induct employees may lead to difficulty in perceiving how the different experiences and perspectives acquired through exploratory learning may be applied to achieve organizational goals or innovation. Our results suggest that where this balance is inadequately managed – or where people have opportunities to learn from new and different experiences (exploratory

> … opportunities to learn from new experiences without clear purpose are unlikely to achieve high levels of innovation

learning) but are not clear about the purpose of so doing (exploitative learning) – organizations are unlikely to achieve high levels of innovation on a sustained basis. Furthermore, employees who encounter a complex environment with many opportunities for skill development may be overwhelmed if the socialization process, which often begins with the use of good induction procedures, is not systematically handled.

This study presents a number of practical implications. If, as we suggest, organizations are more likely to survive and prosper when they promote incremental innovation and engage in sustained efforts to introduce and apply new ideas, it is necessary to consider how best to draw upon the skills and knowledge of the whole workforce. Exploratory people management practices have an important role to play in fostering organizational innovation because they signal to employees that innovative activity is important, and will be recognized and rewarded. Concurrently, therefore, organizations should implement practices designed to exploit existing knowledge. These include induction, training, appraisal and contingent reward systems, designed and implemented effectively to ensure that employees are clear about their tasks and have the basic skills necessary to perform effectively. In this and every context, teams have an important part to play, a role that is perhaps not fully acknowledged, in enabling organizations to both appropriate the knowledge of employees at all levels of the hierarchy, and to facilitate innovative outcomes.

Postscript

In this research, we took into account frequency and incidence of prior innovation to strengthen our case for suggesting that the measured HRM practices promote innovation. By controlling for the effect of size and profitability, we excluded alternative interpretations.

This was, to our knowledge, the first study to directly consider the relationship between HRM systems and organizational innovation while controlling for prior innovation. We believe that HRM practices – effectively designed and synchronized – enhance learning and empower people at all levels to instigate change and innovation. People are central to innovation performance, and the findings of this study suggest that relatively high levels of innovation can be achieved where people are empowered to make changes at local levels through effective HRM practices.

Summary

There are two HRM capabilities that drive change from the inside out:

1. HRM practices that promote exploratory learning
2. HRM practices designed to exploit existing knowledge

Action points

- Be aware of the difference between product innovation and systems innovation in your organization.
- Promote exploratory learning through:
  - Project work and placements to enhance innovation in your products and technical systems
  - Secondment visits to customers and suppliers
  - Training that goes beyond current job requirements
  - Knowledge management practices.
- Exploit your existing knowledge through key HRM mechanisms such as training, induction, appraisal, contingent pay and teamwork to drive higher performance.
- Combine the aforementioned mechanisms appropriately to achieve maximum combined effect – for example, contingent reward combined with exploratory learning.
- Ensure that all members of the organization have the necessary skills and motivation to support change and innovation.
- To help achieve high levels of innovation on a sustained basis, ensure people have opportunities to learn from new and different experiences (exploratory learning) and are clear about the purpose of so doing (exploitative learning).

Self-assessment tool

To what extent are you making use of the following HRM processes to enhance contributions to innovation? (**Tables 1.2**, **1.3**)

Table 1.2   How good are my HRM processes at building innovation capability?

Attribute	Never	Sometimes	Mostly	Always	Cumulative Score
Exploratory work through projects	0	1	2	3	
Exploratory work through placements/ job rotations	0	1	2	3	
Contingent reward combined with exploratory learning	0	1	2	3	
Appraisal combined with exploratory learning	0	1	2	3	
Training combined with exploratory learning	0	1	2	3	
Induction combined with exploratory learning	0	1	2	3	

Table 1.3   Benchmark scores

0–3	4–8	9–13	14–18
In the danger zone!	Some foundations that need development	Good, but room for improvement	Moving toward consistent high performance

Notes

1. This chapter draws on research previously published in *Human Resource Management Journal*. We are grateful to the journal for their support for this follow-on work. We also acknowledge the contribution of Michael West, Jeremy Dawson, Malcolm Patterson and Kamal Birdi – co-authors of the article published in HRMJ – and the medium-sized businesses and their employees who helpfully responded to our various surveys that made our analysis possible.

Further reading

Bach, S. D. (2000) "From Performance Appraisal to Performance Management", in S. Bach and K. Sisson (eds) *Personnel Management*, 3rd edition, Oxford: Blackwell.

Cotton, J. L. (1996) "Employee Involvement", in C. L. Cooper and I. T. Robertson (eds) *International Review of Industrial and Organizational Psychology*, 11, John Wiley & Sons Ltd., pp. 219–42.

Gratton, L. (1997). "A Real Step Change", *People Management*, 24 July, pp. 22–7.

Guzzo, R. A. and Bondy, J. S. (1983) *A Guide to Worker Productivity Experiments in the United States, 1976–1981*, Elmsford, NY: Pergamon.

Guzzo, R. A., Jette, R. D. and Katzell, R. A. (1985) "The Effects of Psychologically Based Intervention Programs on Worker Productivity: A Meta-Analysis", *Personnel Psychology*, 38, pp. 275–92.

Harrison R. and Kessels, J. (2004) *Human Resource Development in a Knowledge-based Economy*, Basingstoke: Palgrave Macmillan.

Lopez-Cabrales, A., Pérez-Luño, A. and Valle Cabrera, R. (2009) "Knowledge as a Mediator between HRM Practices and Innovative Activity", *Human Resource Management – Special Issue: HRM and Knowledge Processes*, 48(4), July/August, pp. 485–503.

McKenzie, J. and van Winkelen, C. (2011) *Knowledge Works: The Handbook of Practical Ways to Identify and Solve Common Organizational Problems for Better Performance*. Chichester: John Wiley.

Schneider, B., Goldstein, H. W. and Smith, D. B. (1995) "The ASA Framework. An Update", *Personnel Psychology*, 48, pp. 747–74.

Simon, H. A. (1991) "Bounded Rationality and Organizational Learning", *Organization Science*, 2(1), pp. 125–34.

Steijn, B. and Tijdens, K. (2005) "Workers and their Willingness to Learn: Will ICT-Implementation Strategies and HRM Practices Contribute to Innovation?" *Creativity and Innovation Management*, 14(2), June, pp. 151–9.

CHAPTER 2

Establishing Organizational Receptivity for Change

Michael Butler

Five factors for responding to change from the outside in

Introduction

The word "complex" regularly appears in discussions of change, strategy and policy implementation. This is especially true in policy implementation because of the successive waves of reform that characterize national and international political arenas.

Concurrently, the notion of an organization's receptivity for change is becoming more pertinent as we consider what makes similar organizations in similar environments respond differently when faced with the same complexity of imminent change.

This chapter explores these two concepts – that of complexity thinking and of receptivity for change – in a "pas de deux" manner to shed light on how

{ ... complexity thinking and receptivity for change }

organizations can prepare and be ready for change. While "complexity thinking" is a term with which most are familiar, "receptivity" may need explanation. For the purposes of this chapter:

Receptivity for change refers to an organization's readiness to respond to the change challenges coming from both outside and inside the organization, to an organization's ability to synchronize appropriate internal organizational practices to meet threats and opportunities.

{ ... receptivity for change, an organization's readiness to respond to change }

Both within the UK and internationally, governments are seeking the holy grail of "achieving high performing public services, delivered at the lowest price, while maximizing participation". The same is clearly true in business for which the equivalent mantra is "achieving strong growth while delivering strong results and maximizing stakeholder satisfaction". In the context of public services, the concept of "complex" is used to refer to the fact that high performance has to occur in a dynamic system, a context in which many stakeholders with diverse roles have a relevant and often very public "say".

Let me step back for a moment. When I left university in 1989, I joined a boutique innovative enterprise as a management consultant. The biggest problem our clients faced revolved around issues to do with the management of change. Specifically, they were taxed by the failure of organizational development programs to deliver the change and benefits for which those programs were originally intended. Change simply did not stick.

The generally accepted approach at that time was to plan interventions that would in themselves drive change, and in particular culture change. Many clients were approaching this from a total quality perspective (TQM), looking for system-wide big change programs that went across the whole organization. At the time, North American solutions dominated the market, provided through the "guru model" like that of Tom Peters. "In Pursuit of Excellence" with its "6S" model typified **the** approach. I became interested in creating new models focused on how we could solve the problem of how to make change stick. This has been the overarching concern of my research.

Allied to this, my underlying philosophy was and remains that organizations exist to satisfy client needs. If they don't do this, they go out of business. By "client" I mean anyone who benefits from the services or products an organization creates, even if that is another organization in the supply chain.

Returning to the reality of policy implementation as an example of change, in order to better understand and, as a consequence, more successfully manage the complexity of policy implementation, the field of organizational theory is increasingly drawing on the field of complex systems. There are, however, few organizational examples of how complex systems thinking applies in practice to the management of change. Indeed, some research (K. Houchin and Don MacLean) critiqued the application of complex systems in the context of change, arguing that organizations are recursive, not adaptive. In other words, organizations going through change will default to stability, will replicate former patterns of behavior and retreat from pursuing the novelty of new patterns. Thus they negate complexity. Notwithstanding the validity of those findings, the concept of complex systems has specifically relevant things to say about how dynamic systems

{ ... complex systems: how dynamic systems operate, how organizations change }

operate. It helps us develop a more sophisticated understanding of how organizations change and in particular how they implement changes in policy.

The process of implementing changes in public policy ("policy implementation processes") should be understood as a self-organizing system in which the ability of the organization to adapt is extremely important. Policy implementation is self-organizing because in almost every instance national policy is reinterpreted at the local level, with each local organization uniquely mixing elements of national policy with their own multifaceted local requirements. As such, policy implementation at the local level becomes unpredictable and compliance with national policy looks increasingly sketchy.

So how do complex systems inform our understanding of how to better drive policy change, how to do it more effectively, and how does it link to the notion of receptivity for organizational change?

If in no other way, by adopting a complex systems perspective, it is possible to explore the concept of emergent processes, which in the context of receptivity to change I have termed "possibility space". More on this later.

New findings suggest that there are two levels of change within an organization and that these two levels continuously interact. One is more mecha-

{ ... two levels of change: mechanistic and organic }

nistic and operates at a surface level while the other is more organic and takes place at a deeper level. It is into this second deeper level that the concept of complexity thinking and "possibility space" speaks. However, unless both sets of processes, the mechanistic and the organic, are considered during policy implementation, the management of change is likely to fail.

Policy implementation and complexity

Policy implementation has recently been revisited as an important issue for public services. The focus of this chapter is on the operational end of the policy process, at the point of implementation where national policy meets local professionals, where the managerial skill and decision-making ability of the local team are what most matters. Jill Schofield and Charlotte Sausman note that the role of discretion at the local level takes the form of street-level bureaucracy. They highlight the role played by complexity as local stakeholders self-organize and apply their adaptive abilities to implement new processes, imposed as new policy, in a locally advantageous and customized way.

Looking from the outside in, however great may be the insights that could be gained from complexity theory, in reality policy formulators and public service managers are inclined to simplify their processes, to reduce the actual level of complexity surrounding the policy changes they need to implement. In the National Health Service (NHS), this has been achieved by closely joining the macro and micro levels of implementation over a sustained five-year period of time. As such, individual changes in policy have been linked in a process that has essentially been led from the top. The strategy is sophisticated in that the complexity of the system has been acknowledged. Different paces and directions of change have been adopted as less receptive contexts resist reforms while more receptive ones adopt change. In many cases, though not always obvious to those within the system (i.e. the NHS) or for that matter at the time when it comes to policy implementation, a clear project management function has been adopted to drive reform programs through the different localities and substrata of the larger organization.

Looking from the inside out, the notion of receptivity for organizational change offers a more traditional view of policy implementation and, on a broader platform, of strategy. Receptivity attempts to reveal the factors that contribute toward an organization's inclination to be low-change and non-receptive or high-change and receptive to change. Receptivity as a concept has been around as a notion since the late 1990s. It was first applied in the private sector to multiple businesses in several sectors before being used to understand change in the public sector, starting with the NHS. Despite that, it is still an emerging, under-developed idea that is now being reapplied.

Let us consider a case in the UK public sector context to exemplify how receptivity to change explains an organization's predisposition to adapt, and to see how change is both complex and contingent upon our organizations' receptivity to change.

During the period following the Second World War, most working people in the UK lived in local authority housing. This changed in the 1980s as Margaret Thatcher's Conservative government promoted home ownership and created the social structures to make this a de facto position for every family unit. A revolution in social expectations occurred. Through the Housing Act 1980, council and Registered Social Landlord (housing associations) tenants gained the "Right to Buy" their homes at a subsidized price. Other privatization measures followed, including government policy that encouraged public sector organizations to downsize and outsource their services. Among the most prominent of those were Compulsory Competitive Tendering (CCT; e.g. Local Government Act 1992), Best Value (Local Government Act 1999) and new reforms to ensure that decisions about housing were taken locally (2011). For purposes of clarification, the intention of CCT was to bring in competition to what was considered a "closed shop" environment. Specifically the drive was to replace existing in-house service providers with new external ones who it was believed would be less biased, more efficient and more professional.

Despite legislation at the national level, there was widespread variation in the use of contractors at the local level. Trafford and Westminster Councils are just two cases in point. In Trafford, CCT implementation culminated in the awarding of five contracts to five in-house contractors on November 13, 1996. In other words, there was no change of contractor. Lip service was paid to the legislation as these newly awarded contractors started trading as independents on April 1, 1997. By contrast, it took Westminster until December 1998 for CCT to be implemented in the manner that was intended. It culminated in the awarding of contracts to three types of external contractors, each licensed to replace the hitherto single in-house contractor.

Receptivity helps us explain the relative success of the two contrasting boroughs and why Trafford manifested as a low-change non-receptive environment for CCT, while Westminster showed-up as a high-change receptive entity.

First level change – four receptivity factors

Beginning at the organizational mechanistic level of change, four receptivity factors are recognized and seen as interconnected. $\left\{ \text{... at the organizational mechanistic level of change, four receptivity factors} \right\}$

- **Ideological vision**: this factor critically analyzes the strategic decisions being made in order to establish and evaluate if they are driven

{ ... establish the strategic context and case for change in the vision }

by a higher-order purpose. High change organizations establish the strategic context and state the case for change in their vision. This drives strategic change, and is shared, accepted and understood by all as being the reference point for evaluating the relevance and importance of any new change.

- **Leading change**: this factor analyzes the actions of key decision-makers to see the extent to which clear leaders for change are

{ ... clear leaders for change are appointed to enable innovation }

appointed to enable innovation to be identified and cascaded across the organization. Through this factor new practices are embedded. In high-change organizations, leaders of transformational change can be spotted throughout the organization and through them good practice started in one part of the organization is shared across the whole.

- **Institutional politics**: this factor explores how decision-making processes originate and continue through formal processes and informal net-

{ ... decision-making through formal processes and informal networks }

works. High performing organizations make formal decision-making processes explicit but also recognize informal networks and influencers that enable or disable change. Social connections and networks within high-change organizations are multi-channeled and operate independently of the hierarchy.

- **Implementation capacity**: this factor explores where decision-making takes place in greater detail by going beyond structural relation-

{ ... necessary skills and knowledge to implement the desired change }

ships to explore which staff has the necessary skills and knowledge to implement the desired change. This factor is about the wider organization's flexibility and awareness to support and accept change as it is being implemented.

Let's see how each of these four factors manifested in the case of our two councils.

Ideological vision looks at the quality and coherence of policy. Following this through our case, the Director in Trafford and the Conservative local councilors in Westminster developed strategic agendas to guide action in their departments. The strategic agendas were associated with a characteristic set of managerial beliefs. In Trafford, a dominant belief was that it was important to keep things "in the family" and to retain tacit knowledge of historic in-house service providers. By contrast, in Westminster, the dominant vision was that service provision could be improved through new actors and the opportunity provided by CCT was seized.

Leading change locates the level within the organizational hierarchy where decision-making takes place – relative to the top of the hierarchy. In Trafford, decision-making was located with the Director who was resistant to the outsourcing strategy. In Westminster, decision-making was located with the Conservative local councilors who, being supportive of the logic of outsourcing, adopted an accelerated strategy. Westminster was viewed as an early adopter, an exemplar of change, and went on to develop a media reputation for supporting outsourcing initiatives. Trafford was judged to be a follower.

Institutional politics points to the extent to which both formal and informal network structures are used to arrive at decisions. In Trafford, an informal structure was used to drive CCT adoption and passivity was generated by the Director's management style. In contrast, Westminster used formal structures. The Conservative local councilors recruited a Director to accelerate outsourcing and residents were assigned a key role during contract negotiations to enable them to demand higher levels of service delivery.

Implementation capacity is associated with who actually makes the change happen and the extent to which local actors carry influence, the extent to which actions of local players can be reversed by top-down decisions. In Trafford, an Area Housing Manager used the opportunity of looser managerial-staff relations and the secondment of a Director (1995–7), to set up initiatives to reduce the number of empty properties in her area. However, the Director, aware that local actors were opposed to this, resisted the Area Housing Manager's initiatives, limiting Trafford's implementation capacity. By contrast, in Westminster, the residents used their key role to reappoint the in-house public sector contractor. The Conservative local councilors, though subject to the higher moral grounds of the residents, used the Contracts Committee to overrule the residents' decision and appoint an external private sector contractor. Implementation capacity at Westminster was upheld.

Moving back to take a systemic view of change, the level of change in the environment is the motor for change in the organization. In the case of our two borough councils, change in the environment (increasing demand for private housing and legislation) provided the case for outsourcing. The four receptivity factors at the organization level influenced how each of the two organizations responded to those motors of change from the environment. The receptivity factors at the organization level then created institutional patterns at the public service level. As was clearly the case in our examples, some organizations will find it easier to slow down or increase the pace of change by adjusting their response to imposed change. As a consequence, they create increased complexity within and across multiple systems.

Let's return then to the topic of complex systems to see how this sheds light on an organizations' receptivity to change.

Complex systems – establishing analytical categories

Complex systems and complexity thinking offer a radical view of organizational change that reveals why mechanistic representations of organizations are insufficient.

When organizations and change are associated with biological processes, an evolutionary view of structure and organization emerges. Change is viewed as the structural evolution of an organization as a result of its on-going dialogue with possible innovations, various contingencies and stresses in the wider environment. In complex systems, as in biological environments, the existing structure either resists

{ ... in complex systems, the existing structure either resists an innovation or changes }

an innovation or changes. The ease with which that happens depends on the receptivity of the organization to the particular change that is presented. Clearly, this involves a complex interaction between the internal nature of an entity, its possible variability and the environment that it inhabits.

Consider a different example: the receptivity to change displayed by automotive manufacturing organizations. Ian McCarthy et al. identified 53 characteristics of a manufacturing organization by examining annual reports and descriptions of organizational changes made by many different companies over the history of automobile manufacture. Using this, John R. Baldwin et al. constructed a matrix of paired interactions between the characteristics in order to examine how they can combine to create emergent organizational forms. The matrix was used to develop an evolutionary simulation model in which a manufacturing firm attempts to incorporate successive new characteristics at a given rate selected by the user of the simulation.

As one can imagine, an incredible range of possible organizational forms can emerge. Each time a new characteristic is adopted within an organization, it changes the receptivity of the organization for any new innovations in the future. This is a consequence of path-dependent evolution that characterizes organizational change. Arguably successful evolution is about the discovery or creation of highly synergetic structures of interacting practices that follow path-dependent trajectories.

Without getting into the detail of how it works, the simulation demonstrates four principles behind complexity thinking: that there is { four principles behind complexity thinking: } (1) no universal organizational best practice, (2) path dependency, (3) choice in the system and (4) constituency. Let's take each in turn.

No universal organizational best { (1) No universal organizational best practice } practice: even within organizational subsections, there may be no simple, single recipe for improving organizations since organizations and subsections of organizations differ in their receptivity. An organization may be made up of different practices and these practices change over time as organizational performance strengthens and weakens. Even when best practice is found, no best practice fits forever. New practices will continuously be available to and evolve within an organization seeking organizational change for competitive success. Ironically, therefore, the most dangerous strategy is to "do nothing different".

Path dependency: innovative practices must inevitably interact { (2) Path dependency } with existing practices. This interaction will produce new emergent attributes and capabilities. Actual success of new practices is predetermined by the practices already present and the change that preceded. The future evolutionary pathway is affected by that of the past. Path dependency corresponds to sensitivity to initial conditions because the new practices must interact with existing practices.

Choice: different simulations lead to { (3) Choice in the system } different structures.

When the simulation is rerun, a different pattern of interactions between the practices emerges. It is therefore impossible to predict what will be adopted and what new practices will succeed. This in itself is evidence that the system has choice. Choice corresponds to Houchin and MacLean's concept of emergent order as it is impossible to predict what change will be adopted and what that adoption will look like.

Constituency: organizations possess individual practices, capabilities and performance levels within which they operate. In other words, organizations perform according to a pattern; the system produces after itself as if it had a reasonably hardwired DNA. Again, when the simulation is run and rerun, preferred organizational modes of operation begin to appear. Going back to McCarthy et al.'s research, different companies over the history of automobile manufacture developed different organizational identities or modes of operation, ranging from craft at one end to extremely sophisticated manufacturing processes at the other. Constituency corresponds to negative and positive feedback processes within the organization that reinforce a preferred organizational mode of operation, that dictate how well any new practice will be received.

{ (4) Constituency }

Second level of change – the new and fifth receptivity factor of possibility space

This provides a way of looking at level change, where the policy changes are relatively familiar and known. It also takes us to a second level of change that must be explained, which occurs when several novel management processes are introduced at the same time. We group the effects of this deeper order of change under the label of "possibility space": the fifth factor in receptivity for change.

■ **Possibility space**: this fifth receptivity factor allows for and encourages creativity in organizational processes, so that existing behaviors can be adapted and new behaviors can emerge – people are allowed to trial new things. Possibility space exists where parts of the organization feel comfortable experimenting, when the organization creates space for this experimentation to take place

{ ... at the organizational organic level ... parts of the organization feel comfortable experimenting } and can then exploit it. Mistakes are accepted as long as learning takes place so those mistakes don't happen again.

It is in this context of possibility space that we continue to assume the four principles of complexity thinking, that there is: no universal best practice, path dependency, choice and constituency. We group these concepts under the label "possibility space" because it captures creativity in organizational processes.

Peter Allen states that any single organizational behavior can only grow until it reaches the limits set either by its input requirements, or, for an economic activity, by the market limit for any particular product or service. After this, it is the "error-makers", the micro innovations and, in the case of enterprises, the outliers that grow more successfully than the "average type", as they are less in competition with the others. As this evolutionary process progresses, the "identity" of the population becomes unstable as the organization changes. In this way it is easy to see from a distance that organizational systems, unlike simulations, evolve in discontinuous steps of instability, separated by periods of stability (Kurt Lewin's "unfreeze, transition, refreeze" stages). So, returning to the metaphor of biological systems, there are times when the system structure can suppress the instabilities caused by the innovative exploration of its inhabitants, and there are other times when it cannot suppress them, and a new population emerges.

How does this apply to a real-life organization? Reconsider our local authority housing case and view it as a macroscopic system. The Government, through national policy, wanted stability throughout the system. In our specific example this meant the widespread take-up of outsourcing. Yet, at the local level, there was instability as the subsystem dynamics of the different local housing authorities kicked in through the variation in their compliance with the policy. At the subsystem level, there was self-organization and coevolution. Coevolution usually deals with the circumstances in which complex systems evolve without a central planner who directs the system to a predetermined goal. In the context of the councils, there was a central planner, the State, but these are also coevolution at the local level, with the local housing authorities taking decisions of their own that enabled or impeded the directives of the central plan.

Our research suggests that staff accepted that there was no universal best practice for outsourcing in local authority housing. Hence the stakeholders within Trafford and Westminster needed to decide on the future strategy for their individual organizations. This became the role of organizational play, which in fact also pointed toward the receptivity factor of implementation capacity as it demanded that each council reflect to learn from their past (path dependency) and to anticipate their future (choice).

The fact that there is no universal best practice acknowledges that there may be no simple, single recipe for improving organizations since they differ in their receptivity. This is an important point because although it may be possible to identify the variables, such as the five receptivity factors, for an optimal performance, it is not possible to predict what should be done with them to achieve that desired performance. Some organizations may have a synergy with central government policy initiatives. These organizations will be early adopters of change and are likely to be referred to as exemplars of best practice by central government. Other organizations may then develop synergy, depending on the experience of the early adopters, and are likely to be referred to as laggards by central government. Who is to say whether it was the early adopters or the laggards that obtained optimal performance for their client populations? Local history and circumstances shape political and managerial ideological beliefs that will underlie the bureaucratic processes and decisions of the organization. Central government can either tolerate local variation or find enforcement techniques to achieve conformity. In our case study, local variation was tolerated. This could be interpreted as a policy failure. More accurately, it is an example of the limitations of government to implement policy in the context of increasing complexity in different societal sectors.

Neither the Director in Trafford nor the Conservative local councilors in Westminster were right or wrong in the strategic agendas that they developed. Instead of imposing good practice, that is, Government-preferred outsourcing activity, public service organizations needed to be allowed to experiment with different practices – to engage in exploratory learning and organizational play/constituency.

Organizational play weighs up two factors: learning from the past (path dependency) and anticipating the future (choice). Focusing on path dependency, innovative practices must interact with existing practices to produce emergent attributes and capabilities. Emergent attributes and capabilities will, in turn, adapt to encounters at the other levels of change.

Example: the innovative practices of reducing empty properties at Trafford and the attempt to reappoint the in-house public sector contractor in Westminster were unsuccessfully launched. Nevertheless, turning to choice, nothing is fixed. Despite laws, regulations and institutional inertia, governments have limits. Processes like coevolution turn complex systems into adaptive complex systems. Another way of expressing this is to acknowledge that in any change there are a very large number of possible futures. There may have been a different future if the innovative practices in Trafford and Westminster had been successfully launched.

The five receptivity factors have been summarized in the following model.

Implications

There are implications for policy formulation and policy implementation. At the national level, local variation in the implementation of government policy initiatives poses a problem. Policy implementation is always concerned with the performance of a large population of organizations. Because of this, central government policy initiatives aimed at improving local service delivery will consist of attempting to force public service organizations to adopt new practices that are believed to improve their performance.

However, in order to benefit from the self-organizing system enabled by the variation in receptivity, central government may be better off limiting its role to that of setting strategic aims and objectives; it may be best advised to refrain from trying to impose best practice through strict regulation (i.e. CCT and Best Value). To some extent, as Ewan Ferlie et al. reveal, this learning has already taken place in the NHS. The Localism Bill (2011) seems to transfer the new learning to local government, but the test will be its eventual implementation. Perhaps the consequence of limiting central government activity is to give local public service organizations greater freedom to manage. In turn, this freedom to manage may encourage innovative public services to grow spare capacity to pursue developmental work. Local services are best placed to tap into knowledge about local practices, to move available resources around the service base to meet hot-spot service demands and to use informal and formal structures to achieve preferred goals. New learning can then be more easily disseminated to assist other public services.

The discussion of possibility space, because of its focus on Trafford and Westminster, might suggest that the two local housing authorities are autopoietic systems, that is to say, there is a boundary surrounding each authority. This is not accurate because policy implementation is a process of self-organization, which contains multi-level interconnections. The adaptive abilities of stakeholders at the $\left\{\begin{array}{c}\text{... adaptive abilities of stakeholders}\\\text{at the local level are extremely important}\end{array}\right\}$ local level are extremely important, so that local needs are addressed during the implementation of national policies. Herbert Simon's near decomposability principle captures the reality of policy implementation when it argues that complex systems can emerge by modular design, through nearly autonomous subunits, units like Trafford and Westminster, which increase complexity and the rate of their adaptive responses.

Organizational practice

A major implication for those leading change is that one must operate at two levels within an organization and these will continuously interact.

Managers are well prepared to operate at the first level, the mechanistic level. In order to get promoted, they will have demonstrated competence in the traditional management processes of leadership, politics, implementation and vision – the first four receptivity factors.

It is unlikely that managers are as well prepared to operate at the second level of change – in the context of the fifth receptivity factor, in the arena of possibility space. Nevertheless, the evidence from Trafford and Westminster indicates that both the politicians and staff intuitively operated at this level.

Five preliminary practical steps can be identified that may lead to success in possibility space.

First, possibility space seems to open up when there is a stimulus for action. Trafford and Westminster responded to the outsourcing agenda. It may be, however, that just being aware of the possibility space will stimulate action because inhabitors of that space will then be able to reflect in that space.

Second, one aspect of reflexivity is to acknowledge that there is no universal best practice, making it essential for managers to reframe the parameters of their decision-making as openly as they need in order to achieve a given task.

Third, as organizational play generates ideas, managers need to know the factors that contribute to learning and creativity, and these may be organizationally based.

Fourth, idea generation is contextualized by path dependency and choice. Path dependency indicates that managers should continuously review past successes and failures to establish an initial pool of ideas for the possibility space.

Fifth, dynamic capabilities suggests that managers exercising choice should go beyond renewing past ideas or reconfiguring organizational structures, and include re-creating how they enact leadership, politics, implementation and vision.

These five steps echo Bill McKelvey's notion of "complexity leadership"; instead of incentivizing followers to implement the vision of the leader, complexity leadership enables the bottom-up formation of effective emergent structures.

The five steps facilitate the formation of emergent change and stress the importance of managing tension in organizations.

The TRANSFORMATION Project

In order to operationalize receptivity and to find practical approaches of applying receptivity to executives and their organizations, The TRANSFORMATION Project, was founded in 2009 within Aston Business School, part funded by the Economic and Social Research Council (ESRC). The aim of the Project is to translate existing academic theory, including complexity and receptivity, into practical management tools for performance improvement. To this end we worked in a collaborative partnership with colleagues from the public, third and private sectors. Founding partners include Catalyst Education (Birmingham Local Education Partnership), Echo Managed Services, NHS Warwickshire, Playgroup (a London advertising agency), Warwickshire Police, Associated British Foods plc, DHL Supply Chain and the Association for Project Management. This Project is being extended into the British Sugar Group, Saudi Aramco and non-government organizations (NGOs). By using action research methodology with our partner organizations, we created The Receptivity for Change Toolset.

The Receptivity for Change Toolset measures an organization's receptivity for change against a set of indicators for each of the five receptivity factors in the Model in Figure 2.1. The indicators have been validated by

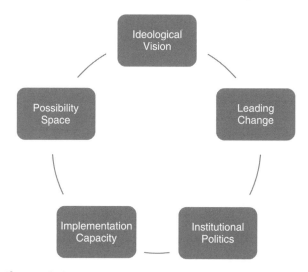

Figure 2.1 Butler's Receptivity for Change Model

research within the Project team. The scores for each of the indicators are translated into a traffic light system:

- Red: indicates performance that needs to be urgently reviewed, improved and monitored to increase an organization's receptivity for change.
- Amber: indicates some foundations that need development.
- Green: indicates moving toward consistent high receptivity for change.

Depending on the level at which the toolset is used, it reveals specifically which individuals, projects and organizations are doing well in the context of change and what their

{ ... toolset reveals development needs to better target change initiatives }

development needs are to better target change initiatives. Future actions can thus be recommended, founded on evidence, in order to maximize potential and target executive development interventions.

By way of example, consider Warwickshire Police. They were an early adopter of the receptivity for change toolset because at the start of the TRANSFORMATION Project the organization was in the process of planning and instigating two new major projects. Many issues existed which undermined effective implementation of the first of these projects: the Automatic Number Plate Recognition (ANPR).

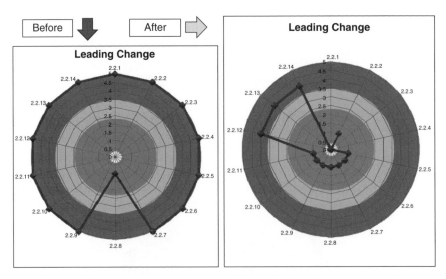

Figure 2.2   Case study – Warwickshire Police (ANPR Project) →
Successful leadership development

- the problematic engagement of key actors within the project
- lack of funding
- minimal training in project management
- a tight timeline as funding would only be available from December 2009 to March 31, 2010
- the departure of a key supporter for the projects

By using The Receptivity for Change Toolset to benchmark change before and after project implementation, we were able to show the development of leadership competencies by the project manager who acted as a catalyst of change (Figure 2.2):

Return on investment was quick. Major improvements were quantified as a consequence of effective change management and project implementation.

Conclusion

This chapter demonstrates that any change, including policy implementation processes, should be understood as occurring in self-organizing systems. Success in this process impinges upon the adaptive abilities of the organization and of the significant individuals within them. Adaptive capability is therefore extremely important for all stakeholders. Policy implementation is self-organizing because national policy is reinterpreted at the local, even individual, level. As such the likes of Trafford and Westminster had different paces and directions of change as they awarded different types of outsourcing contracts. As for Warwickshire Police, a key individual was able to overcome the complexity of that policy environment by addressing specific personal implementation issues to demonstrate greater impact on two major projects.

Complexity and receptivity offer a novel view on the process of policy implementation and organizational change. While stakeholders work to reduce the complexity of implementation, receptivity offers them an explanation of change in the language of traditional management processes.

Reinterpreting data previously published from a complex systems perspective allows us to identify five dynamically interconnecting receptivity factors that enable organizations to navigate successful implementation of change: ideological vision, leading change, institutional politics, implementation capacity and possibility space. The concept of possibility space extends to four characteristics, namely the fact that there is no universal best practice, there is organizational play, there is path dependency and there is choice in the system.

Summary

There are five factors for responding to change from the outside in:

1. Ideological Vision – to establish the change imperative
2. Change Leadership – to drive change throughout the organization
3. Institutional Politics – to effect formal and informal decision-making
4. Implementation Capacity – to implement change in practice
5. Possibility Space – to allow for experimentation and emergent change

Action points

- Have a vision that is: understandable by everyone; aligned to your underpinning philosophy and culture; communicated across all media platforms.

- Instill change leadership by: leading to help others lead; encouraging change leadership through the hierarchy; recognizing effective leadership across all functions.

- Manage institutional politics by: harnessing the power of your formal communication; recognizing your informal connectors; managing your external communication channels.

- Extend implementation capacity by: having sufficient people with the skills to implement change; having people willing to change personally; having the reward mechanisms to encourage change.

- Create possibility space by: ensuring procedures are flexible for evolutionary change; encouraging your staff to change; having the balance right between exploration and exploitation (See Figure 2.3).

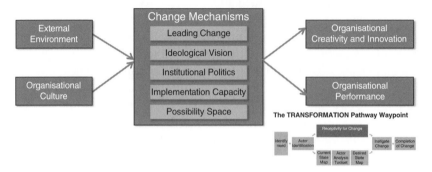

Figure 2.3 Receptivity – a summary in practice

Self-assessment tool

To what extent are you increasing your organization's receptivity for change? (**Tables 2.1**, **2.2**)

Table 2.1 How good is my organization at building our receptivity for change?

Attribute	Never	Sometimes	Mostly	Always	Cumulative Score
Ideological Vision					
1. We have a vision that is understand-able by everyone in our organization	0	1	2	3	
2. Our vision is aligned to the underpinning philosophy and culture of our organization	0	1	2	3	
3. Our vision is being communi-cated across all media platforms and linked to our evaluation of the strategic context and the change we have decided on	0	1	2	3	

Average (divide your cumulative score for Ideological Vision by three and round up to a whole number)

Change Leadership					
1. We lead to help others lead through distributed leadership and empowerment	0	1	2	3	

(*continued*)

Table 2.1 (*Continued*)

Attribute	Never	Sometimes	Mostly	Always	Cumulative Score
2. We encourage change leadership through all the layers of the hierarchy in our organization	0	1	2	3	
3. We recognize effective leadership across all functions in our organization	0	1	2	3	

Average (divide your cumulative score for Change Leadership by three and round up to a whole number)

Institutional Politics

	Never	Sometimes	Mostly	Always	Cumulative Score
1. We harness the power of our formal communication processes	0	1	2	3	
2. We recognize the informal connectors within our organization through whom communication speeds up or becomes distorted – that is, the power brokers positioned throughout the hierarchy	0	1	2	3	
3. We manage the external communication channels for effective inter-organizational working and to protect corporate reputation in the context of change	0	1	2	3	

Table 2.1 (*Continued*)

Attribute	Never	Sometimes	Mostly	Always	Cumulative Score
Average (divide your cumulative score Institutional Politics by three and round up to a whole number)					
Implementation Capacity					
1. We have sufficient people throughout the organization with the skills and knowledge to embrace and implement change	0	1	2	3	
2. We have people throughout the organization willing to change personally	0	1	2	3	
3. We have the reward mechanisms in place to encourage teams to pursue change	0	1	2	3	
Average (divide your cumulative score for Implementation Capacity by three and round up to a whole number)					
Possibility Space					
1. Our procedures are sufficiently flexible to allow for evolutionary change – given path dependency	0	1	2	3	
2. We encourage our staff to input into significant choices for change	0	1	2	3	

(*continued*)

Table 2.1 (*Continued*)

Attribute	Never	Sometimes	Mostly	Always	Cumulative Score
3. We have the balance right between exploration and exploitation in our organization	0	1	2	3	

Average (divide your cumulative score for Possibility Space by three and round up to a whole number)

Now add up all five of your averaged scores for each of the five receptivity factors.

This gives you your overall Receptivity for Change Score.

Table 2.2 Benchmark scores

0–3	4–8	9–12	13–15
In the danger zone!	Some foundations that need development	Good, but room for improvement	Moving toward consistent high performance

To make the score more meaningful, consider which specific receptivity factors you need to address.

For more detail, complete The Receptivity for Change Toolset FOC, available from The TRANSFORMATION Project (www.thetransformationproject.co.uk).

Further reading

Butler, M. J. R. (2003) "Managing from the Inside Out: Drawing on 'Receptivity' to Explain Variation in Strategy Implementation", *British Journal of Management*, 14, Special Issue, December, pp. S47–S60.

Butler, M. J. R. and Allen, P. (2008) "Understanding Policy Implementation Processes as Self-Organizing Systems", *Public Management Review*, 10(3), pp. 421–40.

Butler, M. J. R. and Gheorghiu, L. (2010) "Exploring the Failure to Protect the Rights of the Roma Child in Romania", *Public Administration and Development*, 30(4), pp. 235–46.

Butler, M. J. R. and Reid, M. A. (2011) "The TRANSFORMATION Project – A Case Study of High Performing Inter-Organizational Collaboration, Chartered Management Institute (CMI) and Wiley, Corby". If you are a member of the CMI you can access and review it at http://www.managers.org.uk/toparticles. An expanded version of the case study is available at http://www.thetransfor mationproject.co.uk/wp-content/uploads/Case-Study-Warwickshire-Police-Approved-v2.pdf.

www.thetransformationproject.co.uk.

CHAPTER 3

The Alchemy of Entrepreneurial Business Growth

Mark Hart

Two forces that fuel entrepreneurial growth and sustainable change

Introduction

Understanding business growth, and particularly the growth of small firms, has been the subject of academic enquiry for over 40 years. Yet it still creates debate and controversy as academics and policymakers wrestle with a rich, complex evidence base. This chapter represents a personal journey through this maze from a starting point in 1978 when, as a rather naïve and woefully ill-equipped doctoral student, I commenced my first study of small firm growth and of the entrepreneurial process in the city of Belfast. The motivation was simple. The city was in social, economic and political turmoil, buffeted by the influences of a global recession and resultant lack of inward investment. Job creation was a priority and the emerging evidence suggested that small firms were major providers.

Within 12 months of starting my research, David Birch initiated (albeit unintentionally) what has turned out to be a long-lasting and at times acrimonious debate that continues to this day. Birch sought to answer the

{   ... question: what size firms create the
                       most jobs?

}   question: what size firms create the most jobs?

On average about 60 percent of all jobs are generated by firms with 20 or fewer employees, about 50 percent of all jobs are created by independent, small entrepreneurs. Large firms (those with over 500 employees) generate less than 15 percent of all net new jobs.

This appears a simple enough proposition, so it seems difficult to imagine how it could have become, and remained, so controversial. One of the factors that played an important role in sustaining this debate was that Birch's argument about the role of small business in job creation fitted perfectly with the US government's long tradition of supporting small businesses. In the 30 years since Birch's publication there have been a number of further studies in the US (by Birch among others) and other countries looking at different dimensions of job creation. As yet no consensus has emerged to answer Birch's original question.

The objective of this chapter is to summarize the range of evidence on small firm growth, which has formed the core of my research activities since 1978. In it I hope to identify the determinants of small firm growth and to

{   ... understand how business support
           policy can actually change the growth
           trajectories of individual small firms

}   understand how business support policy can actually change the growth trajectories of individual small firms.

Not an easy task. Thirty-three years of new and innovative projects have added to the growing evidence-base on small firm growth. While firms themselves have often been the focus of attention in my research (i.e. size, sector,

{   ... the role of the individual owner-manager
                       or "entrepreneur"

}   ownership, location) the role of the individual owner-manager or "entrepreneur" and

what they actually choose to do has grown in importance. Indeed, a study which I helped design in the early 1990s was one of the first to attempt to validate David Storey's three spheres of influence on small firm growth: the entrepreneur, strategy and the characteristics of the firms.

Questions such as "Who are the entrepreneurs?" and especially "what differentiates those with high-growth aspiration?" have taken my research journey in the direction of the Global Entrepreneurship Monitor (GEM) project. Commencing in 1999 and now 12 years later, it is the most important available source of international data on individual entrepreneurs. Working in the UK on this project since 2002, based at Aston Business School since 2008, I have gained unique insights into the entrepreneurial process. This in turn has formed an important source of evidence for the UK's development of entrepreneurship and enterprise policy.

Underlying the discussions and debates over the decades on the drivers of small firm growth has been a challenge laid down by policymakers to the research community: can we devise a way to "pick winners" in order to ensure the most efficient and cost-effective delivery of business support schemes and initiatives? Today this manifests itself in the overriding interest in High-Growth Firms (HGFs) and their seeming importance to economic recovery. The justification for this interest lacked strong empirical foundation. With the availability of the new UK Business Demography database since 1998, comprehensive research is now possible. NESTA[1] invited me and some colleagues to provide them with the first analysis of business growth in the UK. Through this we determined the number of HGFs in the economy and their contribution to job creation. Thus, the "Vital 6 percent"[2] was born – a somewhat simplistic metric that has permeated policy documents across the UK Government and provided an opportunity for economists in Aston Business School to develop an international reputation for groundbreaking research on HGFs.

This chapter will highlight two major contributors to small firm growth. First, though, we summarize the recent HGF research and discuss where that had led us in terms of policy conclusions. Then we review the first major contributor: the role of business support policy in stimulating small firm growth, examined through an evaluation of the Business Link offer in England. Finally we look at the second major contributor: the entrepreneur and specifically the profile of high-aspiration entrepreneurs as seen through the GEM UK dataset.

Background: what we know about High-Growth Firms

High-Growth Firms (HGFs) in particular have continued to attract considerable attention from the academic and policy community in recent years. Recent statements from the government in the UK summarized the available UK evidence. There is a perception that the UK and Europe are failing to create innovative new firms that grow rapidly into world leaders, like Microsoft and Google. It has been argued that the main contribution to job creation comes from a small number of HGFs that are also fast-growing companies commonly called gazelles. The Organisation for Economic Co-operation and Development (OECD) suggests that gazelles include large and small firms, young and old firms. While there has been a great deal of research on the characteristics of HGFs (using business demography datasets) in terms of firm size, industrial sector, business age and location, there has been less attention paid to the relative importance of the range of individual characteristics associated with high-growth aspiration of new firms. So, while we are reasonably well informed about the types of businesses that can be classified as high growth, we are perhaps less able to identify the extent to which we can build a profile of those individuals most likely to set up enterprises which might be described as "gazelles".

The literature on gazelles that has appeared in the wake of the Birch and the US Small Business Administration (SBA) studies has been usefully reviewed by Magnus Henrekson and Dan Johansson. Based on a synthesis of 19 studies, they note that there is no general agreement on the definition of gazelles. Many think of them simply as fast-growing firms while others confine the term to only those start-ups that grow very rapidly. Definitions vary in terms of the following: choice of growth indicator (e.g. employment, sales and profits); measurement of growth; length of time-period over which growth is measured; and whether growth through acquisition is included or just organic growth. Birch defined *gazelles* as "establishments which have achieved a minimum of 20 percent sales growth each year over the interval, starting from a base-year revenue of at least \$100,000". This definition, therefore, includes three criteria: (i) growth rate, (ii) sales as the measure of growth and (iii) minimum start-size (to avoid the arithmetic problems associated with growth from a very small base). An alternative approach is to define HGFs as the X percent fastest growing (new) firms. The consensus of opinion favors the first approach, with the OECD seeking to achieve some consistency by proposing that "HGFs are defined as those with an average employment growth rate exceeding 20 percent per annum over a three-year period and with ten or more employees at the start of the period". They can be long-established firms or more recent start-ups (i.e. and it is these that are most often referred to as gazelles).

A number of findings emerge from the literature review of the general term "gazelles" despite differences in method, definitions, time-period, etc.:

1. It confirms the existence of gazelles in that a few rapidly growing firms generate a large share of all net new jobs in the economy, irrespective of the population studied. This is particularly marked in recessionary periods when gazelles (i.e. not just start-ups) continue to grow. Aston's

most recent research for NESTA would tend to support this view for the UK in the post-2007 period.

2. There is less consistency between studies in terms of whether gazelles make a disproportionate contribution to total job growth. The evidence is positive for the US but not for some other countries, such as Sweden. Indeed, there is less evidence of a gazelle effect in Sweden which Per Davidsson et al. suggests may be the consequence of a small country effect which require fast-growing companies to expand by internationalization to a much greater extent than in large countries such as the US. Other possible explanations for this conclusion in Sweden are the time-period (which coincided with recession) and the large government sector that lowers the growth potential of private firms and excludes them from certain service sectors, which in the US are an important source of opportunity for fast-growth firms (e.g. worker health insurance).

3. Gazelles can be of all sizes. Whereas small firms are over-represented in the population of gazelles, large firms can also be important creators of jobs, particularly within a subgroup of "super gazelles" which in some other studies have been called "gorillas".

4. Gazelles tend to be younger on average. Super gazelles are also relatively young.

5. Younger gazelles are more likely to grow organically; hence they make a greater contribution to net employment growth. Larger and older gazelles are more likely to grow through acquisition.

6. Gazelles are found in all industries. They are not over-represented in high-tech industries. If anything, they are over-represented in services.

These findings have provoked a still unresolved debate that is pertinent to policy: is the quality of new firms or the quantity more important? Is it better to have a large number of business start-ups or a few firms that grow rapidly? Davidsson and Frederic Delmar call this the "mice" versus "gazelles" debate. Henrekson and Johansson suggest that it is not an either/or situation. Employment in new firms is just as crucial for total employment growth as the growth of gazelles. The position of the Scottish Business Birth Rate Strategy was that the ratio of gazelles to all new starts-ups appeared to be fairly constant so increasing the start-up rate should produce more gazelles. This approach is in sympathy with the view that "a selective policy of support for small firms is simply unworkable" because (a) it is "not feasible on operational grounds, neither at the business start-up stage nor later on when the small firm has begun to expand into a sizeable company" and (b) because research has failed to identify an absolute list of distinctive or distinguishing features of fast-growth firms (of gazelles).

Not with standing this caveat, in January 2011, the Department for Business, Innovation and Skills (BIS) launched their "Bigger, Better Business Strategy" that signaled a clear departure from an era of blanket support for small businesses in the UK. Going forward, there will now be a greater emphasis on enabling small businesses with growth potential to expand the ranks of the vital 6 percent.

Returning to the subject of gazelles, Zoltan Acs et al. have produced an important study in the US. They refer to gazelles in broad terms as "high-impact firms" which they define as enterprises whose sales have at least doubled over a four-year period and which have an employment growth quantifier (the relationship between its absolute and percentage change) of two or more over the period. Such firms were tracked from 1994 to 1998 and from 1998 to 2002. Some findings deviate quite considerably from Henrekson and Johansson's synthesis. For example:

- The average age of a high-impact firm is 25 years old. Very few high-impact firms are start-ups.
- High-impact firms come in all sizes.
- "Small" firms (less than 500 employees) created about half of the jobs and large firms created the other half in the first two periods (1994–1998 and 1998–2002) but not from 2002 to 2006.
- High-impact firms exist in all industries and are by no means confined to high-technology industries.
- High-impact firms exist in almost all regions, states, metropolitan areas and counties.
- There is evidence of some "super high-impact" firms that double their sales and revenue in more than one time-period and expand their employment over eight years or more. These firms are most frequent in the 500-plus employee firm size class.

The contrasting findings may be attributable to the time-periods, the relative importance of manufacturing, the significance of large firms and the entrepreneurial activity. Improvements in data availability may be another factor. Finally, Acs et al. do not say one way or the other whether growth through acquisition is included: we assume that it is, and this would favor older and larger businesses.

High-Growth Firms in the UK – a new analysis

The analysis of firm-level growth rates and the identification of the proportion of HGFs in the UK are based solely on the Business Structures Database (BSD), which has been accessed through the UK ONS Virtual Micro-Data Lab (VML). We adopt the OECD definition of a HGF as one with average annualized employment growth greater than 20 percent over a three-year period, and with ten or more employees in the beginning of the observation period.[3] Using this employee-based definition, we can arrive at the number of HGFs in two distinct periods – 11,369 in 2002–5 and 11,530 in 2005–8. This represents a very small proportion of the overall number of firms employing ten persons or more: 6.4 and 5.8 percent respectively. Conclusion? HGFs are relatively rare in the UK representing just over 1 percent of the total business population in the analysis or around 6 percent of businesses with ten or more employees – hence the magic "Vital 6 percent". Despite a small absolute increase in the number of high-growth firms between 2002–5 and 2005–8, the proportion of all surviving HGFs in the sample population as a whole had declined (to 5.8 percent).

HGF are found in a diverse range of sectors. They tend to be small (less than 50 employees) and established (five years and over). The vast majority (70 percent) of HGFs were aged five years and over in both the three-year subperiods. Implications? Not only are there very few HGFs but there are even fewer "gazelles" in the population of UK businesses – that is, confining the term to rapidly growing start-ups. The analysis indicates that there are approximately 2940 gazelles in the UK in the 2002–5 period and marginally fewer in the 2005–8 period (2749). It would appear that high growth, therefore, is not an activity of large firms in the UK, nor is it something that is driven by gazelles.

In terms of their economic impact, we can state that in 2008 HGFs employed 1.97 million people who represented approximately 8 percent of the total private sector employment in the UK. This represents an increase of 1.3 million jobs and an increase of £837 million in sales in the three years following 2005. Though 11,530 HGFs in the UK in 2008 may seem a small number, their economic footfall is not insignificant, and they don't all come from the creative industries – knowledge-based and high-tech industries.

With this first estimate of the proportion of HGFs in the UK economy for 2005, we can undertake some international comparisons. The UK has the highest proportion of HGFs in all the G7 or EU15 economies for which data is available. For example, the comparable figure for the United States was 5.2 percent, while for Spain – the highest ranked EU15 economy – it was 4.2 percent. Clearly, the assumption that the UK lags behind the United States in the share of HGFs is misplaced.

Public policy and small firm growth

How then can public policy be used to positively stimulate growth in small businesses that may in turn increase the incidence of HGFs in the UK economy? We provide some observations from our evaluation of Business Link in England. At the outset it should be acknowledged that since the change of government in May 2010 in the UK the Regional Development Agencies (RDAs) were abolished and the decision was also taken to close the Business Link initiative. So a politically driven decision withdrew a comprehensive program of business support in England at a time many firms were struggling to emerge from the worst post-war recession in the UK since the 1930s.What I reflect on here is my experience of the program as a member of the team commissioned to evaluate the program by the Government. This was an independent evaluation and I let the evidence speak on how important such schemes are to drive the growth of the small business population.

The Business Link (BL) program of advice to established firms aimed to improve the contribution made by small firms to the UK productivity growth, and to narrow the productivity gap with the US, France and Germany. There are a number of ways to do this. The program was designed to provide advice, such as marketing advice, which will increase the value of the output to a greater extent than any associated costs and be reflected in sales turnover. It would provide advice, such as operational advice, that cuts costs without reducing the output. If the BL program helps a high productivity firm to grow or aids a low productivity firm to shrink, that would also aid the overall productivity of small firms "sector" as a whole.

Before evaluating the effectiveness of BL per se, it is first important to consider differences in characteristics of firms because of the potential impact these will have on both process and outcomes. If one does not control for the heterogeneity of the small business population, then it is impossible to properly identify the effects of business support interventions. For example, it has long been established that firm size and age are inversely correlated to business growth. { Smaller and younger firms grow faster; a greater preponderance of non-executive directors may increase the growth potential of a firm. } Smaller and younger firms grow faster. We also know that, relative to the characteristics of the management team, a greater preponderance of non-executive directors may increase the growth potential of a firm.

Additionally, the literature on entrepreneurs and small businesses emphasizes the central role of the entrepreneur or the firm's owner-manager, and suggests, among other things, that the older the entrepreneur, the owner-manager, the { ... the older the entrepreneur, the owner-manager, the slower business growth } slower business growth. Serial founders have also a positive association with the growth prospects of firms.

Finally, market characteristics may also play a significant role in shaping firm performance. Studies have found that the general intensity of market competition and the price sensitivity of firms' markets are related to firm growth.

Notwithstanding the aforesaid, evidence from a range of studies suggests that both business planning and strategy choice can contribute positively to small business growth. Based on prior evidence, it appears that both the greater and wider use of formal business planning, often the focus of public policy interventions, and { ... that both the greater and wider use of formal business planning and ambitious strategy spur faster growth in HGFs } ambitious strategy spur faster growth in HGFs.

Let's therefore attempt to isolate the effects of public policy on business growth[4] and work toward some "propositions". We use evidence from the last "national" evaluation of BL to inform that discussion.

Some studies argue that the public sector ought only to provide a time-limited "taste" of business support, signposting firms to further expertise. In response to this, the role of the government-provided business advisers, such as that offered in the past by BL in the UK, was changed to emphasize brokerage and referral rather than direct help. In delivery terms, there was evidence that these changes to the BL network had a positive impact on BL performance and increased market penetration. By 2002, market penetration had increased to 32.6 percent of businesses, positioning BL as the primary source of public sector business support in England. With the change of UK Government in May 2010, the previous regime of BL-fronted business support in England was reviewed and substantially reduced to focus scarce resources on those firms with serious growth potential. Since then as noted previously it has been removed from the business support lexicon in England. More than ever there was, and remains, a need to understand those interventions that work and produce the greatest outcomes for the firms and the economy.

Our interest therefore narrowed to the effect of policy on business growth and how this differs between two forms of BL assistance offered. The first form, "intensive assistance", generally involved ongoing support and regular contacts between a firm and BL over a period of time. The second form, "other assistance" consisted of a one-off intervention, typically the provision of some basic advice. We aimed to separate the impact of the non-intensive signposting service from those generated by more intensive, and expensive, advisory services. We also aimed to identify what the optimal balance between the two types of assistance might be. To this end we looked at BL assistance that was provided between April and October 2003 and its impact on business growth over the following two years.

It should be recognized that although previous research on SME growth and public advisory programs has found only a weak link between the two, many authors adopt the resource-based view (RBV) to understand the impact of advice on the performance of the small firm. Within the RBV, management capability (by definition, and however great, it is, limited) constrains the growth of the firm. Advising managers (increasing their capability) would seem to act upon the key constraint to growth. In this perspective, advice augments the firm's resources and helps to build capability within the firm. Confirming this, Steve Johnson, Don Webber and Wayne Thomas found that growth forced firms to seek advice. However, since managers have different strengths and weaknesses, the theory suggests that the advice will differ from client to client and that the time-period for the outcomes of the intervention may vary. Although the aforementioned emphasizes how difficult it is to provide an effective advice service to small firm managers, the RBV provides a strong rationale for doing so.

The second major element of any intervention is the process through which BL advisory support influences business performance. This process model has a number of steps relating initially to the firms' engagement with BL, decisions about the type of assistance which firms will receive and the subsequent intra-firm processes and capabilities which benefit from assistance and leads to improved performance.

So what kind of firms and how did they know to take up BL's offer?

Studying start-up advice, James Chrisman et al. argued that advice seekers acknowledged a "knowledge deficit". Entrepreneurs lack some useful knowledge and may therefore look around to see whether it is available elsewhere. Of course, owner-managers of new businesses may find it easier to acknowledge a "knowledge gap"; younger businesses are thus more likely to take advice. However, until the small business owner identifies where the knowledge might be available they may not act on

> ... until the small business owner identifies where the knowledge might be available they may not act on their "knowledge deficit"

their "knowledge deficit". Thus, marketing is critical for the take-up of advice. However, Andrew Atherton argued that, in a mature market, heavy promotion of business support services was evidence of dissatisfaction. It was deemed that after the initial promotion that raises awareness, a "quality" service should attract a reputation that subsequently only requires modest promotion. The logic of his position was that the heavy marketing undertaken by BL undermined it in the eyes of possible "clients", reflected the lack of repeat business – repeat business being an indicator of quality.

We are not convinced. First, a new generation of entrepreneurs needed to be reminded of the offer. Second, since taking advice may require a problem to be solved, marketing needs to be "just-in-time". Besides, many "trusted" brands are heavily marketed. A second view concerning which businesses took advice was developed by A. Greene et al. They argued that there was a sense of entitlement felt by new business owners. Those who felt that they were entitled to support for their businesses were more likely to come forward for advice irrespective of whether they felt they lacked knowledge. Sector may also be more important as a predictor of take-up. Nevertheless, this leads to our first proposition, elaborated with specific reference to BL but extendable to other similar services now being developed for HGFs under the new BIS Business Coaching for Growth initiative.

Proposition 1: promotion

Promotional strategies adopted by BL will be positively related to firms' receipt of BL advisory services.

The second element of the BL process model relates to market segmentation. Some firms received basic BL advisory service – "other" assistance – while other firms were selected to receive more "intensive" assistance. What is unclear are the criteria used by BL to select firms for less or more intense support. For example, firms could have been selected to receive BL-intensive assistance where they were seen as winners, as underperforming, or where they faced some short-term strategic or managerial crisis or indeed management opportunity. Selecting winners would boost the expected value added of clients irrespective of the program's effectiveness. Selecting under-performers might result in poor outcomes even if the assistance was highly beneficial. In any case, the characteristics and situation of firms receiving "other" and "intensive" assistance are likely to differ, with different factors likely to have different impact on the firms' ability to act upon each type of assistance. Hence Proposition 2.

Proposition 2: market segmentation

Firm characteristics and operating environment will have different impacts on the probability that a firm receives "other" or "intensive" assistance.

The provision of BL assistance is envisaged to improve the management skills and capabilities of smaller firms, to enable firms to develop internal capabilities to analyze their problems and derive solutions and thereby ulti-mately improve business performance. Hence Proposition 3.

Proposition 3: outcomes

Receipt of BL assistance will, all things being equal, positively relate to improvements in small business performance.

All this involves a process of learning by the enterprise, facilitated by an atmosphere of trust and long-term supportive strong relationships. Chrisman and Ed McMullan distinguished between generic coded knowledge that is widely available and the types of tacit knowledge available from busi-ness support agencies, the latter being highly context dependent and best gained in face-to-face encounters. Such tacit knowledge is associated with "intensive" assistance, and can lead to improved business outcomes. Thus the alternative view that business support should signpost small business managers to the help they need, that the service's aim is to provide basic information but not to be involved with more intensive forms of assistance, would create a lost opportunity for learning and performance that comes from "intensive" assistance, suggesting Propositions 4.

Proposition 4: outcome differentials

Receipt of "intensive" BL assistance will, all things being equal, lead to greater improvements in small business performance than "other" assistance.

In contrast to Robert Bennett, our empirical results based on survey data from over 3000 small businesses provide a broad validation of the program theory underlying BL assistance for small firms in England during 2003, though it suggests more limited support for BL's effectiveness. The program theory underlying BL support argued first that where BL organizations were maintaining a high profile, this was likely to encourage take-up of BL support. A direct contact from BL increased the likelihood of receiving intensive assistance by 33.8 percent.

Our evidence also suggests that market segmentation is beneficial to program success. As already mentioned, the characteristics of firms differed significantly between those firms selected to receive "intensive" versus "other" assistance. BL was more likely to provide younger firms and limited liability status firms with "intensive" assistance. Firms trading for less than five years were twice as likely to receive intensive assistance than those that were over 20 years old. The greater likelihood that younger firms received assistance is consistent with them seeking advice in response to a perceived knowledge gap. The impact on those firms that were limited liability companies was smaller and may be less consistent. The perceived knowledge gap hypothesis by no means implies that those who receive advice were the least knowledgeable – simply that they faced a problem for which they perceived they needed outside help.

What does this tell us? Simply that in terms of the outcomes of BL support we find no significant effects on growth from "other" assistance but do find positive and significant employment growth effects from "intensive" assistance. This provides partial support for the assertion that BL support will lead to improvements in business growth performance and stronger support for the proposition that there would be differential outcomes from "intensive" and "other" assistance. For example, formal business planning improves the employment growth

> ... formal business planning improves the employment growth from "intensive" assistance by 3 percent

from "intensive" assistance by 3 percent. Our evidence suggests that the variation in the outcomes depends not only on the variability of advisers but also on the variability of clients.

Although BL has often been considered as having unacceptable variability, we find "intensive" assistance boosted employment by 2 percent. The fact that positive employment growth outcomes came from "intensive" assistance, even allowing for sample selection, suggests that there was an improvement in the BL network's effectiveness given that earlier studies had suggested that there were no significant growth effects from BL assistance provided over the 1996–8 period.

High-aspiration entrepreneurs – evidence from GEM

To date we have focused on business growth and in particular the incidence and characteristics of HGFs. This leaves unanswered another key research and policy question, namely: who are the individuals who are setting up these high-aspiration new business ventures? The Global Entrepreneurship Monitor (GEM) project provides evidence on this important question. We use pooled GEM UK data to provide new evidence for the UK on the extent to which it is possible to profile those individuals who report that they expect or aspire to grow as measured by levels of employment they envisage in their enterprises in five years' time.

We used the GEM question that asked about the "number of jobs anticipated after five years" as a measure of entrepreneurial ambition. Conceptually, we develop a framework, which argues that the

{ … degree of risk aversion associated with growing a business is related to a bundle of individual characteristics that mediate the probability of aspiring growth }

degree of risk aversion associated with growing a business is related to a bundle of individual characteristics that mediate the probability of aspiring growth. For example, we might imagine that the level of education, migrant status or ethnicity of an individual in the process of setting up a new business venture will impact upon the degree of risk aversion as measured by the anticipated scale of the business and the associated financial returns. More specifically, the degree of risk aversion within a group of nascent and new business entrepreneurs, measured in very simple terms by a lack of desire to move beyond self-employment, may vary according to a person's ethnic background or their stock of human capital, the latter proxied by their level of education.

An individual in the process of establishing a new business venture (nascent or new business) may aspire to be in one of three possible categories with respect to the future growth of the business: just one job (i.e. the respondent only, which we label "one" when we report the results), two to five jobs (labeled "two") and six plus jobs (labeled "six").

Our research suggests that the key variables here are the demographic characteristics of the respondent (age, sex and ethnicity), some personal attributes (household income, migrant status, employment status, education), and attitude to entrepreneurship. This final point is measured by:

■ **confidence** about the possession of start-up skills (fear of failure would prevent them starting a business)

- **perception** of the opportunities for start-up in the local area in the next six months
- whether they **knew**, were acquainted with, **an entrepreneur** in the previous 12 months
- whether they had **previously invested** in another business
- whether they had **shut a business** in the last 12 months

Entrepreneurial attitude, as measured in the GEM survey, is important for our models designed to isolate the individual characteristics associated with high ambition entrepreneurship. The extent to which people think there are good opportunities for starting a business, the level of risk that individuals might be willing to bear and individuals' perception of their own skills, knowledge and experience in business creation are critical.

Our investigation into the characteristics of high ambition entrepreneurs (i.e. in { ... characteristics of high ambition entrepreneurs: "alpha-male" } the 6+ employees category within our analysis) points to a profile that might be termed an "alpha-male". This is an important conclusion in the context of recent policy initiatives in the UK designed to increase the number of growth-oriented women-led businesses. The Strategic Framework for Women's Enterprise published in May 2003 advocates a collective, long-term approach to the development of women's enterprise. Its ambitious objective is to "significantly increase the numbers of women starting and growing businesses in the UK, to proportionately match or exceed the level achieved in the USA". However, almost all the academic literature reflects the fact that "women are not a homogenous group". It is, therefore, important to recognize that there is no one group of women, no one group of { ... no one group of "growth orientated" female entrepreneurs } female entrepreneurs and equally no one group of "growth orientated" female entrepreneurs.

Recent research on the growth orientation of women-led businesses in one English region (East of England) reached the following conclusions. First, previous labor market experience is critical in shaping the businesses which women establish. Career history is vital in providing female entrepreneurs with the skills, networks and confidence to start up a business. It also has a crucial part to play in determining the type of businesses established by women and strongly linked to this is the "high-growth" potential that they might achieve. Second, for many female entrepreneurs the motivations to start up in business are inextricably linked to "the family". The flexibility that business ownership affords is a key driver in this decision.However, these personal factors have a strong influence on the ability of such businesses to be sustainable and grow. Third, it has often been argued that female entrepreneurs tend to locate themselves in sectors where growth potential can be limited. While this is largely the case for the East of England and nationally, our research has demonstrated that there is a stock of large, women-led businesses in the East of England and Hertfordshire, operating across the production and service sectors, making an important contribution to the regional economy and demonstrating significant potential for growth. Fourth, many female entrepreneurs believe that their businesses have "high-growth" potential as opposed to being "high growth". However, few of these female entrepreneurs have any formalized plans for growth. Fifth, only a small number of the female entrepreneurs felt that their gender had a detrimental effect on these aspects of the business. Finally, in keeping with much of the academic literature, there was a general aversion by the female entrepreneurs to take on debt finance. Most of the entrepreneurs were uncomfortable with debt and few accessed external finance in either starting up in business or for any growth plans that they might have. Potential undercapitalization of these businesses at start-up is believed to have significant implications on the future growth of women-led businesses. Further, some women entrepreneurs avoided growth because they did not want to take on debt.

Hunting the snark – business support policy in a time of austerity

This short review of some of my key research projects in recent years, built upon three decades of research on small business growth, demonstrates the current challenge facing the UK economy. The process of business growth is multifaceted and complex. The interaction with publicly funded business support interventions does not always produce the expected outcomes. In the case of our evidence from the "old" BL offer in England, their support intervention provided a significant and positive outcome for employment, but not significantly for revenue and productivity. However, the era of an abundance of taxpayer support for the small businesses sector has now gone and we are increasingly looking to smarter and leaner ways of ensuring business opportunities are exploited. This may be through a combination of improving managerial capability, ensuring access to trade development opportunities, encouraging investment in R & D, IP and innovation and reducing barriers to access to finance. All of these have been shown to be positively related to various aspects of business growth. Small businesses that upgrade their absorptive capacity in these areas are more likely to achieve their growth ambitions.

Allied to this, the GEM analysis has shown that the entrepreneurial process that leads to eventual business growth is very closely related to the motivations and experiences of individual entrepreneurs. That in itself raises another challenge for policy. If we are convinced that increasing the incidence of HGFs is the foundation upon which future business support policy is built, then we must be aware that not all parts of the UK have a similar endowment of individuals who have the requisite high-growth ambition. Therefore, an important dimension of any policy must be to encourage more people to engage with the entrepreneurial process. There are two key dimensions of such a strategy: first, to encourage the movement and settlements of entrepreneurial individuals to the UK (avoiding the zero-sum game in the process) and concurrently to intensify the involvement of individuals, of whatever age, in initiatives designed to develop their entrepreneurial skill set.

Finally, we know that in the last two years in the UK, start-up businesses and small firms (i.e. those with less than 50 employees) have created on average approximately 1.6 million jobs each year. This demonstrates the importance of the thousands of entrepreneurs who even in the midst of a severe economic downturn have been able to exploit many business opportunities. The task is to build on this entrepreneurial dynamism as the economy seeks to move itself away from the trough of an economic cycle that is looking deeper and more prolonged than anyone has anticipated.

Summary

There are two key forces that fuel entrepreneurial growth and sustainable change:

1. Business support policy that can actually change the growth trajectories of individual small firms through intensive assistance
2. The role of the individual owner-manager or "entrepreneur", particularly those who adopt a high-aspiration attitude to their business venture

Action points

Business growth is a complex issue, but there are several underpinning positive actions that support it:

- Seek to improve your managerial capability in areas of weakness
- Engage in activities that will develop your entrepreneurial skill set
- Make a plan to increase your access to trade development opportunities
- Focus on encouraging R & D, increased IP and innovation within your business.
- Investigate ways of reducing barriers to sources of finance

Self-assessment tool

To what extent are you pursuing strategies to strengthen your potential for high growth? (**Tables 3.1**, **3.2**)

Table 3.1 How good is my enterprise at fueling our entrepreneurial growth?

Attribute	Never	Sometimes	Mostly	Always	Cumulative Score
We improve our managerial capability in areas of weakness	0	1	2	3	
We engage in activities to develop our entrepreneurial skill set	0	1	2	3	
We plan to increase our access to trade development opportunities	0	1	2	3	
We focus on encouraging R & D, increased IP and innovation within our business	0	1	2	3	
We invest in ways of reducing barriers to sources of finance	0	1	2	3	

Table 3.2 Benchmark scores

0–3	4–8	9–12	13–15
In the danger zone!	Some foundations that need development	Good, but room for improvement	Moving toward consistent high performance

Notes

1. National Endowment for Science, Technology and the Arts (NESTA).
2. HGF represent just over 1 percent of the total business population in the UK and just 6 percent of sub-10-employee firms.
3. Growth can be measured by the number of employees or by turnover.
4. Small firms can access public advisory support in most OECD countries, even though it is organized differently and justified on different grounds across geographies.

Further reading

Anyadike-Danes, M., Bonner, K., Hart, M. and Mason, C. M. (2009) *Mapping Firm Growth in the UK: The Economic Impact of High Growth Firms*, London: NESTA.

Bridge, S., O'Neil, K. and Martin, F. (2008) *Understanding Enterprise*, Basingstoke: Palgrave Macmillan.

Davidsson, P., Delmar, F. and Wiklund, J. (2006) *Entrepreneurship and the Growth of Firms*, London: Edward Elgar.

Global Entrepreneurship Monitor (GEM) Global and UK reports – www.gemconsortium.org.

Minitti, M. (2011) *Dynamics of Entrepreneurship*, Oxford: Oxford University Press.

Parker, S. (2004) *The Economics of Self-Employment and Entrepreneurship*: Cambridge: Cambridge University Press.

Smallbone, D. (2010) *Entrepreneurship and Public Policy*, Cheltenham: Edward Elgar Publishing.

Storey, D. (1994) *Understanding the Small Business Sector*, London: Routledge.

Wickham, P. A. (2004) *Strategic Entrepreneurship*, Harlow: Pearson Education Ltd.

CHAPTER 4

Linked Data for the 21st Century Enterprise: From Silos to Supply Chains

Christopher Brewster

Six actions for collating collective intelligence to inform and accelerate change

Introduction

We live in a digital age where the effective communication of knowledge is key to the survival and viability of companies and organizations around the world. As companies grow so do the challenges of making knowledge available to all actors.

The need for more knowledge has fuelled and been driven by the accessibility of knowledge and data over the Internet. The immense quantity has given an illusion of abundance when the reality is that most organizations of any size suffer from significant limitations on their activity due to the difficulty of obtaining the right knowledge for the right people at the right time.

{ ... right knowledge for the right people at the right time }

In this chapter, we consider the problem both internally within organizations and externally along the supply chain, and we point to solutions that are being adopted by organizations around the world centering on "Semantic Technologies". We present some of the highlights of semantic technologies and conclude with a future vision that might have alleviated some of the problems associated with the June 2011 *E. coli* outbreak in Germany and its impact on Spanish cucumber suppliers.

Knowledge silos

All organizations develop knowledge silos. As organizations grow, they create different departments, different sections, and naturally people specialize or are hired with expertise in a particular area. Little by little communication between the different departments becomes more difficult.

As organizations move from being start-ups, with five–ten people often working together in one space, to become fully fledged companies with separate departments (development or design, manufacturing, sales, HR, finance, etc.), different bodies of knowledge develop within each department. Finance may know all about the financial state of an organization but not know or understand the new products being developed. The IT department does not understand the needs of the research department. These are typical everyday occurrences in all organizations above a certain size, exacerbated by and made obvious when we consider that most organizations run very large numbers of separate databases.[1]

{ ... different bodies of knowledge within each department }

{ ... exacerbated by large numbers of separate databases }

Communication between departments becomes fossilized in certain specific channels fitting in with defined requirements (which probably made sense originally but are often too constrained today). So typically a particular form is developed to request a specific piece of information or requisition an item. If the information or item falls outside the scope originally foreseen, the systems break down. In an organization with an effective management culture, a telephone call is made and everything is sorted out. In an organization with sclerotic or fossilized structures, getting round such communication bottlenecks can be very time consuming and expensive.

Examples of such knowledge silos exist all around us. A well-known aeronautics company was organized around three traditional departments – design, manufacturing and sales. While design designed, manufacturing would redesign and then manufacture, and then finally sales would sell but sometimes also redesign and manufacture as well. No department would receive appropriate feedback from another as to the suitability of the process they were responsible for.

In the life sciences, one of the major challenges is the large number of laboratories a pharmaceutical company has around the world, and the many different concurrent areas of research being undertaken. Historically, there would occur frequent duplication of effort, or else research that could have given insights was missed because of lack of communication between research teams.[2] This lack of communication has continued to be true until very recently because in spite of an impressive collection of public and shared databases, both of research literature (Pubmed) and of genetic and molecular results (SwissProt, Uniprot, etc.), there was no way to undertake federated queries across data sets.

$\left\{\right.$ ... no way to undertake federated queries across data sets $\left.\right\}$

A very similar phenomenon occurs with the problem of finding who the experts are in an organization. Experts live in their specific subdepartment. Few people know who the experts are in a specific area of knowledge beyond those who collaborate with those experts. It is thus often very hard to find out who knows what in an organization of any significant size. As organizations grow, the problem becomes ever worse. As a great deal of knowledge is undefined, procedural or otherwise tacit, the challenge is magnified.

There are two aspects to this situation. One concerns the mere absence of communication or opportunities for communication. For example, if one is having trouble with the marketing department promoting one's new product (idea, project, event, etc.), it does not follow that one would ask the colleague next door how to solve the problem – as one is typically unaware that they have the necessary skill, experience, contacts, etc. to do so. How could one imagine that the laboratory in Copenhagen is also working on molecule XYZ – but for its use in cardiovascular disease rather than toward one's interest in diabetes? Most organizations try to address this concern with "away days", or "off-site" meetings or other forms of informal gatherings. There is plenty of evidence that informal gatherings lead to serendipitous discovery of solutions to long-standing problems. However, this approach is very hit and miss.

The second challenge concerns the lack of commonality of language. In large complex manufacturing companies, this is very evident in the different labels, tags or names applied to the same object depending on whether it is being referred to by engineering, sales or finance. The same is true in many other areas. Breast cancer specialists describe the same mammogram with different terminology in different hospitals. Confusingly the reverse is also true: life science researchers refer to different entities by the name *gene*, including *DNA sequence, protein, RNA sequence, an allele*. This means, in practice, that even if communication channels exist, knowledge is not shared because it comes under a different heading, a different category, a different label.

{ ... in practice, knowledge comes under different headings, categories, labels }

So far, we have considered the problems mostly from the perspective of communication and knowledge-sharing within a given organization. The problems described are compounded when we consider complex supply chains.

Supply chains

Modern industrial society is highly dependent on complex supply chains, which cross national boundaries, multiple human languages and a myriad of different industrial processes and human cultures. Supply chains are prime examples of structures that suffer from knowledge loss. In principle it is an extraordinary achievement that supply chains work at all given the potential for "Chinese whispers", that is, for the loss of information as it is transferred across or along the chain.

There are many inherent difficulties in sharing knowledge along the supply chain. Consider the many different actors, who all have different priorities and different business models. These actors often come from very different cultures and even when the language is common, breakdowns can occur and have catastrophic results. Simple example: the Mars Orbiter broke up while orbiting Mars in 1999 due to outsourced software that had been written using metric measuring units rather than imperial units which NASA used at the time.

The issue, just as within a single organization, is not only that different actors have different objectives and languages but also that at a purely technical level they are using different databases, with different schemas, and different ways of representing their corner of the universe. Additionally, very often relevant data is not preserved in a manner that allows for subsequent processing and analysis, such as, by recording data in unstructured formats such as PDF or MS Word, such as many fault reports in manufacturing companies are written in MS Word and then saved as PDF documents in a database. A large proportion of universities provide descriptions of their taught courses as PDF documents. In both cases, relatively structured data is made inaccessible as a consequence of technical choices.

If we look back historically to long supply chains like the Silk Road bringing silk and spices to Europe in the Middle Ages, effective supply chains have always required and provided for a transfer of knowledge in both directions (upstream and downstream). But this can be slow. It has sometimes taken decades or centuries for technologies and know-how to spread. Thus the Romans were convinced that silk came from trees.

We now live in a digital age where effective communication of knowledge is essential and possible. We cannot, indeed we should not, wait upon mechanisms for the exchange of information that depend on word of mouth or serendipitous encounters.

In traditional supply chains, each actor only has to talk to their immediate supplier and customer – hence the metaphor of a chain with clear links with

{ ... supply chains – many pressures to increase the flow of data and knowledge }

a trajectory that flows from raw material to end user. This is no longer the case. Not only are chains far more complex, with multiple interconnected players, but also there are many pressures to increase the flow of data and knowledge along the whole supply chain. There are:

- Regulatory pressures for quality or health reasons (Can you as a retailer guarantee the toy manufacturer has not used lead paint?)

- Consumer pressures for ethical or environmental reasons (Is your football manufactured using child labor?)

- Purely commercial pressures where actors need greater information about the origins or final destinations of products (Can you guarantee that that Hermes bag is not reaching the local flea market?)

Furthermore actors across the supply chain need more data and knowledge for their own commercial purposes. Upstream actors (e.g. food producers) need to understand more effectively the behavior, needs and choices of downstream actors (e.g. food consumers). Until now most knowledge has flowed downstream, that is, people have wanted to know who produced a specific product. Historically few producers have really known who consumed their product. Not much knowledge has flowed upstream. Yet increasingly, pressure is rising to integrate data and knowledge given the additional need for product differentiation as well as for rapid responses and greater flexibility in the supply chain. In the food supply chain, for example, there are constant unpredictable disruptive events (crop failures, floods, etc.) and sudden changes in product demands, which need much more agile responsiveness from all actors involved in the supply web. With change spreading ever more rapidly and the increased transparency of our global communication system, availability of correct and appropriate information is more essential than ever for effective operations but also for commercial survival.

Integrating data from different sources in different formats is a substantial challenge and this is where Semantic Technologies are playing an increasingly important role.

Semantic technologies and data integration

The original World Wide Web, the one most of us still use today, whether it is the public incarnation or on a company internal intranet, consists of a vast collection of documents linked together – some of which may be generated automatically from underlying databases. We navigate this structure either by using search engines like Google or by following links from one document to another. This Web is designed for human consumption. Machines to a large extent cannot process all that vast collection of information out there apart from providing an index. Complex questions cannot be answered except through substantial human effort. Even though many web pages are generated from information in databases, the underlying data is largely inaccessible for reuse by a wider audience.

> { The original World Wide Web – a vast collection of documents linked together }

In our document-centric World Wide Web world, we are able to ask questions such as:

- Show me all documents with the words "product recall" or "10 megapixel digital camera"
- Show me all documents with the words "E. coli" and "cucumber" in them

We cannot, however, ask questions like:

- Show me all published articles containing the words "business process" written by faculty in this institution who teach operations management to MBA students.
- Show me reports written in the last six months by members of the new widget development team

Similarly with databases, one can request a report showing:

- A list of all sales made between May 1 and June 30
- All employees employed by the admin department
- All items of expenses charged to Tom Brown

Sadly we cannot ask for reports that:

- List all dentists within 10km who are members of the Royal College of Surgeons and have a free slot next Friday
- List all parts that have had failures used in engine XYZ designed by Tom Brown and sold to client ABC
- Identify all bands from the city of Manchester whose music type is rock and whose date of formation is before 2003

To summarize:

- There are (too) many documents (creating infosmog)
- Documents are designed for humans to read, not for machines to process
- Where data exists, it lies across many databases *within* the organization
- Data also often lies across many databases *across* many organizations

To address these limitations, the concept of the Semantic Web was proposed by Tim Berners-Lee, Jim Hendler and Ora Lassila at the end of the 1990s. The fundamental idea is to create a "web of data", of machine-readable data that sits in parallel to the "web of documents" which already exists.

> … infosmog necessitates a Semantic Web: a "web of data" parallel to the "web of documents"

Berners-Lee's vision is a world where vast quantities of data are published both by the public and internally in organizations, where the format follows certain standard rules, and uses a variety of standard vocabularies or "ontologies", and where different, disparate data can be interlinked to answer questions and to connect both people and knowledge in a manner that was impossible before.

Semantic Web technology consists of a set of technologies each of which are relatively simple, but which in combination prove to be extremely powerful. There are several layers which build on each other and of these the most central are[3]:

1. Objects in the world, whether physical or abstract, have unique identifiers similar to the "name" of a web page, that is, the long address beginning "http:// ...". These identifiers (technically called "Uniform Resource Identifier" or URIs) can be created by anyone so they do not depend upon a centralized database. This is an adaptation of the traditional web page addresses (Uniform Resource Locators or URLs) and is equivalent to proper names for things and people but slightly more systematic and intended to be machine-readable.

2. Statements about the world are made using "triples" such as *London – IsCapitalOf – United Kingdom* where each element in the triple would be identified by a unique identifier (URI). This is equivalent to the everyday idea of simple sentences or statements such as "London is the capital of the United Kingdom". Triples have "subjects", "objects" and "predicates".

3. The triples are expressed in a formal model (the "Resource Description Framework" or RDF) in a machine-readable syntax (of which there are a number, the most commonly used being RDF XML). RDF provides mechanisms to say some things are of certain types. Closely related is the RDF Schema (RDFS), which provides the formal rules so as to define classes and express the concept of "subjects", "objects" and "predicates" that make up a triple. Together RDF and RDFS allow one to express simple taxonomies about the world.

4. Ontologies or formal vocabularies allow more complex statements about the world. One can define formally classes and properties of classes. Ontologies are usually expressed in RDFS or the more formally rich "Web Ontology Language" (OWL). Ontologies allows logical conclusions to be drawn (inference) ranging from the relatively simple (if A isMarriedTo B, then B isMarriedTo A) to the more complex (if A isMemberOf ProjectB, and C isMemberOf ProjectB, then A knows C). There are a great many ontologies that have been established and little by little a considerable number are becoming recognized as *de facto* "standards". One of the most widely used of such ontologies, and one of the most commercially significant, is the "Good Relations" ontology developed by Martin Hepp for the needs of e-commerce.

5. SPARQL is the query language that enables queries to be posed to collections of triples. This is key in facilitating the integration of data from multiple sources.

This stack of technologies, together with a number of others, allows individuals and organizations to publish, either internally or publicly, sets of data. These data sets can be accessed across the Internet (just as one would with a web page), and then integrated with other data, whether in-house or from yet other external sources. All this was technically possible quite rapidly after Tim Berners-Lee's original proposals, but for a certain period of time only limited data was available with relatively restricted access. This all changed with an explosion of "linked data" since 2007.

Open knowledge: linked data

Semantic technologies cannot not have an impact on business and society and on the world in general unless there is sufficient uptake and adoption. A sufficient number of people need to be using the technologies and above all publishing data so that the technology is useful. To further this end, Berners-Lee proposed a set of principles to facilitate the publishing of data on the Web so that a global data space would be created, the so-called Linked Data principles. Linked Data is data published on the Web that "is machine-readable, its meaning is explicitly defined, it is linked to other external data sets, and can in turn be linked to from external data sets".[4] Ordinary links in web pages allow different websites to be connected. Links in Linked Data allow formal statements to be made that link otherwise arbitrary things in the world (See Figure 4.1).

Following the declaration of the principles, there has been an explosion of data available on the Web. The Linking Open Data project brought researchers, universities and small companies together. These were quickly followed by large organizations such as the BBC, Thompson Reuters and the Library of Congress. One of the key developments was the transformation of the publicly edited Wikipedia into a structured set of data called Dbpedia (http://dbpedia.org/). This has acted as a central hub to which many other data sets link, a dizzying array of different types of data mostly freely available for organizations and people to use. Data has been added concerning geographic locations, scientific publications, music, programs on television and radio, all kinds of life science data, including proteins, genes, metabolic pathways, drugs and clinical trials, political and historical data and statistical and census data.

This complex interlinked "cloud of data" provides an immensely rich resource for all { "cloud of data" "data.gov" "data.gov.uk" } types of organizations to integrate with their own data, as well as to provide examples for others to follow. Although the data on the "linked data cloud"

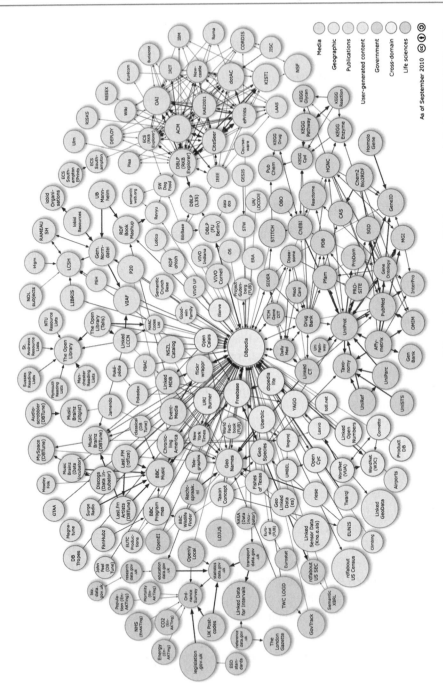

Figure 4.1   Richard Cygniaks's cloud diagram of linked data (http://richard.cyganiak.de/2007/10/lod/)

is mostly open for use by anyone, there are plenty of organizations that offer their data for free when used non commercially, and only charge for commercial usage (e.g. musicbrainz). The open knowledge provided in the "cloud of data" has had substantial impacts in persuading organizations, especially governments, to make more data publicly available in machine-readable formats. The most important initiatives in this regard have been efforts by the UK and US governments to make large quantities of government data available to the wider public for both social and business purposes. This has resulted in the "data.gov" and "data.gov.uk" websites where data has been made available not just in standard database formats (cvs) but also as linked data formats (in RDF) enabling its use and integration in all kinds of projects both commercial and noncommercial projects.

While the development of the linked data cloud is an extraordinary achievement, in reality it is only one step, one part of the wider application of semantic technologies. We now turn to some examples of their application in practice.

Examples in practice

The obvious question with the arrival of new technologies, of new ways of doing things, is whether there has been any uptake of these innovations. Like all innovations that demand a different way of thinking about the world, uptake has initially been slow but has seen a tremendous growth in the period 2007–11. The first users of any scale were pharmaceutical companies. They not only had the necessary resources but also recognized the economic imperative of increasing the flow of knowledge both internally within their organizations and by interacting externally with the very large number of publicly developed databases.

- Domain: health/pharmaceutical
  - Ely Lily uses SW technology for prioritizing drug discovery targets.
  - PharmaSURVEYOR uses SW technology to compose safer drug regimes for patients, to limit drug side effects and interactions. This uses ontologies to specify medical conditions and integrates with data from multiple databases.
- Domain: space exploration
  - NASA uses SW technology for expertise location. Information about employees' work history, affiliation, skills and teams they have worked in is collected by NASA in multiple databases. Identifying the right individual/skill/work history combination has

been revolutionized by the POPS system (developed by Clark and Parsia LLC).

- Domain: media and web publishing
  - ☐ The BBC uses SW and LD technologies to link all its programs, presenters and artists so that website users can easily find what other programs the person "David Attenborough" participates in. Furthermore, all music data is imported directly from the crowd-sourced Musicbrainz website as RDF. Similarly, BBC Nature has URIs for every species it is interested in and aggregates data from a number of external sources (Wikipedia, WWF's Wildfinder, IUCN, etc.). The most recent use of this technology is the sports domain, applying what they call "dynamic semantic publishing", which uses "linked data technology to automate the aggregation, publishing and repurposing of interrelated content objects according to an ontological domain-modeled information architecture".[5] This has been used for the World Cup in 2010 and will be used for the London Olympics 2012.

- Domain: government services
  - ☐ As mentioned previously, the UK government has released a huge amount of data in standard formats on its data.gov.uk website. This was followed by the release of a large amount of geographical data from the Ordinance Survey, for free and in RDF format. These initiatives have spawned a mini industry of applications using the data for creative and commercial ends. For example, applications based on this data include one that compares all cars and their fuel consumption costs http://uk-car-fuel-emissions.findthebest.com/) and another that enables school choices to be based on public data (http://schoolscout.co.uk/pg/customsearch/search).
  - ☐ The Amsterdam Fire Department uses SW and LD technologies to manage fire fighting incidents, by pulling information from a number of different data sources in partner organizations.

- Domain: web security
  - ☐ Garlik.com uses SW technologies to integrate vast quantities of data about people and the data available about them on the Web so as to provide services to protect people's privacy and online security. Semantic technologies enable the integration and reasoning over a very large body of data.

- Domain: e-commerce
  - ☐ The Good Relations Ontology developed by Martin Hepp has enabled a paradigm shift in the way e-commerce websites present their products. Websites using the Good Relations Ontology to mark up their products allow Google, Yahoo and other search engines to display their

products in a much more effective manner. Bestbuy.com had a 30 percent increase in website traffic and a corresponding increase in sales.

The importance of these examples (and there are many others) is exemplified by the fact that Google, Bing and Yahoo recently collaborated to establish a new semantic standard (available at schema.org) for website markup so as to further facilitate the integration of information across the Web at a *data* level rather than merely at the level of web pages read by human beings as has been the case up till now.

The case of the cucumber

In late May, early June 2011, there occurred a major *E. coli* outbreak in the Hamburg area of Germany. Nearly 40 people died and over 3000 people were infected some with severe symptoms. The outbreak was initially linked back to organic cucumbers, tomatoes and lettuce imported from Spain. These were blamed for carrying the E. coli virus. The consequences were disastrous for Spanish farmers who lost tens of millions of Euros in crops that no one wanted to buy. When that line of inquiry was proved wrong, the outbreak was tracked to contaminated bean sprouts produced locally in a farm in Germany. But that too proved incorrect. At the time of writing, the ultimate source of the virus has not been conclusively identified.

The management of epidemic outbreaks like these depends on the rapid collection of data from a variety of sources – patients/victims, retailers, transporters, wholesalers and food producers to name only the obvious. In effect everyone on the food supply chain is implicated as a possible source of the problem.

We can envisage an alternative scenario to that which played out. Let us imagine that all actors along the supply chain were part of the "web of data", of the Semantic Web. After all, the data was there in one form or another. Only the fact that the data silos, the databases, cannot talk to each other prevented a much more sophisticated and rapid handling of the outbreak. We will ignore issues of privacy and data ownership for the present in the following scenario. The complex queries that needed to be posed included:

1. Which cucumbers did persons P_0 ... P_n buy, from which retailers, and where did the retailers obtain them from, using what logistics chain, and from which farm did they originate?
2. What were the growing conditions?
3. Who do P_0 ... P_n have personal contact with?

This data could have been accessed; perhaps we could even postulate that it would have been accessed had the appropriate political will existed. What we do know is that:

- The persons $P_0 \ldots P_n$ were the victims. We know this from the hospital records.

- The victims purchases could have, at least to some extent, been identified from their banking activity, that is, one could have linked bank cards to purchase receipts to retailers and time and location of purchase.

- Cucumber source (retailer purchasing/ordering datasets) could have been identified.

- Journey of cucumbers (truck and logistics data + sensors) could have been established.

- The original farms (based on truck collection, purchase/sales receipts) could have been identified.

- Circle of contacts of $P_0 \ldots P_n$ (social media, Facebook, Twitter, phone records) could have been mapped.

The technologies already exist to facilitate much of this chain of (potentially) linked data. Vocabularies/Ontologies exist to represent individuals (FOAF – Friend of a Friend), health records and to integrate these with clinical results, disease and treatments (e.g. Translational Medicine Ontology), financial transactions (XBRL, Finance Ontology), geographical and logistics data (Geonames Ontology, Logistics Ontology – several others), social networks (FOAF, SIOC Ontology), and more. All of these and many other relevant formal vocabularies (ontologies) exist that would allow data from different actors to be linked together, to enable data to be integrated and for federated queries to be posed, so necessary if we are to meaningfully share knowledge.

The challenge is to actually deploy these technologies in a manner that is beneficial to wider society and business.

{ ... challenge: to actually deploy these technologies to wider society and business }

Like all technologies there will be early adopters who reap early benefits and late adopters who will benefit far less from the power of these tools. Above all, we must recognize that there is inevitable resistance when new technologies arise that have the potential to radically transform the way people collaborate and do business.[6]

Ready for change: semantic technologies

The question arises as to whether a given organization should adopt these technologies. The more appropriate question is whether a company or organization can afford not to. Given the ever growing complexity of our society and the mechanisms by which we collaborate, share knowledge and the implications of failure not to do so, **now** is not early enough to retool our knowledge-sharing technologies.

If your organization has more than a dozen employees, if you depend on knowledge and data as a key competitive advantage in the operation of your business, if you have trouble finding the expert in your company for a particular question or task, if you need to track the performance of products across divisions, if you live in the digital age, then semantic technologies are a must for the survival and future viability of your company let alone its growth.

{ … semantic technologies are a must for the survival and future viability of your company let alone its growth }

Summary

There are six actions for collating collective intelligence to inform and accelerate change:

1. Recognizing the importance of effective communication of knowledge
2. Using standard vocabularies
3. Publishing data using Semantic Web technologies
4. Integrating data with the linked data cloud
5. Increasing the flow of knowledge
6. Adopting semantic technologies as early as possible

Action points

- Ensure your organization recognizes that the effective communication of knowledge is key to the survival and viability of companies and organizations around the world.

- Adopt the usage of standard vocabularies so that different, disparate data can be linked to answer questions and to connect people and knowledge in a manner that was impossible before.

- Assess how Semantic Web technologies will allow your organization to publish data for access across the Internet and for integration with other data sets, whether in-house or from other external sources.

- Explore how the development of the linked data cloud might provide a rich resource to integrate with your own organization's data.

- Consider the economic imperative of increasing the flow of knowledge both internally within your organization and externally with the very large number of publicly developed databases.

- Aspire to be an early adopter of these technologies, in order to reap the early benefits.

Self-assessment tool

To what extent is your organization making use of semantic technologies to improve collaboration and information sharing? (**Tables 4.1, 4.2**)

Table 4.1 How good is my organization at collating our collective intelligence?

Attribute	Never	Sometimes	Mostly	Always	Cumulative Score
We integrate information sources through machine-readable linked data sets	0	1	2	3	
We use linked data to share knowledge across silos	0	1	2	3	
We use linked data to improve supply chain efficiency	0	1	2	3	
We use linked data to improve data integration	0	1	2	3	
We use linked data to increase the flow of knowledge	0	1	2	3	

Table 4.2 Benchmark scores

0–3	4–8	9–12	13–15
In the danger zone!	Some foundations that need development	Good, but room for improvement	Moving toward consistent high performance

Notes

1. Microsoft SQL Server clients have on average over 1700 databases per company (http://www.scribd.com/doc/47442610/oracle-vs-sql-server).
2. The film *Extraordinary Measures* about the search for a drug that would cure the fatal infant disease Pompe describes this clearly.
3. There are other layers of the technology about which further details can be found in the suggested readings at the end of this chapter.
4. Bizer, Heath and Berners-Lee, 2009.
5. J. P. Rayfield (2011) Dynamic Semantic Publishing, Sport and the Olympics at the BBC, SemTech London and http://www.bbc.co.uk/blogs/bbcinternet/2010/07/bbc_news_websites_content_mana.html.
6. This fictional E. coli scenario is very similar to actually implemented work on influenza (cf. Semantic Web Methodologies Provide Access to FLU Data Without Getting You Sick of Searching, Timothy Lebo and Joanne Luciano, AMIA, 2011).

Further reading

On silos

The Silo Effect and Other Productivity Killers, available at http://www.onpreinit.com/2009/10/business-silo-effect-it-software.html.

Bundred, S. (2006) "Solutions to Silos: Joining Up Knowledge", *Public Money & Management*, 26(2), pp. 125–30.

On semantic technologies and linked data

An extensive list of case studies can be found here: http://www.w3.org/2001/sw/sweo/public/UseCases/ and here: http://logd.tw.rpi.edu/.

Berners-Lee, T., Hendler, J. and Lassila, O. (2001) "The Semantic Web", *Scientific American*, May, pp. 30–7.

Bizer, C., Heath, T. and Berners-Lee, T. (2009) "Linked Data – The Story So Far", *International Journal on Semantic Web and Information Systems*, 5(3), pp. 1–22.

Gardner, S. P. (2005) "Ontologies and Semantic Data Integration, *Drug Discovery Today*, 10, pp. 1001–7.

On the E. coli outbreak

Der Spiegel (in English) available at http://www.spiegel.de/international/europe/0,1518,768534,00.html.

CHAPTER 5

Collaborative Decision-Making: Mapping Group Knowledge

Duncan Shaw

Seven steps to collaborative decision-making for robust, innovative, broadly owned change

Introduction

Decisions drive change and change evokes decisions, a seesaw of causality which is a hallmark of leadership.

This chapter focuses on a mechanism for collaborative decision-making, for making shared, robustly defended, broadly considered decisions particularly relevant in mission critical, ambiguous and fast-changing situations.

Many ask: how do we make sure we are making robust decisions in our business? More

{ ... robust decisions consider multiple stakeholders, cause important changes }

specifically, how do we ensure that we consider the multiple perspectives and legitimate issues that stakeholders represent, particularly in mission-critical decision contexts? By inference such decisions almost always cause important changes, and therefore demand rigor and collaboration.

One approach that has been widely adopted in order to ensure this has been to engage in group brainstorming. Extensively deployed throughout organiza-

$$\left\{ \quad \text{... group brainstorming is particularly prevalent in the context of top teams} \quad \right\}$$

tions, this approach has been particularly prevalent in the context of top teams that have sought to work collaboratively and creatively to develop their organization's strategy.[1]

But does it work – does brainstorming lead to more robust decisions?

Our research, on which this chapter is based, has been conducted during authentic strategy development workshops within large organizations. During these sessions, groups of individuals volunteered ideas through brainstorming sessions and built collaborative "causal maps". Using supporting software packages, we subsequently studied the extent to which brainstorming elicits individual contributions and in so doing releases the creativity of the team and encourages consideration of a wider range of issues in more detail.

We concentrated our research on what the literature describes as two-staged brainstorming sessions. The first stage consisted of a quasi-traditional brainstorming session where individuals are invited to present and record ideas, but to initially hold them to themselves. The second stage then asks participants to share all ideas in an open forum and to begin to make linkages. During this second stage, team members have an opportunity to "piggyback" off other people's ideas before being invited to identify causal links in order to build a causal map.

Our research findings suggest that ideas shared through piggybacking are often more highly creative and sometimes more unique to the group than those proposed individually from the start. This approach also provides greater opportunities for collaborative working and individual learning as participants have time to reflect on other people's perspectives and discuss accordingly. We found that using other people's views to stimulate their own thinking helped participants to think beyond the previous limits of their own concepts. Additionally, we found that while the facilitator can adopt a combination of four approaches for structuring and linking the causal map, participants also have preferences for their own structuring. In fact, participants tend to structure and link views with which they are familiar, and avoid linking views with which they are less familiar. Finally we found that these brainstorming events provide good opportunities for both personal and collective learning.

Group workshops are widely used to enable experts to share their knowledge in pursuit of an agreed solution to tackle a problem. That problem might be so complex that a range of experts are needed because they individually bring unique knowledge to inform the action plan, which they collectively are charged to develop. There are several methodologies for facilitating the process of agreeing to an action plan from such group workshops, for helping groups build an appreciation of the relevant issues. Techniques include brainstorming of ideas, voting on options, scenario development and causal mapping.

This chapter focuses on exploring how participants can best share views in a more structured brainstorm format. We concentrate on brainstorming as an activity because it is so central to all methods used in group workshops.

The value of brainstorming sessions

Despite the widespread use of manual workshops (i.e. those that rely on flip-charts and pens or their equivalents) and the rising use of software-supported brainstorming workshops, little attempt has been made to evaluate the effectiveness of such sessions by using empirical data (Finlay, 1998). While there has been widespread use of the brainstorming process as a means of capturing views from a group, no studies have evaluated whether brainstorming is effective, or how it can be improved. There has, however, been a proliferation of studies that evaluate brainstorming from a more positivistic research tradition – from the so-called narrow-band perspective (Eden, 1995). Evaluation by narrow-banders has been based on counting the number of ideas shared by participants and assessing the quality of those ideas (e.g. Dennis et al., 1997; Pinsonneault et al., 1999). By contrast, "wide-band" researchers, (among whom we count ourselves), facilitators and often workshop participants do not prioritize such measures of quantity and quality. After all, are 100 ideas necessarily better than 50 ideas? And what is the measure of a high quality idea? Arguably, to enable the most appropriate result to be generated, and for participants to believe that this is the case, the discussion, negotiation and generation of ideas need to be as inclusive as possible of the entire situation. Wide-band brainstorm evaluation places more importance on the extent to which participants share thoughts on a *variety* of aspects surrounding the problem or issue being considered. They argue that this is necessary to ensure that the outcome of the brainstorming session takes into account the system as a whole. This is an aspect that has not been measured by previous brainstorming research.

Causal mapping of brainstormed ideas

Our research approached the subject of brainstorming as a mechanism for effective decision-making. We started from the wide-band perspective that it is important to improve the process of group work and group decision-making in order to achieve the overall aims of such an intervention. Two major aims of wide-band methods are:

1. To effectively mobilize participants' thinking in order to generate an outcome which is optimally appropriate for the situation while

2. To concurrently develop the participants' cognitive and emotional commitment to that outcome

Our research concludes that the aims of wide-banders can be fulfilled through suitable, rational and robust processes (Checkland, 2001; Friend, 2001; Eden and Ackermann, 1998). Brainstorming is one way of helping participants to appreciate the problem by having an opportunity to contribute views and expand upon them in order to understand the wider context.

{ ... contribute views to understand the wider context, and to grow commitment }

By providing a sensible process that develops sensible outcomes the group members can show and grow their commitment to the implementation of the outcome.

Example of a wide-band approach: the computer-facilitated brainstorming workshop

In a computer-supported brainstorming workshop, computer technology assists the group to share, capture and display views. It also allows the group to vote on the optional ideas that are generated through the process.

For those who have not experienced such a brainstorming environment, walking into a typical room the participant would see:

- Eight to ten laptop computers arranged in a horseshoe with participants to the session inputting with these computers. These would be running a networked brainstorming-type software
- A projector displaying a causal map on a very large projection screen
- A facilitator sitting facing the group and operating two computers (typically one as a back-up)

In such a workshop, normally six to 20 participants use computers to share their knowledge, which in turn creates and populates the causal map. During the brainstorm, participants type their knowledge, views and opinions (in the form of "contributions", phrases consisting of four to ten words in length) into their own networked computer (Eden and Ackermann, 1998). The facilitator, on their own computer screen, moves the participants' views into content-related clusters and projects those clusters onto a public screen for all the participants to read and critique. Participants, stimulated by the multiplicity of ideas, are invited to type in more views and make causal links between the contributions (Shaw et al., 2003). Throughout the session, the role of the facilitator is to encourage and funnel group discussion around the key issue(s) represented on the map. The ensuing discussion will aim to surface more views, add links and refine the structure of the emerging map.

The obvious end product of this collaborative knowledge-sharing will be a structured causal map that reflects the participants' knowledge of the situation.

{ ... end-product: a structured causal map of participants' knowledge of the situation }

With this participants can begin to consider which actions should be implemented within the organization. Two less obvious but probably more valuable by-products of such a session are:

1. The wider and deeper understanding that is gained by all participants into the situation in question

2. The productive and purposeful network of participants that is reinforced by working through a decision in this collaborative manner

This process additionally allows participants to explore the effects of various optional courses of action that could be implemented (Eden and Ackermann, 2001). By enabling the groups to build and negotiate a feasible action plan (and to understand the benefits that could be gained from implementation of the same) the facilitator aims for the group to attain greater commitment to implementation.

Methodology

The gathering formats – how brainstormed ideas are gathered

In our research we contrast three formats for gathering the ideas that create causal maps:

1. *The traditional gathering*: participants are presented with one issue and invited to type ideas into their console. These contributions are automatically and immediately displayed on a public screen. Causal maps are thus created and continually updated with every new contribution that is keyed in. Participants can also contribute causal links at any time given the real-time visibility of all contributions.

2. *The incubated gathering*: this format occurs in two phases. In the first phase, the public screen is switched off (though the facilitator sees all entries) while participants type contributions into their individual consoles. This is also called the "blind session" because participants can only see their own contributions and can only causally link those ideas. In the second phase, during what is referred to as the "piggybacking session", the public screen is switched on for participants to read all contributions, including those shared by other people. Participants are then encouraged to use someone else's contribution to stimulate their own thinking on the issues and to identify new causal links (Paulus et al., 1995).

3. *The multiple stimuli gathering*: participants are given up to ten different stimuli or issues on which to make contributions. The aim here is to help the group converge on themes on which they share knowledge. The facilitator has the option to not update the public screen with new contributions as they are entered, so causal linking might not be automatically encouraged so as to focus contributions toward the different stimuli.

Each format offers different benefits. These include:

- Extending the range of themes that participants consider during the incubated gathering
- Providing insight into participants' preferences for how they link contributions
- Understanding how personal and collective learning occurs

Let us elaborate.

Extending the range of themes through piggybacking

To appreciate the breadth of issues that a brainstorming session might include, we investigated the extent to which each of the three gathering formats affected the ability of participants to share contributions to a wide range of issues (Shaw, 2002). Results of this work (reproduced in **Table 5.1**) indicate that the incubated gathering format was better at enabling { ... incubated gathering was better at enabling contributions to broader themes }

Table 5.1 The number of group themes in different formats

	Incubated	Traditional	Multiple stimuli
Maximum number of group themes	15	11	6
Average number of group themes per gathering	11.6	6.7	5.3

participants to make contributions to a broader range (maximum and average) of themes than the traditional and the multiple stimuli gatherings formats.

From this result, we concluded that if the main aim of the facilitator is to reveal in participants a wide range of ideas, it would be better to use the incubated gathering format. By implication, the outcome of such a discussion is likely to be more actionable as the group will have considered the issues, constraints and consequences more broadly and will have had the opportunity to create greater commitment to application.

Of particular importance was the role played by the piggybacking second phase of the session. These allowed individuals to contribute ideas on issues that they had previously not considered. It came as a pleasant surprise that piggybacked contributions were not merely a rewording of existing contributions; they were new contributions, relative to the individual consoles, and added to the wider group's bank of contributions:

- 64.6 percent of all piggybacked contributions were to **different themes**, that is, comments to ideas made by others. $\Big\{$ ... different themes; themes that were new; really innovative $\Big\}$

- 43.1 percent of all piggybacked contributions were to **themes that were new**, that is, they had not been considered by the group.

- 19.4 percent of all piggybacked contributions were **really innovative** (radically new and relevant within the theme), that is, contributors had thought about an issue in a way that the group had never done so before, maybe through redefining the issue or through considering it from a new perspective (e.g. from a customer's rather than a supplier's perspective)

These results suggest that it is the piggybacking session per se that might be very useful to some group members in stimulating contributions and linkages that either they had not realized were relevant to the problem, or on themes that they had simply forgotten or never before considered. This might suggest that the convergence of their own knowledge with other people's contributions stimulated different, new and really innovative reflections (Pinsonneault et al., 1999; Dennis et al., 1997). By *integrating* (Grise and Gallupe, 1999) these issues into their consideration of an issue, that possible outcome was more informed.

The facilitators' and participants' approaches for linking contributions

Causal linking is done by both the facilitator and the participants. This element of the work sought to explore the approaches both parties adopted in making their causal linking.

Facilitators' approaches for linking contributions

Near the start of every workshop, participants are often unaccustomed to identifying and making causal relationships. Part of the facilitator's role is then to mentor the group through the process, explaining what a causal link is, showing how to enter the link through the computer and "teaching them" how to identify links. To this end, facilitators tend to adopt one of the four approaches to linking.

1. *Interpreting*: the facilitator listens to the group discussion and makes causal links based on his or her interpretation of that discussion. To validate their own linking, the facilitator draws the participants back to the public screen to confirm that the causal relationships he or she has made are valid, that is, that they have linked the contributions correctly.

2. *Responsive*: group members control their navigation of the issues as they wish. Links are explicitly suggested to the facilitator who responds by entering them into the group map.

3. *Directing*: the facilitator focuses the participants' navigation of the map by directing discussion to particular underdeveloped issues. This encourages the identification of links by participants.

4. *Driving*: the facilitator makes causal links without lengthy consultation with the group members. The facilitator expects participants to validate the links and voice objection if they make an incorrect link; otherwise the facilitator assumes that their links are correct. This method is best explained through the statement from one facilitator: "If I am wrong then tell me."

The facilitator uses these methods at different stages in a gathering. *Interpreting* may be used when participants are inexperienced at linking, so while participants discuss the issues the facilitator will link the contributions based on their discussion so that through this participants can learn about the linking process. Also in the early stages of a discussion the *responsive* approach might be used, as participants refer to the screen and suggest the linking of particular contributions. As the session progresses and the clusters become much more linked (or participants are more able to identify links themselves) the facilitator moves into *directing* and begins to focus the group on underdeveloped issues. When the facilitator feels that the group should be moving on, he or she might adopt *driving*, using their own knowledge of the situation (and their own interpretation of the contributions) to inform the linking of contributions that have yet to be linked.

In addition to the facilitator-entered links, participants also share links. On an average, 43 links were made by participants in studied incubated gatherings. Given that facilitators have preferences for how they approach the process of linking ideas, we were interested in discovering if the participants have their own approaches or preferences. We discovered that they do indeed prefer to share links between contributions they know, and avoid those they do not know. The following discussion will explore this work.

Participants approaches for linking contributions

Participants are constrained to six types of linking activity known as link-types. These center on whether the contribution being linked was originally made by that participant or by someone else in the group. Participants' approaches include them linking:

- Two of their own contributions together, that is, oWn to oWn –W>W
- Two contributions that have been made by other participants together, that is, oTher to oTher –T>T
- Their contribution into someone else's (i.e. oWn to oTher –W>T) or the other way around, that is, oTher to oWn – T>W
- Their own contribution into the stimulus contributions/question that has been displayed on the public screen during the blind gathering, that is, oWn to Stimulus –W>S
- Other people's contributions into the stimulus, that is, oTher to Stimulus –T>S
- From the stimulus to their own contribution, or to other people's contributions, that is, Stimulus>oWn, Stimulus>oTher –S>W, S>T

Our research suggests that participants are more confident in and have preference for making links between contributions that they clearly understand.

Participants would be most confident in their own contributions (because they made them) and the stimuli (because it has often emerged as the prime stimulus at the start of the session as a consequence of negotiation by the group members). In contrast, participants may be least confident in other people's contributions because they might not be completely clear about what the contribution actually means.

We calculated the number of own, other and stimuli-inspired ideas being displayed on the public screen during the piggybacking session and found that, on average, 14.5 percent of contributions on the public screen are oWn, 83.6 percent are oTher contributions, 1.8 percent are Stimuli generated contributions. From this we calculated the probability of a participant selecting at random their own, other or stimuli contributions to link (assuming that linking was a random process in that participants did not search for own, other or stimuli contributions to link). With the exception of S>W and S>T links, our results confirm the existence of a "hierarchy of preference" – that participants do prefer, albeit possibly unconsciously, to make links which involve their own contributions, and avoid linking other people's contributions.

The opportunity for personal and collective learning – *learning through piggybacking*

During group discussion that ensued as part of the piggybacking phase of the incubated gathering, participants are exposed to other people's views and new sources of information. Some participants exhibit learning through this phase, evident through their generation of different, new and really innovative ideas (as discussed

$$\left\{ \begin{array}{c} \text{... learning evident through new innovative} \\ \text{ideas and linkages} \end{array} \right\}$$

before), which arise from exposure to new views. It seems that by providing new and diverse stimuli to participants (in the form of ideas generated by others), they were enabled to expand their awareness (and so learn) regarding different aspects of an issue that they had not previously considered relevant or at all. To substantiate this and investigate participants' perception of their own "learning through piggybacking", we collected data through participant interviews, questionnaires, and researcher observations.

By contrast, as a consequence of the piggybacking exercise, some participants reported feeling cognitive overload – the partial inability of the brain to process new information, due to the mass of new information (Grise and Gallupe, 1999) just after the public screen was switched on and ideas were suddenly displayed. One interviewee said how "the more ideas ... that came onto the public screen the more difficult it became to read those ideas".

Another interviewee tried to read the ideas but "got myself in a tangle" due to the large number of ideas on the public screen. For these participants learning from the mass of ideas might be difficult; this could hinder the quality of the individual learning and creative thinking.

For another interviewee, the facilitator's introduction to the themes "was a vital guiding tour around the map as we structured ideas" and "helped to familiarize me with the model". This reduced the potential for cognitive overload. However, for another interviewee it "went right past me as it was too fast and did not register". Clearly, pace is important. Participants need time to read the contributions for themselves. Notwithstanding, some participants did cognitively process the material and share piggybacked contributions without "becoming bogged down by the overwhelming volume of ideas and comments to organise" (Grise and Gallupe, 1999, p. 158).

Several interviewees felt piggybacking was made easier by the anonymity provided through the computers – important in their "hostile and aggressive [work- $\left\{ \begin{array}{c} \text{... piggybacking was made easier by the} \\ \text{anonymity provided through computers} \end{array} \right\}$ ing] environment". They described how they often do "post-it exercises" but because "everyone knows each other's hand-writing" anonymity is eroded and personal relations influence the perception of views. Another interviewee commented that anonymity is good as it ensures that people cannot deliberately undermine the idea of a particular "other". This one interviewee commented on how the piggybacking session provided for the sharing of views "in an uninhibited fashion".

Evidence of learning was also reported by interviewees. One interviewee reflected on how "seeing other people's ideas did not raise new issues ... [however, it did help me] focus on issues that I had not considered in great depth". In effect she learned something in a deeper extent. More generally, from exit questionnaires, participants were in some agreement that the clustering of ideas "helped us to think about bigger issues they had not previously considered". $\left\{ \begin{array}{c} \text{"helped us to think about bigger issues not} \\ \text{previously considered"} \end{array} \right\}$

In summary, cognitive overload might hinder learning in the piggybacking phase. However, some participants did use the piggybacking session to:

■ Learn more about what other people perceived was important and to share their view of those perspectives

■ Learn about issues they had not previously considered relevant and piggyback contributions onto those issues

■ Learn about and share newly formed views on completely new issues, which they had never before considered

Learning through linking?

Linking also provides learning opportunities, as participants consider why proposed links exist between ideas and as the group discusses the legitimacy of these links. In interviews, reflective learning was also evident as most participants expressed concern over the validity of causal linking made between contributions early in the workshop. They commented that they needed more explanation from the facilitator with regards to (a) what a link was, (b) what it symbolized and (c) what its direction indicated.

From observing the group and their discussion, we found that participants do exhibit characteristics of learning during linking. Often during group discussion on the legitimacy of links it is clear that participants learn new details of the situation and develop a richer appreciation of the interrelationships between elements of the situation (supported by Eden and Ackermann, 2001; Shaw et al., 2003). This is apparent as participants often achieve agreement where there was previously divergence – the driver of agreement being the exposure to new persuasive arguments (Burnstein and Vinokur, 1975), which further their awareness of important issues. This exposure is a source of tremendously rich personal learning in that participants can better appreciate the perspectives of others and build their own understanding through these.

Discussion and implications for facilitation

We have argued that through piggybacking and by negotiating causal relationships between issues, participants of brainstorming and causal mapping workshops seem able to expand their understanding of the situation. Analyses of piggybacked ideas suggests that the participants have thought beyond the boundaries of their earlier ideas and so have been creative and have learned more about the issues that other people view as being important.

For a facilitator who is encouraging the free flow of creative thought during an incubated gathering, particularly with a view to making decisions of a critical nature, the piggybacking session offers participants the discontinuous stimuli with which they can modify the paradigms of their thinking. It allows them to break from bounded vision in order to arrive at more robustly considered, broadly informed and widely owned decisions. Our findings suggest that the participants' piggybacked ideas are creative and represent new insights, which the group members have generated in their consideration of the issue. Without the piggybacked session the importance of these ideas might not be realized. During the piggybacking session a facilitator encourages participants to read, learn from, explore and reflect upon the ideas that other people have shared. This opportunity to synthesize other people's ideas into their own views of the situation is a prime opportunity for individual participants to:

- Expand awareness about the differing perspectives brought by other participants
- Reconsider their own views in the light of other people's perspectives
- Refine and share views on other people's perspectives
- Identify potential opposition to own view and prepare (or not) to defend that view
- Influence the views of other participants by new piggybacked ideas

The piggybacking session also prepares participants to enter group discussion with a more informed understanding of what the competing perspec- $\left\{ \begin{array}{c} \text{... more informed understanding of} \\ \text{competing perspectives} \end{array} \right\}$ tives in the group are – because they can identify those in the group map. Therefore undue time will not be needed on group discussion that reinforces issues on which the group members already agree. Instead group members can quickly identify where divergent views exist in order to more efficiently and effectively discuss and resolve the issues that underlie that divergence.

Facilitators are also likely to be interested in using the piggybacking session to enable participants to share more views of the causal relationships between ideas. By sharing causal links, and capturing the discussion of interrelationships on the causal map, and by structuring/restructuring the map, the group members debate issues that underlie the shared views. Thus they are constructing a more detailed awareness of the interrelationships between the issues. This seems to be another prime opportunity to identify unfamiliar causal relationships between issues, to discuss the supporting rationale for those relationships, and to learn more about the situation and its wider implications.

We believe that the facilitator should encourage participants to share as many links as they think are correct. While participants might prefer to link their own contributions (from the "hierarchy of preference"), the facilitator might like them to also link other people's contributions, in order for them to integrate other people's views into their own consideration of the problem. By linking other people's views, they will reflect on, and maybe critique the views more diligently than they might if they opted to overlook those contributions and only link their own. Participants and facilitators should not be too concerned over the accuracy of participant-entered links, for even inaccurate links can offer some indication of the clusters that might appear. Also, making and discussing links encourages reflection, under-standing and learning.

By using the approach of an incubated gathering, the outcome of these sessions should be the broadest and most all-encompassing possible. Also, by encouraging linking the participants will be able to reflect on the legiti-macy of the interrelationships between the issues. This will have positive consequences for the rigor of the generated outcome.

Conclusion: the implications for executive development

We have evaluated a new format of "decision-making": the incubated gath-ering. In this format, participants are first encouraged to express, in an incubated manner, their own views after which all participants' ideas are exposed to each other and piggybacking off the ideas of others is encour-aged (Figure 5.1). It is safe to conclude that once views are shared and the causal links are identified, participants:

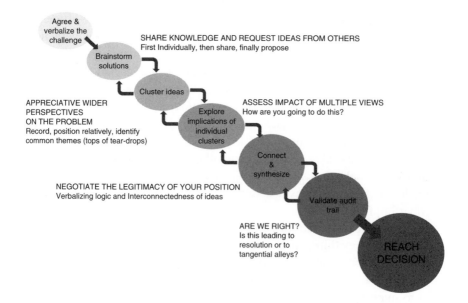

Figure 5.1   A process for collaborative decision-making

- Can piggyback effectively to raise new ideas
- Perceive that the new format is helpful to increase understanding
- Learn from each other during the incubated format

Our evidence suggests that participants can work, reflect, learn and share a broader range of views during the incubated format than during the other formats ana-

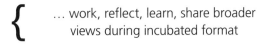

... work, reflect, learn, share broader views during incubated format

lyzed. In particular, the techniques that we have outlined earlier deliver the following benefits. They

1. Help members of senior decision-making teams understand that the world is ambiguous, and how and why.
2. Enable individuals and teams to deconstruct the problem, and identify and understand the different factors that they consider important.
3. Equip a team to reconstruct the important factors underlying a decision and understand the conflict and tensions inherent between them: that is, you can get the safest or the cheapest – but rarely both in the same offering.
4. Encourage individuals and teams to make evidence-based decisions. Evidence can be as simple as: "there are 14 knowledgeable and experienced people in the room who agree and have substantive rationale underpinning their opinions".
5. Persuade decision-makers to realize that difficult problems can be understood.

Applying these techniques provides executives with a methodology for collaborative thinking, decision-making, and structured analysis that creates a culture in which knowledge is shared, perspectives on problems are broadened, and multiple legitimate views are assessed. The outcome can only be that better decisions are made.

Summary

- Decisions can be taken collaboratively to provide a more robust, broadly considered and widely owned result.

- A more structured form of brainstorming can be pursued to encourage deeper and more innovative individual thinking and contributions.

Action points

You can follow this chapter's methodology to arrive at significant decisions in mission-critical environments:

1. Use incubated causal mapping workshops to generate the broadest and most all-encompassing possible outcomes.

2. Empower workshop participants to think beyond the boundaries of their earlier ideas, be creative and learn more about the issues other people view as important.

3. Set up piggybacking sessions to offer participants opportunities to modify the paradigms of their thinking and arrive at more robustly considered and widely owned decisions.

4. Encourage piggybacking participants to read, learn from, explore and reflect upon the ideas that other people have shared.

5. Facilitate the sharing of views on the causal relationships between ideas, by sharing causal links and capturing the discussion of interrelationships on the causal map.

6. Promote linking of views between participants to stimulate reflection on the legitimacy of the interrelationships between the issues.

Self-assessment tool

To what extent are the following critical decision-making stages adhered to in your organization? (**Tables 5.2**, **5.3**)

Table 5.2 How good is my organization at collaborating in decision-making?

Attribute	Never	Sometimes	Mostly	Always	Cumulative Score
We realize that difficult problems can be understood	0	1	2	3	
We share knowledge and request ideas from others	0	1	2	3	
We appreciate wider perspectives on problems	0	1	2	3	
We assess the impact of multiple views	0	1	2	3	
We negotiate the legitimacy of each position	0	1	2	3	
We check whether ideas are leading to resolution or to tangential alleys	0	1	2	3	
We make evidence-based decisions	0	1	2	3	

Table 5.3 Benchmark scores

0–4	5–9	10–15	16–21
In the danger zone!	Some foundations that need development	Good, but room for improvement	Moving toward consistent high performance

Notes

1. Ironically, a raft of research findings suggest that the typical format of brainstorming sessions actually hinders the very individual representation/ creativity it seeks to release.

Further reading

Bryson, J., Ackermann, F., Eden, C. and Finn, C. (2004) *Visible Thinking Unlocking Causal Mapping for Practical Business Results*, Chichester: Wiley.

Eden, C. and Ackermann, F. (1998) *Making Strategy: The Journey of Strategic Management*, Sage: London.

Osborn, A. F. (1953) *Applied Imagination*, New York, NY: Charles Scribner's Sons.

Shaw, D., Eden, C. and Ackermann, F. (2009) "Mapping Causal Knowledge: How Managers Consider their Environment during Meetings", *International Journal of Management and Decision Making*, 10(5–6), pp. 321–40.

Shaw, D. and Edwards, J. S. (2005) "Building User Commitment to Knowledge Management Strategy", *Information & Management*, 42(7), pp. 977–88.

Shaw D., Westcombe M., Hodgkin, J. and Montibeller, G. (2004) "Problem Structuring Methods for Large Group Interventions", *Journal of the Operational Research Society*, 55(5), pp. 453–63.

Further references

Burnstein, E. and Vinokur, A. (1975) "What a Person Thinks upon Learning that He has Chosen Differently from Others: Nice Evidence for the Persuasive Arguments Explanation of Choice Skills", *Journal of Experimental Social Psychology*, 11, pp. 412–26.

Checkland, P. (2001) "Soft Systems Methodology", in J. Rosenhead and J. Mingers (eds) *Rational Analysis for a Problematic World Revisited*, Chichester: John Wiley and Sons, pp. 61–90.

Dennis, A. R., Valacich, J. S., Carte, T. A., Garfield, M. J. and Haley, B. J. (1997) "Research Report: The Effectiveness of Multiple Dialogues in Electronic Brainstorming", *Information Systems Research*, 8, pp. 203–11.

Eden, C. (1995) "On Evaluating the Performance of Wide-band GDSS", *European Journal of Operational Research*, 81, pp. 302–11.

Eden, C. and Ackermann, F. (1998) *Making Strategy: The Journey of Strategic Management*, London: Sage.

Eden, C. and Ackermann, F. (2001) "SODA – The Principles", in J. Rosenhead and J. Mingers (eds) *Rational Analysis for a Problematic World Revisited*, Chichester: John Wiley and Sons, pp. 21–42.

Finlay, P. N. (1998) "On Evaluating the Performance of GSS: Furthering the Debate", *European Journal of Operational Research*, 107, pp. 193–201.

Friend, J. (2001) "The Strategic Choice Approach", in J. Rosenhead and J. Mingers (eds) *Rational Analysis for a Problematic World Revisited*, Chichester: John Wiley and Sons, pp. 115–50.

Grise, M. L. and Gallupe, R. B. (1999) "Information Overload in Face-to-face Electronic Meetings: An Integrative Complexity Approach", *Journal of Management Information Systems*, 16, pp. 157–85.

Pinsonneault, A., Barki, H., Gallupe, R. B. and Hoppen, N. (1999) "Electronic Brainstorming: The Illusion of Productivity", *Information Systems Research*, 10, pp. 110–33.

Shaw, D. (2002) "Releasing the Sharing of Knowledge in Groups – Evaluating the Use of Group 'Brainstorming' Software", European Conference on Knowledge Management, Dublin, Ireland. 20 pages. ISBN: 0-9540488-6-5.

Shaw, D., Ackermann, F. and Eden, C. (2003) "Sharing Knowledge in Group Problem Structuring", *Journal of the Operational Research Society*, 54(9), pp. 936–48.

CHAPTER 6

The Essence of High Performance Teams

Michael West

Eight characteristics that drive high performance and team-delivered change

Introduction

You might ask what inspired my research into the topic of high performance teamwork. Quite simply, it was the observation, backed later by much research evidence, that teams are the basic structure of human endeavor.

{ *... teams are the basic structure of human endeavor* }

Take for example our research in the UK's National Health System (NHS), which is based on staff surveys from 2003–11. As part of that we asked staff in the NHS whether they worked in teams and explored how teamwork affected their well-being and the quality of care patients received. To this end we asked a few simple questions:

"Do you work in a team?"

If yes (91 percent) ...

- Does your team have **clear objectives**?
- Do you **have to work closely together to achieve these objectives**?
- Do you **meet regularly to review** your team effectiveness and how it could be improved?

The results showed that 38 percent of 1.4 million employees saw themselves as working in real teams, 50 percent reported that they worked in pseudo teams – groups that call themselves a team but that do not satisfy all three of the criteria listed above – and 12 percent indicated they did not work in a team.

What was the impact on "performance"?

Errors, stress and injuries to staff were higher in hospitals where more staff worked in pseudo teams (where pseudo 1 meant that one of the three conditions of true teams was missing, pseudo 2 that two were missing and pseudo 3 that all three were missing) (Figure 6.1). In fact,

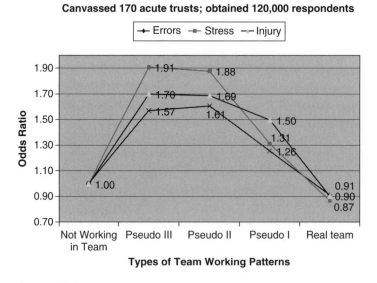

Figure 6.1 Working in team and errors, stress and injury

unless you were in a real team, it was better for "performance" { ... unless in a real team, it was better for "performance" to not be in a team at all }

to not be in a team at all. As for patient care, the study identified that 5 percent more staff working in real teams was associated with a 3.3 percent drop in the mortality rate. This alone represented about 40 deaths a year in an "average" hospital.

Such powerful findings are consistent with the argument that the activity of a group of people working cooperatively to achieve shared goals by taking on specific roles and communicating effectively with each other is basic to the survival, social development and progress of our species. The current enthusiasm for teamwork in organizations reflects a recognition that teamwork offers the promise of greater success than that which can be achieved through individual endeavor or through mechanistic approaches to work.

Human beings work and live in groups because groups enable survival and reproduction. By living and working in groups early humans could share food and could more easily find mates and care for infants. By working in teams early humans discovered they could hunt more effectively and better defend themselves against their enemies. "Over the course of evolution, the small group became the survival strategy developed by the human species" (Barchas, 1986, p. 212).

The fundamental human drive to form and maintain lasting, positive and significant relationships helps us to understand the functioning of teams at work. Research strongly suggests that satisfying this need to belong requires that our team relationships be characterized by:

- Frequent interaction
- Temporal stability and likely continuity
- Mutual affective concern
- Freedom from conflict

This motivation to belong therefore shapes much human behavior and for our purposes helps to explain reactions within teams. The absence of one or more of these characteristics of belongingness (frequent interaction, likely continuity and stability, mutual affective concern, and freedom from conflict and negative affect) will favor disintegration of both relationships and teams. Sadly, our tendency to concentrate on task characteristics and organizational contexts often blinds us to these fundamental socio-emotional requirements for effective team-based working.

A second motivator that fuelled my research into high performing teams

{ innovation is the best barometer of team functioning }

was the conviction that "innovation is the best barometer of team functioning". Though this remains a matter of opinion, we rarely see effective teams that are low in innovation. The two go together.

Whether the context is producing TV programs, training for war, managing health and illness in hospitals, developing new products in manufacturing organizations or providing financial services, the use of teams is both ubiquitous and increasing. Fundamentally, teams are deployed because (a) some tasks require that a variety of people work together to achieve a larger end result than the individuals in that team could achieve by working individually and (b) some tasks require significant innovation.

Innovation is fundamental to organizational survival and prosperity. Innovation has been at the root of the development of our species from our primitive beginnings to our recent stunning advances in technology, communication and social interaction. It has also been at the heart of the development and implementation of improved processes, products and procedures. Yet despite the fascination with individual creativity, innovation has not often been the result of one solitary activity delivered by one single vigorous champion. Innovation has seldom been the result of only one individual's idea. It is more usually the result of concerted activity by teams that develop and implement their ideas over a period of time. Beyond this, the diffusion of successful innovations throughout organizations or societies has been the consequence of teams, bringing their diversity to bear on the presenting need or opportunity, working in the context of high external demands. This has surprisingly, yet consequently, driven high levels of internal integration and psychological safety. Put succinctly, creativity requires safety while implementation of innovation requires high external demands (whether in the form of threat or large reward). Teams will be creative primarily when their task is sufficiently interesting, motivating and challenging and when the team members work well together with a high level of trust and safety. In general, creative cognitions occur when individuals are free from pressure, feel safe and feel positive.

Notwithstanding, several challenges stand in the face of effective teamwork and obstruct the creation of high performance teams. Evidence from many studies suggests that teams are often created without careful thought about the task, the skills those tasks require, the people who have those skills and the people whose prime skill is the ability to join those disparate individuals into a team, through appropriate structures that effectively support the team in its functioning.

Pitfalls of poorly formed and pseudo teams

Specifically, when teams are poorly formed, or when they constitute "pseudo teams" (teams in name only), major failures of function typically follow.

1. The team task doesn't actually get done. Example: a group of people worked in the same office on a disparate collection of tasks all vaguely to do with addressing customer complaints. There were no team objectives and no regular team meetings. Despite that fact, managers decided to refer to the group as the "customer complaints team" and left them to their own devises. As a consequence, the level of customer complaints, far from falling, continued to rise steadily. Many of the complaints began to revolve around how customer complaints were dealt with in the first place. The "team" members tended to sit around the office making negative comments about customers and celebrating their obstructiveness with customers who persistently tried to pursue their complaints. The job of dealing effectively with customer complaints did not get done and the firm began to lose market share as a result. Lesson: don't call a collective a team if you don't introduce clear individual objectives that collectively represent those of the group as a whole.

   > Lesson: don't call a collective a team

2. Individual team members do not deliver to individual objectives or team objectives. Managers sometimes assume that by creating a team, they don't need to manage individual or team performance, believing the team should take care of itself. Example: the financial services customer support team started out well with clear team objectives and individual objectives. Then one member of the team, Richard, began taking time off for minor illnesses. Even when at work, he did much less with customers than the rest of the team. Tensions built up. Some team members expressed strong resentment when the team bonus was shared out equally at the end of the year. Some expressed the view that it was stupid to work hard when Richard was clearly "taking them for a ride". Team effort slackened and customer satisfaction plummeted. Team members were resentful toward their manager who seemed not to recognize or be prepared to deal with the problem. Lesson: managers must manage individual performance and ensure that team performance as a whole is tracked and on track.

   > Lesson: manage individual performance and track team performance as a whole

3. Teams do not have clear objectives or even have none at all. This is the most serious problem we encounter with teams, and one that is astonishingly common. Example: team members often assume that having a vague sense of what the team is supposed to be doing is sufficient for good team functioning. However, having six or seven clear objectives that are challenging and measureable is the surest way to ensure team success. From these one can derive individual team-member objectives based on their team roles. Though managers think they achieve this, check again. Ask team members individually to list their team's key objectives for the year (granting them access to their computers or files). Typically there will be as many variations on this list as there are team members. Lesson: lack of clear, challenging, measureable objectives is, according to our research, the major cause of team ineffectiveness.

    > { Lesson: lack of clear, challenging, measurable objectives is the major cause of team ineffectiveness }

4. Malfunctioning can start with one individual who is not fulfilling their potential. Proverbially, one person pushing a boulder downhill rather than uphill can stop the whole team getting that boulder up the hill, and can prevent a Stonehenge from being constructed. Example: team members may not have the training they need to do the job; they may find another member of the team too aggressive; (more usually) they may not have a clear role definition which would enable them to contribute effectively to the team. When the team fails to perform to expectations, all team members are dissatisfied. The other teams with which they have to interact within the organization also become demotivated also since they are prevented from effectively fulfilling their own team objectives. Lesson: because teams interact with other teams, underperformance of one widely hampers the performance of others.

    > { Lesson: underperformance of one team hampers the performance of others }

5. People waste time and effort trying to work in a team when the task does not require a team in the first place. Example: in one call center, we found a "team" of five call operators who answered insurance queries. They each dealt with different areas – car, household, travel, buildings and professional indemnity. There was no sense in which the task required a team; but management insisted on having team meetings and rewarding the individuals through team bonuses. Team meetings were boring,

nonproductive affairs at which team members rarely spoke – apart from giving a summary of their work over the previous week. Instead, they listened to updates from the manager on other developments in the organization – barely able to conceal their half-hearted involvement in the meetings. Lesson: don't call a group a team if members don't need each other to deliver against individual objectives.

> Lesson: don't call a group a team if members don't need each other to deliver

Conclusion: teams (a) that have a clear purpose which engages team members (such as a breast cancer care team) and (b)a strong sense of identity tend to produce far more and be far more motivated and innovative than teams that don't have these characteristics. When teams are well structured, well led and have clear purposes and objectives – synergy results: $1+1+1+1=5$.

First analogy – the dance of teams

Kenneth Tharp, the former Director of the National Youth Dance Company, founded and worked with the original dance Troupe, training often and hard-to-reach performance perfection. All members of the Troupe were committed to working together effectively, working out their roles and communicating constantly and effectively with each other. Through coaching, they encouraged each other. Together they built a shared vision of the performance they would portray at their first professional gig. They worked hard and supportively for many weeks ahead of opening night. Facing their family and friends and the many people in the audience, they were understandably nervous. Not long into the show, the music CD unaccountably skipped a section. Amazingly, only Kenneth Tharp and the dancers noticed anything. For the dancers intuitively and spontaneously danced their way through the chasm. They drew on the many hours of rehearsals (alias: teamwork) and the mutual understanding that they had built. Attuned to each other's roles and styles they managed the crisis professionally and brilliantly, not only succeeding in their opening performance but building further confidence and efficacy as a team. That ability to work intuitively, backing each other innovatively while reading each other's roles accurately is a hallmark of high performing teams, enabling teams to perform and improvise effectively, particularly in a crisis.

Clarity of purpose

Focus on "home team"

Clear objectives

Shared meaning

Clarity of role

Strong sense of belonging

Clear communication

Strong reflection

Figure 6.2   The problem boulder

Keys to team effectiveness

Essentially, the effectiveness of teams increases when the following eight practices are in place (See Figure 6.2):

1. Clarity of purpose: team members need to be inspired by a clear and motivating purpose. People at work are not inspired by "maximizing value for shareholders". They are inspired by ensuring customers are delighted by the service they are given. Of course, you would think that purpose is much easier to articulate for a health care or teaching team – but even in these contexts, managers can sabotage purpose by adopting a machismo or target-obsessed approach. The role of leaders is to provide a motivating and engaging purpose around which members of their teams can cohere.

2. Shared meaning: team members must have a sense of shared ownership of the stated purpose. People buy into missions that they are involved in articulating. A wise team leader works with the team to enable them to sculpt a statement of purpose so that they "own" that purpose. A truism of human behavior is that people are much more committed to, and motivated by goals they have set themselves rather than goals they have had imposed upon them.

3. Clear objectives: the absence of these is the single most damaging characteristic of teams in modern organizations. Without clear objectives, team motivation is low, team members are unclear about roles and team performance cannot be measured. Team learning suffers and there is little evidence of team innovation. Not that setting team goals is a simple process. Goals must be clear, aligned precisely to organizational objectives, challenging (setting goals that the team is going to achieve anyway is a waste of time) and they must be agreed on by team members. Ensuring measures can be derived to assess team performance against their objectives is part of this and also critical.

4. Clarity about the roles required to fulfill the team task: teams are not about people first and foremost – they are about tasks. Arguably, we should only create a team when there is a task that needs a team to do it – not because a group of people work in the same office, have the same job title or like each other a lot. Once we have identified a task that needs to be done and once we know it will require a team to do it, we then have to identify the skills needed to get that task done effectively (R & D skills, marketing skills, customer relationship management, etc.). To that template we match the individuals with appropriate skills or train those we think are capable of acquiring them. Then we form a team with each person having clear roles derived from the task, with the skills needed for the team **to work**. Too often, teams are formed without reference to the task, which is completely the wrong way around. This results in a lack of role clarity such that team members can be forgiven for asking, "what is it that I am supposed to be doing?" Members give unequal efforts (those who are clearer about their roles work harder or appear to) and that creates resentments about free riders in the team, potentially resulting in turn in reduced effort by other team members.

5. Strong communication: this is not just a question of how effective we are at communicating but also of the extent to which we are engaging sufficiently frequently, spending enough time together to communicate. Team members also need to exchange information effectively with each other, sharing information relevant to the achievement of their team objectives. (If it affects more than one of us, it should be on the table). This too is part of communication. With the widespread use of the Internet, e-mail, teleconferencing and videoconferencing, team members are increasingly reducing the amount of face-to-face time together. Yet the more complex the task, the less effective are those impersonal forms of communication in enabling teams to make the right decisions, to process information to the point of understanding and to develop new and improved processes, products and procedures. Face-to-face interaction should be overdone rather than underdone. Yet the clear tendency in modern organizations is for the latter. Teams that take time to regularly meet face-to-face are much more effective, productive and innovative than teams that do not. Think of a sports team whose members withhold information from other team members and the picture becomes clearer. The dance team described earlier was brilliant in a crisis precisely because they had a shared mental model of their work as a result of months of constantly sharing information. For deep understanding to exist, all members must have influence over significant decisions. Of course, "airtime" and expertise should be highly correlated. Beware of dominant team members or directive leaders as they can subvert team communication and effectiveness.

6. Sufficient time for reflection: high levels of motivation and workload can lead to teams becoming "busily foolish", working ever harder to achieve the wrong goals. Teams are more effective to the extent that they take time out from their work to reflect. This involves reviewing and reflecting on what it is they are trying to achieve and how they are going about it. Just as sports teams take time-out at halftime to review their performance and adjust their strategy, so too teams at work need to regularly review their objectives and performance in order to ensure and improve effectiveness. This can take the form of regular "away days" – and for most complex decision-making teams, this should be at least twice a year – but it is also relevant in the context of daily performance. Typical signs of failures to reflect upon are excessive workload, team members unable to find time to meet together and team meetings feeling unproductive. Team meetings should also involve reflection, even if only at the end of the meeting. Consider posing helpful questions such as: what has contributed to the meeting being useful, productive and effective? To what extent were all team members fully engaged? Did we use the time well? Without an orientation of reflexivity, teams are likely to become ineffective at best and destructive to organizational performance at worst. Moreover, the team is unlikely to learn from mistakes and condemned to repeating them, further damaging team performance and morale.

7. No fear of rejection: team members are willing to constructively point out a discrepancy between the required and actual performance of the team, whether that be in relation to objectives, meetings, leadership, communication, inter-teamwork or in terms of the effectiveness of the decision-making process. Bringing areas of poor performance to the team's attention does not feel threatening, even when individuals are challenged or confronted as a result of underperformance. Team defense mechanisms do not kick in when the motives are supportive and constructive. Creating a climate where team members feel safe to raise issues of poor team performance is therefore important to counteract the natural tendency to suppress bad news.

8. Focus on the "home team": in modern workplaces, people tend to be members of several teams. However, simply because of cognitive time and limited emotional capacity, the more teams one is a member of, the less effective we can be as a team member in any one of those teams. The solution is to identify and engage more with a "home team". This is likely to be the team that has the most influence over the work we do in all the other teams. Investing most time in the activities, development

and reflection of the home team will ensure that the individual is able to maintain a grounded approach to teamwork amidst the demands of all the different teams and to ensure that contributions to other teams are strategically focused and effective. It is also helpful to be clear with all those teams – whether membership is core or peripheral – so that expectations can be effectively managed.

Second analogy – the problem boulder

Imagine that we want to push a huge boulder to the top of a hill. No one can do it alone. It will take five individuals working collectively to push it. First question surely to be answered is: why? Second question is: push it where? Unless these two questions are clearly agreed (purpose and shared meaning), the five could push it in the wrong direction (objectives) or not move it at all because they are all pushing in different directions. Additionally, we need to ensure we have team members who have the skills to push the boulder as a team to the top of the hill. That requires strength, cooperation, a commitment to teamwork and preparedness to persist until the job is done. After all, if they stop halfway, the boulder will only roll back down the hill, potentially causing great collateral damage!

Implications of our analysis

Many teams head in inappropriate directions. The demands of the workplace and customers can lead teams to work very hard together to respond and be effective. However, a failure to carefully define team objectives leads many teams to work hard at the wrong things and to disappoint customers and managers. Teams need to have clear purpose and objectives that all agree on if they are to not dissipate their efforts pursuing the wrong goals.

Very often mistakes are made. When teams do not have clear objectives, when members are not clear about their roles or the roles of their colleagues, when teams do not take the time and care to communicate with each other fully, errors and omissions occur. In health care teams, this leads to higher patient mortality.

Assumptions about who is taking responsibility for what tasks can leave critical tasks undone. Confusion about what is the priority in the team's work grows and conflicts increases within the team, further undermining team functioning.

Disagreements about the causes of errors exacerbate team conflict and undermine trust. Team members will tend to blame particular individuals rather than recognize that the conflicts are a result of lack of clarity of objectives, roles and communication processes. Commitment declines and team members become less involved in their work because of the disappointment of working in a failing team characterized by tensions and recriminations.

Of course, in situations such as these where there is heightened anxiety and growing anger, there is little or no innovation. Introducing new and improved ways of doing things involves creativity and risk, both of which are suppressed when there is tension or hostility in a team.

These problems are not restricted to the one team. They spill over into relationships with other teams, which are often blamed for contributing collateral problems of their own making. Moreover, clients or service receivers are affected by these noxious team processes. In the NHS, assaults on staff by patients and other members of the public are much more likely to occur in teams that are not functioning effectively. Tensions within the team communicate themselves to patients and others, raising anxiety and hostility all round. Within the NHS, research shows a direct relationship between poor team functioning and quality of care – particularly influencing higher levels of patient mortality.

Third analogy – deep-sea diving

Among deep-sea diving crews, someone has to have the specific responsibility of checking divers' valves. If they are not checked, a diver may die. Clarity about roles and responsibilities in teams is vital and this clarity should be reinforced on a regular basis in team awaydays. Team members should take the time to clarify their objectives, roles and responsibilities, for themselves as well as for all other members of the team. Teamwork is about communication, more communication and yet more communication.

What then are the implications for team functioning? Consider applying the following steps for each team to which you belong:

1. Agree together as a team on an inspiring and motivating core purpose, expressed in a single brief sentence. This should reflect the purpose that the team as a collective can own.

2. Agree on six or seven key objectives aligned to that purpose. There should be no more than six or seven (this is an issue of prioritization) and they should be clearly stated. Objectives should be challenging because there is no motivational or performance value in setting objectives that are going to be achieved anyway. Achievement of objectives should also be measureable so that the team can know how well it is progressing in

its aims, to ensure it is not deluding itself about performance. One of those objectives should focus on improving the team's effectiveness in working with the other teams within and beyond the organization – other teams with which it has to work to deliver services, to produce products, to deliver its wider purpose. Objective setting is not an easy process – it takes careful thought, debate and consideration of alternatives to get the objectives exactly right. Given the influence of objectives on how the team uses its resources, it is vital to ensure they are right.

3. Agree on who is taking responsibility for what areas of activity and performance in the team and how they will work together to achieve the objectives.

4. Come together regularly, face-to-face, to review your collective purpose, objectives and progress to achieve these in order to adjust and adapt as required. Such reflexive practice lead to much better team performance, lower team members' stress and workload and higher levels of team innovation.

5. Communicate compulsively. Teamwork involves sharing ideas, successes, concerns and coaching each other and the team as a whole toward better performance. Repeated communication overtime about these issues enables the team to "do the dance", whatever crises and challenges come along.

6. Make sure you have shared meaning. Underpinning the team's work should be a clearly stated value base, the source of shared meaning. Examples include providing outstanding service to customers, supporting the development of staff within the organization, providing the best engineered products in the market, delivering high quality, compassionate and safe care for patients and ensuring the finances of the organization are sufficiently stable to enable the organization to flourish. Underpinning values provide the root into the emotional commitment of team members to their work and to the team.

When as a team you make time to put the previous steps into place, you:

1. Contribute to the development of trust and respect, which often comes as a consequence of working well together. Trust is at the heart of effective teamwork. To be effective we have to trust that team members will follow through with commitments, can be relied on, will back each other up when the going is tough for one or more members, will fulfill their roles effectively and will raise issues that threaten team performance as and when required. Teamwork is about trust; it is about members saying to themselves: "I take the risk of relying on you to do your job effectively, and I don't have to check on this. In so doing I can get on with

my task to the best of my ability, confident that the team task as a whole will be performed effectively and safely as each of us gets on with the task to which we have committed."

2. Ensure there is a level of challenge but in the context of bounded trust. Such a climate provides the safety for team members to raise issues that threaten the team's performance. It allows for all to respect those challenges because all share, are committed to and are emotionally engaged with the core purpose of the team. A climate of mutual respect and trust ensures that challenge and disagreement are received as professional and helpful rather than personal and painful.

3. Reduce the level of constant thrust, parry and high conflict. Most people don't work well when anxious about potential team conflicts. Effective teams have a high ratio of positive to negative interactions. They also have a high ratio of internally sourced inquiries, with team members spending a high proportion of time eliciting information from each other as opposed to advocating individual positions and opinions. Teamwork is about sharing, learning and exploring, not about dominating, asserting and competing.

{ *Teamwork is about sharing, learning, exploring, not dominating, asserting and competing.* }

4. Acknowledge team members. In effective teams, people explore because they feel sufficiently safe. That enables them to divulge their anxieties about their and the team's performance, to explore ideas for new and improved ways of doing things and to share the belief that there is no problem that cannot be solved and no status quo that cannot be bettered.

Fourth analogy – secure relationship

Have you ever observed a child in the park with a parent with whom they have a strong, safe attachment based on love and guidance? They stand out. Within wide but strong boundaries, they freely explore the park. The child returns to the parent frequently, but ventures a little further with time, knowing there is a safe base to which to return. Contrast this with the child who has an anxious attachment so never leaves the parent's side. The relationship is intermittent and unpredictable so the child never feels safe enough to explore far away and constantly seeks reassurance. Even more obvious is the punitive parent who creates a situation where the child neither stays near them nor do they have the motivation or sense of safety to explore. Instead such children hover some distance away, engaging obsessively with a stick or crisp packet. Such anxious, avoidant and secure attachments, in reverse order, are evident in teams also.

Summary

There are eight characteristics that drive high performance and team-delivered change:

1. Clarity of team purpose
2. Clear shared objectives
3. Clear roles and responsibilities
4. Excellent communication
5. Focus on the home team
6. Sense of shared meaning
7. Sense of belonging
8. Ability to reflect and evaluate performance

Action points

- Establish your team's purpose and its clear, challenging and measureable objectives.

- Define the roles and allocate responsibilities, ensuring that there is shared understanding of these and of their implied interdependencies.

- Schedule meetings and team-reflection events on a regular basis. Build agendas around team objectives for strong governance and to look to the future. Seek to establish quality exchanges, reviews and reflection processes – in which everyone engages and has a sense of time well spent.

- Invest in quality of relationships – built on trust, respect, presence/ mindfulness. Members value their strong working relationships with each other and work to maintain and develop them.

- Create a safe and supportive environment for sharing, exchanging ideas, exploring improvement, endorsing others and celebrating achievements.

- Recognize the team's processes and understand the team's challenges including areas for development.

Self-assessment tool

To what extent do teams you lead possess the following eight key attributes of high performance? (**Tables 6.1, 6.2**)

Tables 6.1 How good is my organization at working in high-performance change-driving teams?

Attribute	Never	Sometimes	Mostly	Always	Cumulative Score
We have clarity of team purpose	0	1	2	3	
We have clear shared objectives	0	1	2	3	
We have clear roles and responsibilities	0	1	2	3	
We engage in excellent communication	0	1	2	3	
We focus on the Home Team	0	1	2	3	
We have a sense of shared meaning	0	1	2	3	
We have a sense of belonging	0	1	2	3	
We have the ability to reflect and evaluate performance	0	1	2	3	

Table 6.2 Benchmark scores

0–5	6–11	12–17	18–24
In the danger zone!	Some foundations that need development	Good, but room for improvement	Moving toward consistent high performance

Further reading

Wageman, R., Nunes, D. A., Burruss, J. A. and Hackman, J. R. (2008) *Senior Leadership Teams: What it takes to make them Great*, Boston: Harvard Business School Press.

West, M. A. (2004) *The Secrets of Successful Team Management: How to Lead a Team to Innovation, Creativity and Success*, London: Duncan Baird Publishers.

West, M. A. (2010) *Effective Teamwork: Practical Lessons from Organizational Research – 3rd Edition*, Oxford: Blackwell Publishing.

West, M. A. and Markiewicz, L. (2004) *Building Team-based Working: A Practical Guide to Organizational Transformation*, Oxford: Blackwell Publishing.

Further references

Barchas, P. (1986) "A Sociophysiological Orientation to Small Groups", in F. Lawler (ed.) *Advances in Group Processes*, Volume 3, Greenwich, CT: JAI Press, pp. 209–46.

CHAPTER 7

The Case and Context for Quality Working Relationships

Robin Martin

Seven enablers of leader-follower relationships that sustain impetus for change

Introduction

People's choice of research topic is often triggered by personal events. This was certainly the case for me with respect to my research into workplace leadership. My personal "events", experiences shared broadly by others in the context of work, concerned in each instance the quality of my relationship with my manager. For the sake of simplicity, I will speak in the first person through the first part of this chapter though the "I" concerned is a fictional character, a composite of my personal experiences, of many stories I have accumulated from observations and of individuals whom I have coached over the years. So, continuing in the first person.

The central issue in each event was the variability in that one very special work relationship: the one with my manager. The core issue was the fact that with some managers I had both positive and negative experiences, with the same individual manager at different points in time. Nothing drastic in this, but the variability was sufficient to make certain periods of work more uncomfortable than when I was working with managers with whom my relationships were good **and** steady.

My analysis of these situations led to a number of observations about the leadership process that has very much shaped my research, teaching and consulting in this topic over the last 20 years.

The work relationships that form the launching pad for this chapter were critical in shaping my thoughts on leadership, particularly as I considered their oscillating quality, which ranged between very good and very poor! Up until the first of these events, I had enjoyed predominantly good and consistent relationships with my managers, so much so that I had almost taken "good and reliable boss-subordinate relationships" for granted as a *de facto* standard. In fact, it was actually only on the second occasion that my relationship with my boss started to vary that I began to understand the inordinate effect that just one relationship, the one that one has with one's manager, has on one's personal well-being and performance at work.

> $\left\{\begin{array}{c}\text{...inordinate effect that just one relationship,}\\ \text{the one that one has with one's manager,}\\ \text{has on one's personal well-being and}\\ \text{performance at work}\end{array}\right\}$

Before I draw nine observations about my experiences from these particular leadership situations, it is important to clarify what I mean by "relationship quality", a phrase that I will repeat through this chapter.

Within the leadership literature, researchers usually focus on four dimensions to describe the quality of the relationship between the leaders (managers) and his or her subordinates (followers). These four dimensions are:

1. *Affect*: mutual affection that they have for each other based on interpersonal attraction. This refers to the extent to which each person likes the other person in the relationship.

2. *Loyalty*: extent to which the leader and the follower publicly support the goals and personal character of each other. Loyalty is closely related to the concept of trust.

3. *Contribution*: perception of the amount, direction and quality of effort each person puts into work-oriented activities, toward achieving mutual goals.

4. *Professional Respect*: extent to which each person has a reputation for achieving high levels of performance in their work.

Based on the aforesaid, a good working relationship would be one that is characterized by the manager and subordinate liking each other, publicly supporting each other and through that demonstrating high levels of trust, perceiving that each puts a significant amount of effort into work activities to attain work goals, and recognizing each person's reputation for high levels of work performance. A poor working relationship, by contract, would be one that is characterized as being low on these four dimensions.

So how did this apply in my contexts with my "difficult" managers? How does my research expand on our understanding of the outworking of the previous dimensions?

Nine observations – effects of poor relationship quality between manager and subordinate

My experience with previous "taciturn" managers has led to nine observations that offer insights into how one can develop effective (or ineffective!) leader-follower relationships. These observations are particularly interesting given the fact that my relationships with said challenging managers each had periods when, using the four dimensions, they could have been described as being good and other periods when they could only be described as being poor. Let us first focus on the nine consequences of the poor relationships in order to then generalize to the seven enabling practices that could be pursued to improve and manage relationship quality.

My first observation related to a shift in the direction of my thinking in periods when the relationships were bad. A manifestation of the up and down nature of relationships is that I spent, some might say wasted, a considerable amount of time thinking and talking to other people about the quality of the relationship I had with said managers, especially when the relationships were poor (#1: Poor manager-subordinate relationship quality is a focus of a lot of attention).

> { #1: Poor manager-subordinate relationship quality is a focus of a lot of attention. }

It seems a truism in life that when things are going well, we tend not to question the reasons why. (On the occasions that we do question this, we often conclude that it is because we are "good" or behaving correctly.) The same is not true when things go badly. Under negative situations, we tend to look for reasons why the situation is not going so well. Such contemplation can lead to self-doubt and self-blame, which can hinder effective performance. Ensuing under confidence can inhibit an individual's and therefore the team's capacity to engage positively with change.

This is the way I felt as a consequence of these situations with managers. When the relationships were good, and my managers were meeting my primary needs of affirmation and belonging, I took for granted the good relationships and focused on the duties of my task. I was therefore better able to perform simply because I was free to concentrate on the challenges of the job before me. I was not introspectively consumed with my "self" and my capabilities. By contrast, when the relationships were poor, I spent ages in deep thought trying to understand the reasons why, what I or (more often) what they had done to cause this rupture to the relationship. I became what is sometimes referred to as a "naïve scientist", trying to identify patterns of events or causes that could predict when and why the relationships would be good or poor. Mentally I tested various hypotheses that might explain the variations in the quality of my relationships with my managers. All this was an attempt to bring understanding and predictability to the situations.

My second observation concerned my attitude toward the job. As a consequence of experiencing poor relationship quality with a few managers, I realized that my levels of job satisfaction, commitment to the organization, stress and morale were closely correlated to the quality of those very important relationships, and that my performance was an extension of the same. In particular, when the relationship quality was poor, I felt very unhappy at work and experienced high levels of stress (#2: Manager-subordinate relationship quality affects subordinate's psychological well-being and performance).

{ #2: Manager-subordinate relationship quality affects subordinate's psychological well-being and performance. }

In these situations, I tried to avoid my managers, which led to more negative interactions. Communications became more formal and occurred more often by e-mail than face-to-face. Misunderstandings often resulted from suspicions of the motives behind each other's behaviors. I found it difficult to feel a sense of commitment to my work and I am sure that this detracted from my performance. I was also increasingly unwilling to take personal risks for the benefit of the team or organization, becoming increasingly change-averse as a consequence.

Fortunately, despite the angst that pervaded those periods of time, I was often able to discuss these feelings with my managers, to try to understand why the relationships between us often became unsatisfactory. I recall one of the first of such meetings. It is not easy to go to one's manager to say, "Things aren't working between us, we have a poor working relationship and I feel unsatisfied and stressed as a result!" However, I was almost always pleasantly surprised with how willing my managers were to discuss the situations. Moreover, I was often comforted by the fact that more often than not they also felt stressed due to the poor relationship.

This led to my third observation. A poor manager-subordinate working relationship can affect the manager too, albeit in different ways and not possibly to the same intensity as it affects the subordinate (#3: Manager-subordinate relationship quality

> #3: Manager-subordinate relationship quality affects manager's psychological well-being and performance.

affects manager's psychological well-being and performance). This was a revelation to me. I had focused so much on the negative personal consequences of such relationships that I had forgotten (perhaps conveniently) that a relationship involves two people, and that typically what impacts one part of the relationship, one individual in the relationship, has consequences for the other part, the other individual, also. The realization that poor working relationships have negative impacts on *both* parties increases empathy and the commitment to improve the situations.

The reasons why the quality of the relationships I had with these managers was poor was central to much of my thinking and discussions with my managers. On almost every occasion, many reasons were identified that related specifically to work issues. These included factors such as different interpretations of work duties and problems with role ambiguity. Although not always relevant, but certainly important in many situations that I have observed, relationship quality can also be determined by nonwork factors such as how much the manager personally likes or dislikes the subordinate. This then became my fourth observation (#4: Manager-subordinate relationship quality is

> #4: Manager-subordinate relationship quality is based on work and nonwork factors.

based on work and nonwork factors).

Before continuing let me clarify that the formation of workplace relationships is similar to that of nonworkplace relationships (such as friendships). Research into relationships supports the "similarity-attraction" hypothesis, which shows that when people have similar feelings or ways of thinking on dimensions that are important to them, they are more likely than not to develop friendships. Translating this to the workplace, we know that the more a manager believes that he or she is similar to their subordinate on how they think and feel about work and nonwork-related issues, the more likely they are to develop a good quality working relationship. Though it may be somewhat worrying that workplace relationships can be significantly determined by similarity on nonwork place factors, it is a reality that we need to bear in mind for healthy adult-to-adult relationships.

Relating this to the conversations with my managers that led to observation #3, what became increasingly interesting is that although we agreed that our poor relationships were due to work-related factors, it had become easy to subconsciously see our poor relationships as being the result of personal reasons ("you don't like me and that's why we have disagreements about work!"). We "attributed" our issues to personal characteristics instead of recognizing that they emanated from job-related matters. Indeed, while the discussions with my managers were often prefaced by both of us with "this is not personal", it often felt as if it was. There is a real danger in most people's working situation that difference in opinion surrounding how work should be done (task conflict) can be misunderstood as reflecting personal issues (relationship or personality conflict). Interestingly, at least to some extent, it might be a protective mechanism to think "my poor relationship with my manager is because he does not like me personally" (for reasons beyond my control) than due to work reasons (which are within my control).

That brought me to the next observation, which came from the ability, and often inability, of both my managers and me to recognize the times when the relationship was good or poor. Not surprisingly we often concurred when the relationships were good. By contrast we often had different perceptions when the relationships were poor (#5: Managers and subordinates are often inaccurate in perceiving relationship quality). I suspect this is due to three

$$\left\{ \begin{array}{c} \text{\#5: Managers and subordinates are often} \\ \text{inaccurate in perceiving relationship quality.} \end{array} \right\}$$

main reasons. First, I have largely only had one manager at a time while each of these "difficult" managers had multiple subordinates concurrently. So while all of my attention in terms of the quality of my principal work relationships was focused in each of these instances on just one person and by default one relationship, my managers had to divide their attention between many. Second, in each occasion, the consequence of having a good or poor relationship was much greater for me than it was for my manager in terms of my working experience and prospects. Third, because of the second point, when the relationships were poor I would initially be more likely to use a variety of presentation management strategies to try and disguise any negative feelings (to avoid communicating problems to my managers). The inability of both my managers and me to jointly recognize, in the moment, the times when relationship quality was poor became in itself a source of conflict between us! If we could not agree when the relationships were poor, we found it difficult to examine potential reasons for the paucity of the relationships and to correct the issues quickly. At those times it was very easy to underplay the further impact that these multiple factors had upon on our relationships.

The aforementioned were easy observations. The next and final three emerged more slowly.

When I thought about the quality of the relationships I had with my managers, I often thought about the comparison about how I perceived their treatment of my colleagues, the other people in my managers' work teams (#6: Subordinates compare their relationship with their manager to that of other people in the work group).

> #6: Subordinates compare their relationship with their manager to that of other people in the work group.

This in itself brought much greater complexity than I can do justice to in this chapter but let me elaborate briefly. When my relationships with my managers were good, I did not seem to be overly concerned with how they treated other people in our work teams. I use the term "overly concerned" with caution. Of course, I did not like to see other team members have a poor relationship quality with our managers; but it was easy to fall into the trap of thinking that I deserved my "good" relationships with my managers and that others probably didn't because they didn't work as well as I did. Indeed, I came to realize that people with good relationships with their managers often actively seek out the personal weaknesses in those perceived as experiencing bad relationships with the same manager in order to "justify" why they by contrast are favored. However, when my relationships with my managers were poor, I became acutely concerned with how they treated others. I began to see those who enjoyed good working relationships with our managers as being unfairly favored, and those with poor relationships, like myself, as victims! (While the logic backing these judgments may or may not be true, we know human beings are masters at interpreting the world to make it fit what they want.)

When this happened, this subliminal attitude also had an interesting effect on my relationships with other members of the team. On one occasion, when I had a public disagreement with one manager, I was visited by some team members (who I knew also had a poor relationship with that particular manager) to go for a coffee to discuss our problems! Colleagues who were united by the poor relationship with the same manager (albeit for different reasons) formed a cohesive support group. Clearly, seeking out others who also have a poor relationship with managers can be reassuring, affirming that "it's not me but the manager who is to blame"! On the other hand and concurrently, I began to feel excluded by those who had a good relationship with said manager. It seemed as if they thought that being associated with me might taint their own status within the wider reporting group.

There is sometimes a clear distinction in terms of membership between those who enjoy good relationships and those who experience poor relationships with their manager. Such subgrouping can lead to perceptions that there is an "in group" and an "out group". This in turn leads to different degrees of status and further exacerbates conflict within the group. The situation is typical in work groups, especially in very large ones, and underpins my next observation. If managers have different quality relationships with individual members, team members can perceive that the manager is treating them inequitably – even if such a perception is not justified. This can create team conflict (#7: Different manager-subordinate relationship quality can lead to increased team conflict).

{ #7: Different manager-subordinate relationship quality can lead to increased team conflict. }

My penultimate observation is that relationships between managers and subordinates have consequences beyond their immediate manager-subordinate level (#8: Poor manager-subordinate relationship affects many aspects of the work situation beyond the manager-subordinate dyad). I

{ #8: Poor manager-subordinate relationship affects many aspects of the work situation beyond the manager-subordinate dyad. }

know that, on some occasions, my managers had to make adjustments to work group activities as a consequence of poor relationships with direct reports. This was the case even though the relationships, which had been poor in many respects, had not reached a level where outside intervention had become necessary – a frequent occurrence. (It is not uncommon for poor manager-subordinate relationships to need intervention by senior levels of management, HR or other resolution agencies. When these interventions are necessary, the impact becomes much wider than the manager-subordinate dyad, often extending beyond the work team and into the wider organization.)

That in fact leads to my final observation: relationships between managers and their subordinates are dynamic and can change over time (#9: Manager-subordinate relationship quality is dynamic and changes over time). I have been

{ #9: Manager-subordinate relationship quality is dynamic and changes over time. }

fortunate that I have had managers who were willing to discuss our relationship and prepared to work toward one of better quality. These conversations required, and evidenced, a lot of honesty on both sides. On most occasions, through these discussions, we were able to identify the main reasons for the poor relationship and the key factors that caused the relationship to turn from good to bad. With that better understanding we were able to identify core factors and agree ways to overcome the ones that most ruptured our exchanges. Indeed, as a result of such discussions, working relationships ended up being good far more often than they remained poor! This final point is as simple as it is profound: that the quality of a relationship can change for the better – but this requires brave, mature and honest dialogue on the part of both the manager and the subordinate.

To recapitulate, my nine observations from collective experiences are:

1. Poor manager-subordinate relationship quality is a focus of a lot of attention.
2. Manager-subordinate relationship quality affects the subordinate's psychological well-being and performance.
3. Manager-subordinate relationship quality affects the manager's psychological well-being and performance.
4. Manager-subordinate relationship quality is based on work and non work factors.
5. Managers and subordinates are often inaccurate in perceiving relationship quality.
6. Subordinates compare their relationship with their manager to that enjoyed by other people in the work group.
7. Different manager-subordinate relationship quality can lead to increased team conflict.
8. Poor manager-subordinate relationship quality affects many aspects of the work situation beyond the manager-subordinate dyad.
9. Manager-subordinate relationship quality is dynamic and changes over time.

Experiences such as those described previously were the catalyst for my research into leadership. Let me reiterate that while I have positioned the observations as personal, and some were indeed based on my own visceral experience, each of the nine points listed earlier have not only been anecdotally validated by others who I have coached over the years but have also been and continue to be verified through formal research. Most of this research utilizes as a framework the Leader-Member Exchange (LMX) theory, which proposes that managers develop different types of relationship quality (from very poor to very good) with each of their subordinates.

LMX proposes that relationship quality is determined by both work and nonwork factors. As with social relationships in real life, work relationships develop over time through the social exchanges that occur between the leaders and subordinates. In these, as in other relationships, early experiences are particularly important, especially how the subordinate reacts and behaves toward the social exchanges "initiated" by their manager. Through a variety of stages, relationship quality becomes defined and often increasingly difficult to change. Relationship quality is known to correlate very highly with reactions to work (such as job satisfaction and organizational commitment), task performance and employee loyalty (employee turnover). It is also known that teams led by managers who have relationships of different quality with different team members tend to experience high levels of conflict and to underperform.

A view from the other side

So far we have looked at the effect of relationship quality from the perspective of the employee. Given that there are at least two sides to all situations and in light of observation #3, consider the following mini case study of poor work relationships as seen from the point of view of managers.

When I lived in Australia, coaching of managers became a rich activity that informed my research. Part of the coaching process, appropriate to my coachee's situations, was to explore through in-depth discussion the quality of the relationships these managers had with each individual in their teams. (Teams usually consisted of eight to ten people.) Our coaching process was often informed by 360-degree feedback from team members. It was clear that while most managers/coachees had mainly good relationships with the majority of their team members, many had at least one notably poor relationship with a subordinate. Managers in these coaching sessions were very honest in their assessments of such individuals, in admitting that they did not enjoy the company of such individuals and that they often avoided such individuals in the work situation. Through careful discussions it became clear that the negative personal views that managers had of the individuals with whom they had a "poor relationship" were shaping the managers' perception of those individuals' work performance and work behavior. When those subordinates performed well, the managers attributed that good performance to something *external* to those persons (e.g. they had been lucky or had received help from others). By contrast, when such subordinates performed badly they (the managers) attributed that poor performance to reasons *internal* to those persons (e.g. they were simply lazy or suffered from a lack of appropriate skills). By recognizing this "attributional bias", managers realized that their personal dislike for these individuals was creating a bias in the way they perceived the work performance of those individuals. Worse still, in cases where team members detected the bias, the "poor performing" subordinate's feeling of being under-appreciated was exacerbated. Not surprisingly what then became general antipathy toward an individual team member reduced that subordinate's work motivation and had knock-on effects on performance. Sadly I have observed on several occasions the outworking of this self-fulfilling prophesy.

In my experience, by giving managers the opportunity to reevaluate the performance of individuals with whom they have a poor relationship, managers can become aware of previously unspoken perceptions – where these exist. They can be encouraged to recognize personal biases more generally and to work against such by focusing their evaluation of individuals on "hard" performance measures, accrued through multiple assessments from independent parties. Over time, dealing specifically with the subordinates with whom they have difficult relationships, managers were able to change the way they attributed the causes of those particular subordinates' performance and were able to develop better quality relationship with many of them.

The earlier case is based on many real-life examples that I have witnessed in my years as an occupational work psychologist and through my research into manager-subordinate relationships.

Seven enablers of relationship quality between leaders and followers

My personal experiences amplified by my research and coaching examples demonstrate that the quality of the relationship between managers and subordinates is crucial to determining well-being and performance, and to creating a team that feels "safe" enough in its interpersonal relationships to have the capacity to absorb change. This applies not only to the individual subordinates concerned but also to the teams and ultimately, depending on the seniority of the managers, to their organizations as whole entities. There are seven simple practices that managers should undertake in order to improve and ensure the quality of the relationships they have with their direct reports:

1. **Be aware of interpersonal issues and engage in honest dialogue**. If you suspect that the quality of the rela-tionship between you and one or several of your direct reports is poor, take the initiative to discuss it

> Be aware of interpersonal issues and engage in honest dialogue.

privately with the individual concerned – manager to subordinate, directly and exclusively. Frankly, in a mature relationship, taking the initiative should be the responsibility of both the subordinate and the manager – such that one or the other brings attention to and addresses issues before those issues create a problem.

2. **Be consistent in your multiple relationships**. As a manager, endeavor to be consistent in your relationships with your individual { Be consistent in your multiple relationships. } ual direct reports. This consistency is important at both an individual level (how you deal with each person as an individual over time) and across the group (how you deal with different individuals within the group – relative to each other).

3. **Assess the differences in your relationships**. Recognize the "natural" exchanges that you have with different individu- { Assess the differences in your relationships. } als who report to you in order to better manage the tacit differences between those relationships that come from the undeniable human element in the equation.

4. **Acknowledge your natural biases**. Be honest with yourself about the biases, positive and negative, that you are likely to { Acknowledge your natural biases. } have toward the different individuals in your team. Regulate yourself in terms of the relationship differences that ensue.

5. **Be objective in performance assessment**. Regularly measure individual performance on a transparent basis, doing so as { Be objective in performance assessment. } far as possible on a factual basis. Measure delivery against objectives that are within the sphere of control of the individual members of the team and on multiple "assessments" from other different individuals to ensure more than one perspective.

6. **Evaluate team perceptions of relationships**. Consider conducting regular (annual) 360-degree evaluations of the { Evaluate team perceptions of relationships. } working relationships between members of the team and you as their

manager. This form of "reflective assessment" provides a mirror for evidence-based self-evaluation.

7. **Maintain wherever possible a positive note**. While it is important for fairness that you base the quality of your work

$$\left\{ \text{ Maintain wherever possible a positive note. } \right\}$$

relationships with individuals on their actual performance against objectives, recognize that people have to feel positive about themselves as human beings, to feel trusted and to have a sense of belonging, in order to perform at their best and be receptive to embrace change.

Summary

Most managers naturally have different quality relationships with those they manage and this is sometimes a consequence of managing diverse or very large groups. In that context:

1. There are nine significant consequences that follow from poor manager-subordinate relationships.
2. There are seven enablers that help you build and maintain good leader-follower relationships.

Action points

To ensure that the differences remain healthy, managers need to be able to:

- Accurately recognize the quality of the relationships they have with members of their team
- Engage in open and honest dialogue that encourages an examination of relationship quality from both perspectives
- Acknowledge that you will have a different perception of relationship quality than your subordinates
- Try to understand your biases (both positive and negative ones) as these can shape the interpretation of relationship quality
- Be aware of personal nonwork-related biases (e.g. negative stereotypes) affecting your judgments
- Be aware that managers need to be "authentic" (open, transparent and ethical) to encourage good working relationships
- Be prepared to change your mind

Self-assessment tool

To what extent are your team and leadership relationships aligned with good practice? (**Tables 7.1**, **7.2**)

Table 7.1 How good is my organization at fostering change-sustaining leader-follower relationships?

Attribute	Never	Sometimes	Mostly	Always	Cumulative Score
By making a point of being aware of issues and engaging in honest dialogue	0	1	2	3	
By doing our best to be consistent in our multiple relationships	0	1	2	3	
By regularly assessing the differences in our relationships	0	1	2	3	
By acknowledging our natural biases	0	1	2	3	
By endeavoring to be objective in assessing the performance of our direct reports	0	1	2	3	
By evaluating the team's perceptions of relationships	0	1	2	3	
By seeking to maintain relationships on a positive note	0	1	2	3	

Table 7.2 Benchmark scores

0–4	5–9	10–15	16–21
In the danger zone!	Some foundations that need development	Good, but room for improvement	Moving toward consistent high performance

Further reading

Graen, G. B. and Graen, J. A. (2006) (eds) *Sharing Network Leadership*, Charlotte, NC: IAP

Lewiciki, R. J. and Bunker, B. B. (1996) "Developing and Maintaining Trust in Work Relationships", in R. M. Kramer and T. R. Tyler (eds) *Trust in Organizations: Frontiers of Theory and Research*, Thousand Oaks: Sage, pp. 114–32.

Martin, R. (2010) "Vertical Dyad Linkage Model", in J. M. Levine and M. A. Hogg (eds) *Encyclopedia of Group Processes and Intergroup Relations*, Thousand Oaks: Sage, pp. 947–49.

Martin, R., Epitropaki, O., Thomas, G. and Topakas, A. (2010) "A Critical Review of Leader-Member Relationship (LMX) Research: Future Prospects and Directions", *International Review of Industrial and Organisational Psychology*, 25, pp. 35–88.

CHAPTER 8

Organizational Change and Development: A Case Study in the Indian Electricity Market

Pawan Budhwar, Jyotsna Bhatnagar and Debi Saini

Five principles for accommodating cultural nuances to accelerate envisaged change

The Indian economic context

The present economic growth of India is largely an outcome of the liberalization of its economic policies in 1991.[1] Since gaining independence in 1947, India adopted a "mixed economy" approach (emphasizing both private and public enterprise). This had the effect of reducing both entrepreneurship and global competitiveness. Despite the formalities of planning, the Indian economy reached its worst in 1990 and witnessed a double digit rate of inflation, decelerated industrial production, fiscal indiscipline, a very high ratio of borrowing to the GNP (both internal and external) and a dismally low level of foreign exchange reserves. The World Bank and the IMF agreed to bail out India at that time on the condition that it changed to a "free market economy" from what at the time was a regulated regime. To meet the challenges, the government announced a series of economic policies, followed by a new industrial policy supported by fiscal and trade policies. A number of reforms were made in the public sector that affected trade and exchange policy. At the same time, the banking sector together with activity in foreign investment was liberalized.

The economy responded positively to these reforms and India is now considered to be one of the largest global emerging markets. The World Bank forecasts that by 2020 India could become the world's fourth largest economy. In the last few years, further substantial reforms have been made in the telecommunications, financial and shipping sectors, as well as in direct tax structure and industrial policy. Significant reforms have already been initiated in the insurance sector by the present (2011) government. However, India still has to go a long way before it can compete fully with some of the more economically advanced Asian nations. For details on the challenges facing future Indian economic growth see Budhwar and Varma (2011a).

Liberalization of the Indian economy has resulted in sudden and increased levels of competition for Indian firms from international firms. At the same time it has also created opportunities for resource mobilization from new sources. Human resource management (HRM) issues have now become more important with the firms' adoption of strategies of expansion, diversification, turnaround and internationalization. These developments have direct implications for people management in India. The human resource (HR) function across all Indian organizations is under severe pressure to bring about large-scale structural changes in order to cope with the challenges brought about by economic liberalization. Not least it has to develop a domestic workforce capable of taking on the challenges thrown up by the new economic environment. Given such conditions, the core focus of the Indian HR function has been on the development of their human resources (HRD) in order to bring about requisite and major organizational change (see Budhwar and Varma, 2010).

In the present Indian business context, firms are more than ever required to make changes in order to survive and flourish. As a result, the trend in Indian industry encourages organizational change and development practices. The emerging evidence indicates that a number of Indian organizations and managers are making serious efforts to deal with issues of transformation and growth. Topics such as restructuring, reengineering, realignment of systems and structures, modification of tasks and adoption of new technology seem to have become the new success imperatives. These are putting pressure on all organizational functions to both rationalize and professionalize (Budhwar and Varma, 2011b). In this regard, there has been some evidence of a general need among the managerial cadre to build capabilities, resources, competencies, strategies for both macro as well as micro HRM/HRD activities. Also, researchers have raised the need for relevant people development and Organization Development (OD) interventions to deliver quality improvements, cost-efficiency, to improve corporate ethical practices, to provide for employee development and enhance motivation, to build team functioning and to deliver change management programs.

Developments in OC and OD in India

Management of change refers to the process or strategy by which resistance to change is significantly reduced. Organizational change (OC) can occur in many forms – but fundamentally always in the context of growth, transformation or decline. All forms of change need to be managed. In the growing literature on OC, transformational change has attracted most attention. It is referred to as reinvention, radical or frame-breaking change and involves simultaneous alterations in strategy, architecture and culture of an organization.

> Management of change refers to the process or strategy by which resistance to change is significantly reduced.

A number of researchers have prescribed different mechanisms that can facilitate OC in Indian organizations. For example, Ramnarayan (2003) attempted transformational change in several Indian government organizations and found that a combination of both psychological and leadership-related impediments affect change efforts. He also presents a case of unsuccessful transformational change in a large engineering organization. This research found that transformational changes in large Indian organizations fail if managers do not address three important factors: mindsets and routines, architecture and the final

> ... a combination of both psychological and leadership related impediments affect change efforts

> ... three important factors: mindsets and routines, architecture and the final destination of change

$\left\{ \begin{array}{c} \text{... successful change management requires} \\ \text{effective leadership at the top} \end{array} \right\}$ destination of change. Undoubtedly, success-ful change management requires effective leadership at the top and sensitization of the top-level executives.

Further, in order to tackle resistance to change, prescriptive suggestions (such as raising people's awareness, understanding, acceptance of and commitment to the change process) are made by researchers (see Burnes, 2006). By contrast, others prescribe solutions that involve "architecting" and "processizing" the change management process (e.g. Kotter and Cohen, 2006). Clearly change strategy is known to trigger HRD/OD interventions, be they focused on structural, technological or behavioral change strategies.

Not surprisingly, OD has grown tremendously in the West over the last five decades or so. In India, its emergence would appear to be more recent, especially where it has been used to bring about changes in people, in technology and in organizational processes and structures. In the post-liberalization scenario, Indian organizations were forced to change to survive and flourish. In order to tackle such challenges, a strong HRD movement developed in India over the last 15 years or so that has been merged with wider OD efforts (see Budhwar and Bhatnagar, 2009). Although many Indian organizations have been using OD interventions (either via their managers as internal change agents or by help of external consultants) to bring about change, not many cases have been documented in existing literature. Moreover, except for few researchers who have highlight OD failures in India, it is largely the successful OD experiences that have been documented.

Existing literature on OCD (organizational change and development) in India then suggests that the terms "change management" and "OD" have been used interchangeably. Corporate transformation and organizational transformation have also been used as a synonym for change management. As indicated earlier, change management in India is a relatively new discipline that focuses on the why and how of organizational change. Some researchers (e.g. Sharma, 2007) have highlighted the cost and risks associated with change, while others have come up with the concept of "Institutional Development" (ID) where an institution may be simply defined as an "organization of organizations", for example, the Federation of Indian Chamber of Commerce and Industry (FICCI).

Effectively, the roots of OD in India can be traced back to early 1960s when a group of Indian professionals trained at the National Training Laboratories at Bethel, Maine in USA brought OD technology to India. At that time, "grid programs" were initiated at Larsen & Toubro. By the mid-1960s T-groups were initiated and widely used at the Small Industries Extension Training (SIET) Institute, Hyderabad; at the State Bank of India; and in the Indian Institute of Management (IIM) programs. These few initiatives, despite being seen as isolated efforts, formed the basis of OD in India. In the 1970s, OD was incorporated as a formal part of the HRD department of Larsen & Toubro. This was not carried forward by other organizations that operated in very protected and secured environment as they felt less compulsion to change. Hence, till lately, OD has been largely restricted to academic institutions.

As an interesting aside, there has been some debate regarding the extent to which HRD and OD interventions are considered to be the same in the Indian context. Sharma (2007) summarizes such debates while incorporating contributions of a number of Indian scholars. For example, Dayal states that both OD and HRD are two different concerns, they may be related but are not the same. Singh on the other hand, states that HRD and OD are not only highly compatible but also complimentary to each other. While all HRD efforts are aimed at bringing about performance improvement and/or personal growth, OD is focused on improving the work environment through planned, long-term and group-oriented change in organizational structures or interpersonal relations. In Pareek and Rao's model of HRD department, OD has been conceived as one of the main tasks of the HRD department. Thus, the intention has been to institutionalize OD through HRD departments. According to McLagan, OD, training and development and career development are components of HRD. In fact training and development have been proved to be an effective means for successfully pursuing various OD interventions in India. This is mainly because training raises the consciousness of participants, makes people aware of the gaps between reality and ideals, provides a common language to articulate shared problems and difficulties, generates ideas for change and creates greater energy for change. Thus, over the last few decades a variety of OD/HRD interventions have been used in Indian organizations.

An analysis of the Indian literature then highlights that: (1) OD interventions have been practiced in a variety of Indian organizations over the past few decades; (2) a number of different OC initiatives and OD interventions have been adopted in the Indian context; (3) there is less research related to strategic HRD audits and the resultant transformational organizational change that it creates; (4) hardly any research exists on recently privatized Indian companies and the key role of HRD and related functions in transforming the same and (5) there is still a strong scarcity of OCD research in the new Indian economic environment.

Realizing this gap in the literature and the growing importance of HRM/HRD in the journey of improving a firm's performance, this chapter zooms in on the extent to which HRM and OD/OC practices are pursued systematically to facilitate major change in the Indian organizational context and the extent to which HRM audits validate the role of HRM as an agent for organizational change.

{ ... extent to which HRM audits validate the role of HRM as an agent for organizational change }

To this end we documented a case study with an HRM/HRD audit in an Indian organization that was undergoing radical change: North Delhi Power Limited (NDPL). Its conclusions give us significant insight into a successful change program in a significant and critical Indian infrastructure organization.

Research method

We adopted a case study research design with a mixed method approach that included 30 unstructured in-depth interviews with different stakeholders of the case company. Those interviewed included the CEO; HR Head, HR managers; heads of main functional areas; line managers and customers of the organization. Additionally we conducted a survey with the employees. The key themes along which the interviews were conducted included: organizational culture (before NDPL was formed) from both management and employees' perspective; key HR and strategic OD interventions to be used for change; key strategic HR themes (e.g. flexibility, empowerment, leadership building, job enrichment, work culture interventions, human resource information systems, team building, etc.); and identification of concrete cases, events, reflecting claims of the management in support of these HR/OD interventions.

The case of NDPL: transformation via OD interventions

The power sector in India has been passing through an extended phase of major transformation. Huge losses incurred by state electricity boards caused a heavy burden on the exchequer. Major contributors to these losses include inefficient systems, large-scale corruption, pilferage of power, inability of boards to collect revenue and general lack of accountability of employees. In the present economic context, India can't afford the losses enjoyed by electricity boards over the past decades.

In a north Indian state, the process of privatization of the power sector was initiated in March 1999 with the establishment of Delhi Electricity

Regulatory Commission (DERC). Following this, in March 2001, the Enactment of Delhi Electricity Reform Act came into existence. Delhi Electricity's reform transfers scheme rules were notified in November 2001. The process was completed in May 2002.

The Delhi Vidyut (electricity) Board (DVB) had been split into six companies – three distribution companies and separate holding, transmission and generation companies. Historically, DVB's high losses had particularly been attributable to its distribution activities. In order to control the losses, DVB transferred ownership of the first distribution company to two private companies, Tata Power Company (TPC) and Bombay Suburban Electric Supply (BSES) on July 1, 2002. In August 2002, the two distribution companies of BSES were renamed as BSES Rajdhani Power Limited (South-West region) and BSES Yamuna Power Limited (Central-East region). TPC renamed the North-Northwest Delhi Distribution as NDPL. Two of the chapter's authors were invited to conduct an empirical investigation (participant observation, interviews and a questionnaire survey) to understand the change process initiated at NDPL in order to reduce losses, improve efficiency within the organization, raise customer satisfaction and increase revenues and shareholders' value as per its new strategy. In 2002 the annual aggregate technical and commercial (AT&C) losses of all state electricity boards had reached a whopping Rs 25,000 crore (£1 = Rs 75). The critical commitment of NDPL was to bring such losses down to 31 percent from a level of 53 percent at the time of privatization, with an expected load growth at the rate of 7–10 percent in the following five years.

The NDPL case focused on the management of change in the acquisition of an ailing government-run public utility company by a public-private partnership (PPP), in this case between DVB and NDPL. It shows how efficiencies were attained through the introduction of basic functional structures and formal performance management and change management processes. The nexuses between different interest groups (such as slum dwellers and industrial/commercial consumers), which had partly led to malaise in the earlier organizational setup, were substantially diluted by sagacious leadership as well as by pressures to change.

Organization structure at the time of takeover was chaotic (e.g. in some cases even the existence of persons in whose name salaries was disbursed were not always known). To sort this out, a manpower mapping exercise (mainly in the form of meetings) was initiated for the entire organization in September 2002. Two executives were exclusively assigned to this task. An analysis of the secondary data, along with detailed discussions with senior executives about the existing patterns of reporting and manning levels were undertaken. One important outcome of this exercise was the appointment of 482 new NDPL employees (which included 300 engineers to facilitate the operations and maintenance work and 15 MBAs in different functional areas) to expedite the change effort. As per the MOU (memorandum of understanding) signed at the time of acquisition, NDPL inherited 5368 employees from the DVB. The CEO devised an attractive voluntary retirement scheme. Out of the total DVB workforce, 1794 employees sought retirement under the voluntary retirement scheme. This included about 90 percent of the meter readers. The union was involved in the rightsizing process throughout. The DVB-scheme employees continued to be governed by the old DVB pay structure as per the MOU. They were also entitled to pension and retirement benefits as per the DVB structure. A number of changes were also made to the job titles such that an operator became a "service associate", and the chief engineer of erstwhile DVB came to be considered equivalent to a deputy general manager.

To a great extent the new employees acted as key change agents in the transformation process as they did not have to face the reengineering impact like the DVB employees. Also, the existence, knowledge and role of the new employees in the organization went a long way in working toward changing the mindsets of those associated with the DVB culture. They also put the requisite peer pressure on those affected by the anxieties and fears of the reengineering decision and consequently made them realize that quite simply they had to learn to adjust with the new dispensation or leave.

Role of top managers as the main change catalyst

The CEO of NDPL was respected by his entire team for his charismatic and visionary leadership qualities. His technical competencies and soft skills proved to be one of the important change management "tools". Similarly, with personal competence, experience and a proactive mindset, the HR General Manager facilitated the transformation by articulating and implementing NDPL's people management strategy.

The CEO led from the front. He knew that in order to exponentially improve the pre-takeover work culture, which was absolutely pathetic, he had to demonstrate a concern for urgency as well as detail. One of his main goals for example was to achieve corporate excellence through customer satisfaction. His strong technical background proved very helpful throughout the change process. He was even seen explaining a circuit diagram to the members concerned in meetings. Some of his meetings, with the engineers got converted into training sessions as the situations so demanded. This helped to promote a sense of urgency and the commitment to change on the part of the senior management. He conveyed to the team members his pressing concerns and laid down the standards of his expectations in these meetings. He also reminded them of the need for and his determination to take on issues head-on rather than avoiding or suppressing them. Most of these managers were erstwhile DVB people who were initially docile in these meetings. The CEO used both soft and hard measures to enhance their performance and raise their commitment levels.

The CEO's working style showed his determination to acclimatize the DVB-scheme employees into the new ethos of NDPL. He succeeded to a reasonably good extent. His belief that corporate performance is determined not just

> { ... corporate performance is determined not just by customer care, but equally by focusing on employee care }

by customer care, but equally by focusing on employee care and on their involvement in decision-making was useful in order to promote employee commitment and, to a great extent, legitimize his change agenda. His humane approach to downsizing and redeployment was admired by the common employee. In

> { ... humane approach to downsizing and redeployment and regular communication with the employees }

the fortnightly meetings with his team members, the CEO emphasized the need for regular communication with the employees, which helped to direct the change effort. He gave significant priority to the issue of removing fear among employees that is usually witnessed in merger and acquisition situations. This was

> { ... removing fear among employees that is usually witnessed in merger and acquisition situations }

more significant in the takeover of an Indian government-run enterprise, as within these employees enjoy lifetime employment without much accountability. His willingness to listen and allegiance to transparent working practices were

> { ... willingness to listen, open approach toward redressing grievances, sense of transparency }

seen as positive by most employees and the union, which helped dilute their adversarial feelings toward organizational issues. His open approach toward redressing grievances created a strong impression on the employees in general. The "meet the CEO scheme" demonstrated his sense of transparency, and added to his stature as a leader. His positive stance on three of the burning

> { ... positive stance on employees' burning issues secured consent to change }

issues from employees' point of view – uniforms, widow fund and time-bound promotion – could be seen as a *quid pro quo* for securing the employees' consent to the change agenda.

Modernization and rationalization of performance management system

Adoption of performance measurement methods (such as the balanced scorecards) sent signals that

$\left\{ \begin{array}{c} \text{... performance measurement supported} \\ \text{by reliable data} \end{array} \right\}$ claims of better performance need to be supported by reliable

data. These efforts included devising the performance management system, a system of zonal performance, and sending zonal performance data through e-mail to relevant people and departments. The MIS (built through software programming) was fully internalized and considered as a necessity for knowing where the company stood. The centralized control room located in one of the grid stations circulated the report on operations to all concerned functional departments via e-mail. A performance-monitoring cell was specially created to directly report to the CEO. The respective functional heads prepared the functional reports on a monthly basis; this included, among others, the monthly human resource information system (HRIS). An HRIS is made up of a set of activities that has *inputs* (an application for employment in the finance department, for example), *transforms* them into useful items (a hiring approval from the HR department), and then *outputs* in the form of new items where they can be used (e.g. sends the approval to the finance department). It also has a feedback or *control* mechanism (the finance department sends back a completed new employee report) that helps supervisors to manage the operation of the system.

This collection of initiatives built pressure on weaker zones to improve their performance and change their existing ways of working. Further, one of the present authors along with his HR team conducted work optimization studies on "manpower norms" to find out the productivity ratios, working efficiency and employee engagement level. The findings of such studies were collated in June 2003, November 2003 and January 2004 respectively. The HR department also undertook a comparative study with similar utility providers in India such as Tata Power Centre, NTPC and Powergrid to develop a benchmark for roaster, shift timings and the manpower requirements for grid stations. The findings were replicated for district/circle/common functions, taking into cognizance the expected variance in the workload.

The initiative to change the organization structure gave signals about the core values of NDPL, most of which had been adopted from Tata Power (the parent company). The resulting changes can be exemplified as follows: every circle/zone, which was responsible for operations and maintenance of the area in its jurisdiction, used to be manned by 30 to 40 people. In the post-takeover scenario, just five people were necessary to manage a circle. This was made possible by the use of appropriate technology, computerization and organizational restructuring. Also most of the job titles were changed from executive engineer, assistant engineer, etc. to manager, assistant manager, office associate, work attendant and so on. Expectedly, new job titles aroused considerable resistance initially from most DVB-scheme employees, including senior officers – but things fell into place after a while.

One of the other primary aims of the planned change was to focus on functional requirements and to align them with performance demands and customer needs rather than putting importance on hierarchical supremacy. The expected standards of performance were made clear from the outset. The company's investment into welfare issues and improving working conditions helped legitimize the employer brand of NDPL. The entire change effort demonstrated seriousness of purpose, which sent a clear message to all that old habits and inefficient ways of working would no longer be tolerated. Thus, those DVB-scheme employees who did not want to avail themselves of the voluntary retirement scheme were compelled to demonstrate a higher degree of commitment. Communication and knowledge management initiatives also helped to internalize the new performance culture, which was based on measurement of performance through implementation of key result areas. (This contrasted with analysis of earlier practices that revealed a disappointing picture of no proper system of performance appraisal and review. Ratings had been based on religion, caste and personal relations. The very few promotions that took place were based on existing seniority and were generally manipulated by the administration.)

When employees were asked to give Key Result Areas and their job descriptions, it led to a lot of heartburn within the rank and file of the organization. The CEO and one of the present researchers had to work very hard to get information in this regard. They organized a series of workshops and finally 240 Key Result Areas for 70–90 managerial positions were agreed on.

The HR team comprising four members completed the manpower mapping that was technology driven. It also proposed a two-tier appraisal system.

1. **Organizational performance management system**: Based on the targets set by the company, this included business performance such as

financial performance, commercial targets, consumer billing, capital expenditure, engineering billing, etc.

2. **Individual performance management system**: In this system, performance of individuals was judged on the basis of their Key Result Areas, given to executives up to the level of assistant managers. For each set of positions, certain levels of competency are desired. Poor performance had an adverse effect on final remuneration.

A "perform or perish strategy" is presently followed at NDPL. A special reward scheme was introduced to recognize ingenuities and promote talent. The scheme has four categories of awards: "extra kilowatt award", "extra megawatt award", "grid award" and "the CEO award". More than 40 awards were given under the scheme in a single year. Employees who successfully achieve their targets are rewarded with appreciation certificates and target mementos. Further, special quarterly awards and monthly awards have been institutionalized and nonperformance letters are also given to employees.

The CEO along with the research team proceeded to establish a fairer assessment of individuals' performance linking it with the reward and incentive system. Further, they decided to institutionalize a web-enabled Performance Management System, which would be fully aligned with the organizational goals and evaluation criteria of the individuals. The intention of such a Performance Management System is to track individual performance, track organizational and divisional performance (for a set of well-defined parameters that would be eventually linked to the balance scorecard) and to develop a link between the two systems.

The CEO further initiated a top management forum, which aimed at fostering multipronged communication among management members and also at facilitating performance monitoring.

Though Kotter and Cohen (2006) do not focus on performance management as a key factor for change management, in the context of NDPLs' goals and

$$\left\{ \begin{array}{c} \text{... performance measurement: a key aspect} \\ \text{of change management in the Indian context} \end{array} \right\}$$

working it should be noted as a key aspect of change management in the Indian context, and more so when dealing with a workforce imbued in a strong bureaucratic culture. The company had to deal with public sector mindsets,

$$\left\{ \begin{array}{c} \text{... and more so when dealing with a} \\ \text{workforce imbued in a strong bureaucratic} \\ \text{culture} \end{array} \right\}$$

corruption and inefficiencies, and needed to deliver an immediate message: that it was capable of stemming the rot that was plaguing DVB.

Apart from these strategies, the company also used paternalism in managing business excellence to overcome employee diffidence. As a result, NDPL improved its functioning on several

$$\left\{ \begin{array}{c} \text{... paternalism in managing business} \\ \text{excellence to overcome employee} \\ \text{diffidence} \end{array} \right\}$$

operational parameters. For example, it benchmarked itself against the top five utilities in the world. In particular relation to billing errors, substantial reduction had taken place since the time of the takeover, but this remained an area of concern.

To better understand and manage performance, NDPL hired a market survey firm to understand and accurately measure its consumer preferences. It is now benchmarked on various parameters: for example, its equity indices with international standards. The hired market survey firm now conducts the market survey every quarter. Issues related to customer requirement analysis, reliability of services, price and ambience of customer care center have been identified and resultant amendments have been made. For example, avenues for bill payment have been increased from 22 to 1150 in two years. Power interruptions have been reduced from 50 to 16 per year. Average waiting time for bill payment went down by a factor of four. Customer confidence in paying bills by checks has increased to 50 percent. In remote areas where collection centers were less in numbers, mobile catch vans have been made available for collection of bills. Customers are also increasingly using the Internet to pay their bills.

Such initiatives were followed by regular audits of the distribution network, which has resulted in the rationalization of the billing system, replacement of faulty meters and aggressive enforcement activities. All these actions demonstrated the seriousness of the company's purpose to one and all. The performance of the new recruits put pressure on the DVB-scheme employees to perform or leave. Attempts toward adoption and implementation of the Tata Business Excellence Model also facilitated performance.

HRD initiatives as an OD intervention

To achieve such ambitions, the company made HRD a strategic priority by also investing in training. Training need analysis was instigated to assess skills and knowledge required for different levels of the organization. For example, initially in July 2002, for the 5000 employees in the organization there were 100 individuals assigned exclusively to salary preparation. NDPL management decided to reduce this number and to that end introduced computers into the salary department. To facilitate such a move, it was necessary to train the retained employees. Additionally, quality improvement training was provided to the concerned employees. This improved general technical proficiency in the organization. Moreover, some old transformers were replaced with new transformers and in this regard training was provided to technicians for maintenance of the new equipment. Training for team building was also designed following a brainstorming session.

Since the creation of NDPL, a record 9000 plus man-days of training has been imparted to 4500 employees under a planned and sustained training schedule covering operational, technical and IT skills and also fundamental programs on consumerism and communication. However, NDPL has miles to go to fully develop HRD as a determinant change management tool.

Like that of the CEO, the role of the HR head in facilitating the change was important. Internally there were burning issues of setting the right tone of affection and care for internal people, reducing fear and increasing trust. His leadership was marked by a concern for acclimatizing the employees to the core values of the company. The policies and OD interventions devised and implemented by the HRM department helped to determine industrial harmony. They helped employees integrate to adopt the Tata culture within the company's industrial relations (IR) policy.

OD interventions were designed at the individual, team and organizational levels. They encompassed a complex interaction of many issues and challenges that are handled simultaneously by the CEO and the head of HR. Two DVB employees, retained as consultants, helped the company articulate the employee expectations and devise ways to meet them within the limits of acceptability. Internal communication through employee newsletter and "Joint Interaction Forum" helped to nurture acclimatization of the DVB-scheme employee into the new-organization ethos to a reasonably good degree. Also, the HRIS and Key Result Areas developed by the HR department were some of the most important work accomplished. Their initiatives on framing and implementing a quality policy were also appreciable. The HR department's decision to send union leaders to Tata Steel at Jamshedpur to observe labor-management cooperation made a good impact on developing an atmosphere of cooperation and encouraged the leaders themselves to play the role of change agents.

Further, the researchers carried out an independent strategic HRD audit to gauge the role of HR department in the change process and to gauge the perception of employees, line managers and HR managers about the HR/ OD interventions administered. The findings of the survey were used by the

HR department to diagnose the perception of employees regarding existing problems versus different functions at NDPL. Demographic analysis was further used to gauge the acceptability of the various interventions undertaken by the HR department.

Content analysis of the qualitative information indicates that the HR department played three strategic roles well. These roles were:

1. To introduce a forward-thinking organization. Employees believed that a progressive organization had brought about many changes in a very short span of time.

2. To be a strategic partner. The strength of this perception may be due to the fact that the strategic role played by the HR department in most organizational contexts had not been clearly visible to all within Indian organizations.

3. To present a coherent and holistic approach to change. In order to bring effective and efficient organizational change, it is important that the principle of coherence exists and is practiced among the concerned functions (e.g. HR, customer care, marketing, finance) so that the core change agents have a comprehensive approach to change.

Conclusions

The previous analysis and discussion highlights the main developments in the fields of OC and OD in the Indian context and the need for more empirical investigations regarding how Indian firms are changing to adapt to the pressures created by the economic environment. Like most successful organizational transformations, the case of NDPL reiterates the need to pursue correlated strategies (such as an efficient top management team, identification of core problems, clear targets for change, clear benchmarks to follow and appropriate OD interventions). NDPL invested much effort to improve the performance and turn the company around. The usefulness of each actor (such as the top management, new employees), each action (e.g. new job titles, identification of core problems) and each initiative (such as adoption of computer, IT, MIS, balance scorecards, manpower norming, HRD audits) is clearly evident from the earlier analysis in changing NDPL into an efficient company. NDPL needs to build on these successes to further ensure long-term efficiency at NDPL. In this regard, the HR department needs to remain a true business partner and its activities need to continue to be inextricably aligned to the business strategy.

From the research it is clear that HR in NDPL is moving from a functional to a strategic HR role. All three strategic HR roles are present at NDPL, though at a moderate level. The transformation may take some time. If these efforts are continued, NDPL will be able to attract, retain, motivate and develop the necessary human resources and thus to continuously position itself as an organization that instigates and responds to emergent change according to current and future requirement.

The research highlights the growing strategic role of HRM in the Indian context and also significantly contributes to the field of OCD. OD interventions perhaps require effort, as does the marketing of HR as an agent for change. HR on the other hand needs to aggressively market itself – both its image and initiatives – to showcase to internal customers the impact that HR interventions can have and are having on the business.

This research also suggests a growing need for the institutionalization of talent management, specifically in the way it is anchored to the entire HR value chain within the organization. Further, it suggests a need to establish the entire HR architecture with an emphasis on first establishing a climate of trust and the removal of fear from employees' minds regarding adverse impacts of change. The widespread establishment of more sophisticated HR subsystems like balance scorecards and talent management is perhaps only a question of time in the present Indian context.

Summary

There are five principles for accommodating cultural nuances to accelerate envisaged change:

1. Raising commitment levels across the organization and promoting a sense of urgency
2. Focusing on employees care and involvement in decision-making
3. Carrying out regular training need analysis and delivering relevant programs that address these needs
4. Institutionalizing talent management
5. Establishing a climate of trust

Action points

- Use both soft and hard measures to enhance performance, raise commitment levels and promote a sense of urgency on the part of senior management.
- Determine corporate performance not just by customer care, but equally by focusing on employee care and involving them in decision-making.
- Carry out training need analysis regularly to take into account skills and knowledge required for different levels of the organization.
- Pursue correlated strategies such as:
  - ☐ Establishing an efficient top management team
  - ☐ Identifying core problems
  - ☐ Setting clear targets for change and clearing benchmarks to follow
  - ☐ Launching appropriate OD interventions
- Aim to institutionalize talent management, to anchor it in the entire HR value chain within the organization.
- Build the entire HR architecture with an emphasis on first:
  - ☐ Establishing a climate of trust
  - ☐ Removing fear from employees' minds regarding adverse impacts of change

Self-assessment tool

To what extent is your organization adopting culturally sensitive HR practices to manage change more effectively? (**Tables 8.1**, **8.2**)

Table 8.1 How good is my organization at accelerating culturally nuanced change?

Attribute	Never	Sometimes	Mostly	Always	Cumulative Score
By raising commitment levels and promoting a sense of urgency on the part of senior management	0	1	2	3	
By focusing on employee care and their involvement in decision-making	0	1	2	3	
By conducting training needs analysis regularly	0	1	2	3	
By institutionalizing talent management, to anchor it in the entire HR value chain	0	1	2	3	
By establishing a climate of trust and removing fear from employees' minds	0	1	2	3	

Table 8.2 Benchmark scores

0–3	4–8	9–12	13–15
In the danger zone!	Some foundations that need development	Good, but room for improvement	Moving toward consistent high performance

Notes

1. The research outlined in this chapter was originally published as the following journal article: Bhatnagar, J., Budhwar, P., Saini, D. and Srivastava, P. (2010) "Organizational Change and Development in India: A Case of Strategic Organizational Change and Transformation", *Journal of Organizational Change Management*, 23(5), pp. 485–99

Further reading

Budhwar, P. and Varma, A. (2011a) (eds) *Doing Business in India*, London: Routledge.

Budhwar, P. and Varma, A. (2011b) "Emerging HR Management in India and the way forward", *Organizational Dynamics*, 40(4), pp. 317–25.

Budhwar, P. and Varma, A. (2010) "Guest Editors' Introduction: Emerging Patterns of HRM in the New Indian Economic Environment", *Human Resource Management*, 49(3), pp. 343–51.

Budhwar, P. and Bhatnagar, J. (2009) *The Changing Face of People Management in India*, London: Routledge.

Burnes, B. (2006) *Managing Change*, Harlow: FT Prentice-Hall.

Clardy, A. (2004) "Toward an HRD Auditing Protocol: Assessing HRD Risk Management Practices", *HumanResourceDevelopment Review*, 3(2), pp. 124–50.

Kotter, J. P. and Cohen, D. S. (2006) *The Heart of Change: Real-life Stories of How People Change their Organizations*, Boston: Harvard Business School Press.

Ramnarayan, S. (2003) "Changing Mindsets of Middle-level Officers in Government Organizations", *Vikalpa*, 28(4), pp. 63–76.

Sharma, R. R. (2007) *Change Management: Concepts and Applications*, New Delhi: Tata McGraw-Hill.

CHAPTER 9

Leveraging Relationships to Get Ready for Change

Paula Jarzabkowski, Michael Smets and Paul Spee

Four strategies toward key external relationships to effectively implement strategic change

Introduction

At its most fundamental, businesses are built by establishing relationships with customers.[1] Such relationships enable you to capture more of their patronage by better evaluating and servicing their needs. High-volume industries with fragmented customers, such as supermarkets and other retailers of fast-moving consumer goods can use rich purchasing data points and information technology to develop customer relationship management systems based on mass customization. They need little actual contact with consumers to understand their needs and buying patterns, to better understand how to secure more of what they spend. Much has been written about these industries, and about how they can capture value through advanced customer relationship management systems.

By contrast, industries that are characterized by relatively low-volume but often high-value transactions with a limited number of market participants (such as professional service firms, many investment-based financial service organizations and the reinsurance industry) require deep knowledge of clients in order to evaluate the quality of their business proposition

> { ... deep knowledge of clients, "relationship-intensive" industries }

and tailor packages to their often complex needs. We term these "relationship-intensive" industries because deep relationships that involve significant investment of time and resources are critical to establish and maintain the basis for doing business. Less has been written about effective relationship management to add value and support growth and change in such industries. This chapter is a contribution to stimulate that end.

In relationship-intensive industries, strategic decision-makers in the respective companies have a range of opportunities to meet and build relationships with others. Road shows, conferences and social outings like golf days, sport events and theater visits all enable the development and maintenance of relationships. While these events can be pleasant, they are also time consuming, involving a small number of key people within the company whose time is a scarce resource. The point of all this personal contact is to garner valuable information and gain impressions that tacitly inform strategic

> { ... personal contact tacitly informs strategic thinking }

thinking about the business relationship. As these relationships are also personal, often developed through prolonged contact and trust between specific individuals, it can therefore be hard to distinguish between a quality business relationship and a good personal relationship. Additionally, much relationship behavior is tacit, unrecognized by the individuals in question even as they forge and maintain relationships and make business decisions based on them.

It is thus critical to develop a strategic approach to relationship management in relationship-intensive industries that both identifies the best ways to meet, and which levels of strategic decision-maker in the company should be meeting in different situations. A strategic approach can help to distinguish between clients and allocate firm resources appropriately to support the development of a portfolio of business relationships that align with the firm's strategy and appetite for growth or change.

In this chapter, we offer recommendations for managers in relationship-intensive industries to think more deeply about how to take a strategic, portfolio-based approach to their corporate relationships. We will

{ ... how to take a strategic, portfolio-based approach to corporate relationships }

illustrate our chapter with examples from our two-year global study of the major players in the reinsurance industry – a relationship-intensive finance sector industry. We offer a framework to think systemically about business-to-business relationships and to manage them in ways that support current and future business, particularly in relationship-intensive industries, that are based on deep and often personal relationships with a relatively small number of market participants.

Such relationships are often based on personal contact that builds trust. We shall first unpack the association between trust and information quality, in order to provide greater insight into how being selective about relationship activities can support information and help to build trust in business relationships. We will then introduce the two key dimensions of our framework, which are (1) long-term business value and (2) information quality. These two form a matrix of four distinct relationships that should be managed very differently. It is critical to understand what type of relationships you want to have, with whom and how that relationship is best managed. We will use the information-value matrix to outline how to establish a portfolio approach to managing business relationships for growth and change.

Case examples that contextualize our recommendations

The global reinsurance industry is both an important sector in its own right and one with application to other relationship-intensive industries and services. The reinsurance market is of great economic significance with reinsurance companies holding invested assets of some US$ 927 billion in stock markets (IAIS, 2009). It also has great social significance, supporting the pricing and protection of insurance cover for the policy-holding public at large. Reinsurance is effectively the insurance of insurance companies. Reinsurance markets enable insurance companies to better leverage their capital by providing financial cover in the event of a big loss, such as hurricanes, floods and terrorism, which involve large-scale insurance claims. This lowers the cost of capital for insurance companies, helps to keep direct insurance prices more affordable and ensures the liquidity of insurers to pay out in the wake of a loss. For example, in recent world events, such as the 2010 oil leak in deep-water horizon, the earthquakes in Chile (2010) and

New Zealand (2011), or the 2011 tsunami in Japan, the reinsurance industry underwrote significant proportions of the risks that insurance companies had taken. The reinsurance sector paid out for much of the losses experienced.

Global reinsurance markets represent an ideal context in which to study relationship management. Reinsurance firms must make judgments and allocate significant capital to high-value, high-severity risks, such as earthquakes, hurricanes and floods, where the quality of information and probability of events is uncertain and difficult to model accurately. Hence, in addition to quantitative modeling, reinsurance underwriters are continuously looking for "soft" information to supplement their knowledge of the risks they are underwriting and their confidence in their clients, the insurance companies that they are underwriting. In turn, the insurance companies that are clients are looking not only to purchase risk cover at a good price, but to know that the reinsurers they are working with will be both financially solvent and willing to meet their commitments to pay claims in the event of a major and unpredictable loss, such as a tsunami. Both business parties are thus looking to establish deep relationships that provide information about and trust in each other. They gain this information through a protracted decision-making process that involves multiple opportunities for reinsurers and clients to meet at conferences, on-site visits to the insurance premises, on road shows where the clients visit their reinsurers, and at social events such as golf days, sailing and ski trips and dinners. At these meetings, managers at different levels from underwriters to CEOs meet to discuss business, socialize and often meet each other's partners. The aim of these meetings is to develop sticky, long-term relationships that can be sustained over many years, providing reinsurance cover in both good and bad years. As the COO of a leading reinsurance company notes about his meetings with key insurance clients:

If you are friends, it's very nice. We have friends in the industry but we try to keep that separate. I could spend three months a year sailing, golfing and skiing because of the invitations I get but we normally don't accept. We're talking about business; it's a serious thing and we are exposing a lot of money from our shareholders and our decisions are not based on who is giving you the best golfing experience. It's based on a business relationship and that is important for us. We make sure that someone at senior management level visits the senior management of our key clients around the globe at least once a year. All that this is doing really is ensuring there is sufficient activity, that there is the right type of behavior going on in our company in relation to extremely important people in our client company.

COO, European Reinsurance Firm

Relationships: personal or corporate? Based on trust or information?

At first glance, using relationships to get ready for change seems odd. Relationships thrive on – and provide – longevity, reliability and stability: features of our lives that are

> { Relationships thrive on – and provide – longevity, reliability and stability; the exact opposite of change. }

the exact opposite of change. Relationships make the future seem a little bit more certain and foreseeable. In a relationship, what is to come seems more likely to be like what has gone before, which is a comforting idea in a turbulent business environment in which tomorrow rarely looks much like yesterday and we are forced to adapt to change at an ever increasing pace. But maybe it is that idea of comfort that is the problem when we come to think about relationships from a business perspective – and in the context of getting ready for change.

At a closer look, relationships are not only a good instrument for making (business) life more predictable and reducing the need to adapt, but are also a great tool for shaping the future, which allows those who use it skillfully to proactively shape their future business environment. Rather than adjusting reactively to the future, why not shape a brighter future by building it with existing relationships? These relationships can involve a variety of stakeholders, such as suppliers, staff, competitors or regulators. The most critical, however, are relationships with one's customers. It is critical to establish a picture of the future that resonates with their needs and to build your growth and strategic portfolio around these client relationships. In order to create a desirable future, you need to understand what customers need now and how to adapt (reactively). Equally and more importantly, you need to appreciate what customers are likely to need in the future and to shape that future (proactively). Essentially, good relationship management is about creating a joint and coherent understand-ing of what the future

> { ... good relationship management is about creating a joint and coherent understanding of what the future will and should look like for mutual organizational business benefit }

will and should look like for mutual organizational business benefit. Hence, whatever your time horizon and however radical the change you may con-sider, you can use your relationships to get ready for it.

Relationships come in a variety of shapes and sizes. Instinctively, all of us maintain a host of personal relationships with families and friends and many business relationships start from a personal link. Therefore, it is not surprising that many people take their understanding of personal relationships into business, particularly when the business context for relationship-intensive industries provides many opportunities to develop personal relationships between decision-makers in client and supplier businesses.

A number of industry-based events are specifically designed to develop personal contacts between key operatives. For example, there are industry conferences in exciting locations that are conducive to developing personal as well as professional contacts. In the reinsurance industry, there are annual global conferences held in Monte Carlo, Baden-Baden and different venues in USA, as well as more regional events at which the key players gather to discuss business, drink champagne, attend cocktail parties, dine, play tennis and golf and develop not only market knowledge but also personal relationships. These conferences are only one point of contact each year. There are also meetings between clients and reinsurers in each other's offices, at which detailed questions about business practices, financial management and strategy can be examined. Such meetings are often followed with lunch or dinner to further the relationship. Additionally, there are various forms of corporate entertainment offered by suppliers, from corporate boxes at key sporting events, to ski trips, golf days, sailing and theater tickets, at which the managers of client and supplier firms can socialize.

At these various meetings, both parties gain an impression that they "know" each other and this knowledge provides some reassurance about the quality of both the people in the business and the business itself. The value of such meetings is often expressed as: "When you spend time with someone over golf and dinner, you get to know what he is really like, whether you trust him, much more than if you just meet in the office to talk about business." At the same time, much of business is based on generating a positive feeling toward a client or supplier. These meetings provide people with an opportunity to find out whether they like each other: "At the end of the day, people are going to do more business with people they like." Thus, opportunities for meeting not only provide an opportunity to gain business information, but also to develop positive feelings and liking for business partners. This liking is perceived to be valuable and is often expressed as: "I know him"; "He's a good guy"; "I trust him".

While such meetings undoubtedly do add value and can be very important in the strategic formation of relationships, often people are confusing the dimension of personal liking with the purpose of business relationships and the different ways

> { ... people confuse personal liking with the purpose of business relationships }

that they add competitive advantage. It is important for managers to understand that perceptions of liking and trust are actually grounded in informational proper-

{ ... perceptions of liking and trust are grounded in informational properties }

ties, which can be developed in many ways, not all of which are dependent on personal relationships. Trust is critical to business relationships and is likely to be devel-

{ Trust it critical to business relationships }

oped through repeated, long-term engagement. However, the real basis of this trust is not based on the personal likability of the respective managers, but on trust in their business practices and their business context.

When we unpacked what managers in relationship-intensive business were saying when they talked about trusting, knowing and liking particular business partners, we found that there are three important informational aspects to this trust: (1) personal, (2) pro-cessual and (3) institutional. These three aspects should

{ ... three important informational aspects to this trust: (1) personal, (2) processual and (3) institutional }

not be confused as they indicate different approaches to, and reasons for, business relationships. Successful companies are those that know how to exploit business relationships according to these different informational aspects of trust. Explore this with us.

Trust as a proxy for information

When clients and suppliers meet, they are each looking for information on which to evaluate the other and, importantly, the viability of the other's business, and their suitability for a business relationship. Much of this information is conveyed personally and, so, is equated with personal trust and liking. However, while quality information on a partner is indeed a good basis for trust, there are many ways that information can support the development of trust, not all of which is grounded in personal liking. Our research indicates that there are three types of trust with unique informational properties: (1) personal or goodwill trust, (2) processual trust and (3) institutional trust. Not all of them are dependent on personal relationships. Rather, we like to think of these as three complementary lenses that progressively zoom out from the personal relationship to the wider business context.

{   ... personal or "goodwill trust"   }

First there is personal or "goodwill trust". Traditionally, in business relationships, personal ties play a strong role. In personal relationships we intuitively base impressions of trustworthiness on personal "likability".

{   ... impressions of trustworthiness on personal "likability"   }

Getting to know each other over drinks, dinner, golf and sailing provides an opportunity to develop personal knowledge and liking; quite simply, managers will not want to spend as much time on social activities with people that they do not like. Likeability and personal knowledge therefore provide a good initial point for a business relationship. Furthermore, they are enhanced by repeat behavior. That is, the longer the relationships last, the more we trust the people with whom we have those relationships. We have faith that they will prioritize the common good of the relationship over some self-interested benefit they might otherwise gain. This is the essence of trust. In long-term business relationships, goodwill trust is thus not just about personal likability but is also based on information, built up over the lifetime of the relationship, about the transparency with which a business partner acts and their honesty in past behaviors. It may supplement the other forms of trust described next.

Generic belief in a person's benevolence or likability is not, on its own, sufficient for a good business relationship. As one Lloyd's CEO put it:

Some people want to prolong relationships. You get to know them quite well and there becomes this sort of bond and almost friendship. There's an element of potential protectionism in there of one's mates.

CEO, Lloyd's Reinsurance Firm

History is full of lovable rogues and there is no shortage of charismatic conmen in the recent and current business context. Thus we need to recognize that trust depends on a range of ways to access high-quality information about the business partner. This is particularly important as personal relationships are displaced by corporate relationships in an increasingly competitive, accountable and regulated business environment. Understanding that trust in a business relationship is essentially a proxy for high-quality information about business behavior directs attention to other forms of trust, decoupled from personal likability, and information that exist in business relationships.

A second dimension is "process trust", that is confidence in an organization's

{ … "process trust": confidence in an organization's operating standards, governance, control and policies }

operating standards, governance, controls and policies. This view on trust and information zooms out from the personal relationship and anchors trust in the context of the organization. Process trust addresses two fundamental questions. First: "Does the organization actually have the capability to deliver on the commitment that the individual made on its behalf?" and second: "If the individual was inclined to cheat or be dishonest in the relationship, how likely is it that organizational policies or structures will protect against that?" By asking these questions, organizational characteristics such as governance, financial management and oversight come into view. For example, in business meetings, reinsurers typically ask prospective insurance partners about their underwriting procedures, claims management practices, strategies for growth and financial security. Furthermore, we observed that smart reinsurers used this information to grade firms on the quality of their organizational practices:

Understand the company, understand what they do and understand how they do it, how they make decisions, get inside how they underwrite, how they select risks, how they adjust claims, what risks they're taking on and how they're taking those risks on.

Chief Underwriting Officer, Lloyd's Reinsurance Firm

Such information can be obtained through personal contact, but it does not necessarily involve golf or drinks. Rather relational activities such as a site visit, detailed discussion of the current firm position and any recent loss history, and some auditing of the prospective partners' books are more likely to provide information that supports process trust. Where this information suggests trustworthy practices and procedures, there is less need to base business decisions on your assessment of the personal qualities of your counterpart; you can put your faith in the company's processes to deliver good results. Your business partner may be a teetotaler with different personal and social interests to you. But even someone you find socially boring could run a tight company with which you wish to do business.

Lastly, to predict current and future behavior, you can zoom out further and look at the institutional context in which your partner organization

{ ... "institutional trust": legal and political systems, professional standards or reputational networks would discourage dishonest behavior }

operates. This perspective can instill "institutional trust" in a relationship based on the judgment that legal and political systems, professional standards or reputational networks would discourage dishonest behavior. For example, people prefer to do business with partners in countries that have low corruption, stable political systems and regulatory policies that provide reasonable standards of assurance about business practices. Furthermore, it is preferable to do business in contexts where public information is of good quality and easily available, because of information standards. Such contexts provide some surety about the quality of information you can access about a business partner and also indicate the minimum standards with which a partner company will comply. Examples of such institutional trust sources are rating agencies that independently assess the creditworthiness of organizations or government databases on insured risks. Both provide independent, verifiable information on whether a borrower can be trusted to repay his debt or, respectively, whether a portfolio of insurance policies is actually worth what an insurer claims. For example, much of North America and Western Europe have consistent, fine-grained, publically available information on insured properties, and insist on corporate governance standards. These regions have robust regulatory systems that subject companies to scrutiny and provide retribution for those that fail to comply. Indeed, one of the key insurance markets, Lloyd's of London, derives much of its reputational assets from the strong financial and regulatory assurance that underpins membership in Lloyd's; an insurance company cannot operate out of Lloyd's without meeting these standards. While there are bound to be relatively stronger and weaker companies within Lloyd's, a reinsurer may be assured that any Lloyd's insurance company has at least acceptable operating standards and robust financial and regulatory backing.

Adopting such a multifaceted understanding of trust, has two benefits:

{ ... trust is really a proxy for information }

First, it makes clear that trust is really a proxy for information. The close link between relationships and information, however, has not often been made explicit. If, so far, to try and predict future behavior you have relied on past experience and your trust in your business partner as a person, think how much more accurate and reliable your predictions could be if you deliberately included the organizational and institutional context in your assessment.

Second, if you orient your relationship management toward acquiring more information about what your customer values, how the firm operates and what institutional networks it is tied into, you get much closer to sensing the "next big thing" on their agenda. For example, a good insurance client, with tight organizational processes and a strong portfolio in stable markets is a good bet to work with when they penetrate emerging markets. Similarly, in markets where the institutional context does not inspire confidence, a strong knowledge of the specific insurer's organizational processes can help with selecting the best clients in such markets and learning how best to operate within that market. As a senior executive at one leading reinsurer notes, the longer you work with such clients, the more that you can benefit from mutual learning and information exchange, and that facilitates a stronger business relationship:

> It's two-way. They need to know that you're partnering with them but for you to do that, you need to really understand them. We're getting to that level of dialogue which isn't one-way; it's: "come and help me with my business plan. Does it look sensible? What are the risks that I can run?" And it's that sort of dialogue which is superb. That's where we want to be.
>
> *Global Account Executive, European Reinsurance Firm*

To position your firm for the future and get ready for change, you should shift the focus from interpersonal relationships to business relationships at the corporate level with a view to gaining and sharing information that helps to create a desirable future *with* the client.

Appraising relationships: the information-value matrix

Relationship management is time intensive and costly, but can also be a very valuable business tool. There fore, it is important not to indiscriminately apply the same relationship management techniques to all existing and potential clients without distinguishing exactly what a relationship can add, and how to best foster each type of relationship to gain the appropriate benefits. Let us consider how to differentiate business relationships according to their ability to provide competitive advantage, and illustrate the relationship management techniques appropriate to different relationships.

Unpacking the different types of trust according to the different types of information behind them opens up opportunities for more strategic relationship management. While it is always easy to lose someone's trust, building it up – especially quickly – is very difficult. Essentially, any measure directly targeted at enhancing trust can be exposed as such and dismissed as a tactical move. Sharing information from which different forms of trust can flow is easier. A focus on acquiring and sharing information rather than developing trust strengthens the relationship and facilitates current business, but also opens up mutual learning opportunities to understand the ramifications of future business.

As different forms of information underpin different forms of trust, the management of different relationships should differ according to information availability and quality. That is why "information quality" forms one dimension of our relationship management framework. For simplicity, we measure information quality on a "low-to-high" continuum. If information is only accessible through personal contact, it forms the low point. The availability of detailed, independently verifiable information, in combination with other, personal and organizational ways of accessing information comprises the maximum on the scale. The relative importance of contextual and organizational information can vary anywhere in between.

On the other dimension, relationship management should differ by the value you attribute to different customers. Business relationships differ from personal ones not only in the role that trust and information play, but also in the form of payback we expect. Maintaining meaningful relationships takes a lot of effort. In this respect business and personal relationships are alike; but in business relationships we expect a measurable, value-adding payoff.

> { ... in business relationships we expect a measurable, value-adding payoff }

If a customer is of low value for us, it is unlikely that investment in a long-term relationship will pay off. Understanding relationship value ensures that those relationships which generate the most solid returns to a firm receive the highest levels of relationship management, including entertainment such as sailing, golf, skiing and dinner. At the same time it guards against over-investing in personal relationships and other time-intensive and costly mechanisms of relationship management where opportunities for value-adding payoff are limited, no matter how congenial the individuals concerned.

As intuitive as it sounds that more substantial investments should focus on relationships with valuable customers, there is an easy pitfall: too often, business relationships are evaluated on the basis of current business value.

This is bound to be shortsighted, especially if we want to use our relationships to get ready for change. If we want to shape a positive future business environment, we need also to team up with those customers who are likely to be valuable in future. Business prospects, recent growth rates, market potential and strategic orientation provide good indicators for which customers are likely to be valuable in the future – and they need not be the ones who are valuable today.

Developing a portfolio approach to business relationships

Different types of relationships serve different purposes. One type of relationship serves the need to get good quality information in order to build a good understanding of each other. Another type of relationship exists to make ourselves more attractive to each other. Organizations need to segment relationships on the basis of what they want or need to get out of them and then decide how they will pursue such relationships and through whom.

Consider the following tool, the relationship portfolio matrix shown in Figure 9.1, based on the two dimensions we have defined: information quality and relative value. The quadrants distinguish four distinct, idealized types of relationship with associated typical forms of interaction that fall into two broad categories: high engagement strategies for high-value clients and low engagement relationships for low-value clients. Managers can use

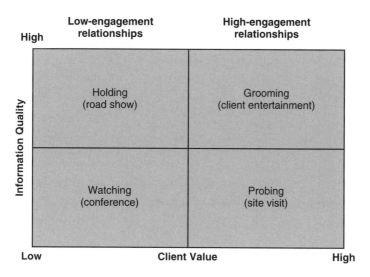

Figure 9.1   Relationship portfolio matrix

this matrix for evaluating relationships and developing a portfolio approach to their management.

A *watching relationship* is appropriate for clients whose development you want to "watch from a distance". They might be firms in regions where institutional information is of poor quality and there is little transparency with which to assess the quality of the company's practices, or its longer-term viability. Many firms in emerging markets fall into this bracket. People may know that these regions will develop, but it is hard to generate sufficient information to select particular firms to partner, and the size of current and potential business is not sufficient to invest in a closer relationship that could overcome informational deficits. Quite simply, until these clients grow in potential value or information quality, they are not worth a great deal of relationship investment. Naturally it pays to keep an eye on them; in order to spot those companies that might have potential to grow into one of the other quadrants – in particular, if they can learn to improve the quality of the information they provide, they can move up the left-hand side of the matrix. Meeting at one of the annual industry conferences is usually sufficient to stay appraised of the client's business development without committing serious resources. If executives target a particular emerging market as a potential area for growth, they could even attend a regional conference in that market, in order to gain information about the market and the potential players, so that they have an idea of which client firms to watch for development potential. As a Lloyd's reinsurance underwriter noted, after attending a Latin American insurance conference: "It was a useful fact-finding trip. Every client appreciated that we were there. Many of them don't travel because of financial constraints." Such conferences are also a way for the company to signal its potential interest in that market and so flush out any clients that might have potential to grow in information or value.

The *holding relationship* is typically a case of maintaining small but well-managed clients who provide good business information and operate in relatively stable institutional contexts. While such clients may have limited potential for growth, each one can still be a sound bet that is profitable within its own financial parameters. These clients make up an attractive part of a portfolio, because they earn steady rents and the relationship can be maintained over many years, providing stability and predictability in the overall firm portfolio. It is important to maintain a sufficiently close relationship to profit from any change in growth or potential value. This can be done through road shows. For example, where the insurance company visits reinsurers to explain their business portfolio and attract reinsurance funding, such visits might be accompanied by dinner while the client is in town, particularly if there are any new business developments to discuss. Deeper personal engagement is inefficient because there are no information deficits to be addressed through extensive face-to-face interaction and client value does not warrant such investment:

> *It's an hour of talking about the business, what they've been doing in the last year, what is important in the next renewal. But if it's a client I know I don't want to grow further with, I avoid the dinner.*
>
> *Chief Underwriting Officer, Bermudian Reinsurance Firm*

Nonetheless, such relationships can be important in an overall firm portfolio, because each one is a small but sound piece of business and thus comprise attractive elements of a portfolio because they yield relationships of sufficient value, given their relatively low cost to maintain.

The purpose of a *probing relationship* is to develop sufficient confidence in large-scale, potentially valuable clients to counteract the lack of publicly available information. This type of client is likely to be the one in either an unusual line of business that is less knowable or in an unknowable market place. In reinsurance, this might be clients representing credit, terror or nuclear risks, or an insurance company in a region where it is difficult to get quality information, such as a large client in a new or emerging market, where political, legal and cultural systems are still not well understood. For example, imagine reinsuring the London Olympics for a terrorism risk. A reinsurer would want information on the security systems available, the capability for responding to and containing terror threats, the experience of the insurance company in appraising such risks, their knowledge of the potential size and scale of damage from different types of terror acts, and the possible payout. Place that same risk – a major global sporting event – in a less known global region and the informational problem is exacerbated. The purpose of a probing relationship is thus to get more granular information about the client's procedures for appraising the risks that they underwrite. This type of relationship requires high engagement to generate information. It is best managed by visiting client premises and probing their work practices, so-called kicking the tires: "I want to see the risks. I want to talk to them, meet their people, know that they know what they are doing" (Underwriter, Lloyd's Reinsurance Firm). The costly investment of time spent conducting site visits is warranted by the value of the client.

The objective of a *grooming relationship* in which there is both high-quality information and high value, is to "get more of what everyone wants", that is, to maintain or grow the share of large-scale clients doing business that is supported by good information. Where information is considered good and verifiable, such as in North American insurance firms, where fine-grained data on insurance risks are widely accessible, there is less need for managers to personally probe the client's practices. However, where quality data is widely available, all players in the market can access that information to evaluate the attractiveness of the client. This is thus the business – those leading global clients – that everyone wants to partner with. Here relationships that involve intensive personal time serve a different purpose.

> ... relationships that involve intensive personal time serve to establish personal liking and goodwill as a differentiator from other potential partners in the marketplace

They are not to gain better information, but to establish personal liking and goodwill as a differentiator from other potential partners in the marketplace: "Relationships to make business more sticky are probably more important than the knowledge of the underlying risk. I think you can get that [knowledge] without a relationship" (Chief Underwriting Officer, Bermudian Reinsurance Firm). Managers should use high-engagement strategies, such as golf weekends and sailing trips to "groom" or get to know their clients better and firmly establish themselves as the partner of choice in the client's mind. Furthermore, this engagement should be multi-level, with contact between CEOs and senior executives as well as between middle managers; "We did a sailing event on the south coast of the UK just because one of our clients liked sailing" (CFO, Bermudian Reinsurance Firm). Such relationship strategies allow managers to protect and grow their participation in business with these firms. That is, high-engagement, grooming relationships can create a barrier to entry for other market players. These relationships are where corporate entertainment has its place as a legitimate tactic to exploit competitive advantage. Keeping in touch in a nonbusiness environment is an important signal of willingness to invest in a relationship.

Summary

There are four strategies toward key external relationships to effectively implement strategic change:

1. A watching relationship, appropriate for clients whose development you want to "watch from a distance"
2. A holding relationship, for small-scale clients that provide good business information and operate in relatively stable institutional contexts
3. A probing relationship to develop sufficient confidence in large-scale, potentially valuable clients
4. A grooming relationship in which there is both high-quality information and high value to "get more of what everyone wants"

Action points

Consciously select which business relationships to proactively pursue:

- That will enhance the information you have about the client organization
- With key individuals in client organizations that present significant growth potential
- With strategic individuals in strategic organizations where rapport, personal goodwill and affinity already exist
- Where robust processes exist that enhance trust in the client organization
- Within organizations that operate in strong institutional governance structures
- Purposefully nurturing the opportunity to create greater mutualy beneficial business gain.
- Building greater trust and enlarging the comprehensive nature of the information that underpins the business activity
- Increasing and securing the potential size of the business overall

Self-assessment tool

To what extent are you selecting which business relationships to proactively pursue? (**Tables 9.1**, **9.2**)

Table 9.1 How good is my organization at targeting change-enabling external strategic relationships?

Attribute	Never	Sometimes	Mostly	Always	Cumulative Score
That will enhance the information we have about the client organization	0	1	2	3	
With key individuals in client organizations that present significant growth potential	0	1	2	3	
With strategic individuals where rapport, personal goodwill and affinity already exist	0	1	2	3	
Within organizations where robust processes exist that enhance trust in the client organization	0	1	2	3	
Within organizations that operate in strong institutional governance structures	0	1	2	3	

Table 9.2 Benchmark scores

0–3	4–8	9–12	13–15
In the danger zone!	Some foundations that need development	Good, but room for improvement	Moving toward consistent high performance

Notes

1. The authors gratefully acknowledge support from the following bodies in conducting the research that informs this chapter: The Insurance Intellectual Capital Initiative; the Economic & Social Research Council: RES-173-27-0163; RES-186-27-0020; British Academy: SG091192.

Further reading

Bachmann, R. and Inkpen, A. C. (2011) "Understanding Institutional-based Trust Building Processes in Inter-organizational Relationships", *Organization Studies*, 32(2), pp. 281–301.

Galford, R. and Seibold Drapeau, A. (2003) "The Enemies of Trust", *Harvard Business Review*, February.

Kramer, R. M. and Lewicki, R. J. (2010) "Repairing and Enhancing Trust: Approaches to Reducing Organizational Trust Deficits", in J. P. Walsh and A. P. Brief (eds) *The Academy of Management Annals* (Volume 4), Abingdon: Routledge, pp. 245–77.

Lewicki R. J. and Bunker, B. B. (1996) "Developing and Maintaining Trust in Working Relationships", in R. M. Kramer and T. R. Tyler (eds) *Trust in Organizations: Frontiers of Theory*, Thousand Oaks, CA: Sage.

Tomkins, C. (2001) "Interdependencies, Trust and Information in Relationships, Alliances and Networks", *Accounting, Organizations and Society*, 26, pp. 161–91.

Vosselman, E. and van der Meer-Kooistra, J. (2009) "Accounting for Control and Trust Building in Interfirm Transactional Relationships", *Accounting, Organizations and Society*, 34(2), pp. 267–83.

Zucker, L. G. (1986) "Production of Trust: Institutional Sources of Economic Structure, 1840–1920", in B. M. Staw and L. L. Cummings (eds) *Research in Organizational Behavior*, Greenwich, CT: JAI, pp. 53–111.

Further references

IAIS (2009) *Global Reinsurance Market Report 2009*, end-year edition, International Association of Insurance Supervisors, available at http://www.iaisweb.org/Global-Reinsurance-Market-Report-GRMR-538.

CHAPTER 10

"Marketing is all about T-Shirts and Posters – Right?"

John Rudd

Five questions for conducting marketing as a profession that ushers in strategic change

Rationale behind this line of research and knowledge creation

"Marketing is all about T-shirts and posters – right?" The statement from the student was earnest, but my "Introduction to Marketing" course had clearly taken an early wrong turn. However, and possibly more importantly, those present were clearly in the right place.

As the nominated speaker fed back the summation of the group's discussions on the marketing case study, I reflected on my own experiences of marketing practice and the reasons why I had embarked on an academic career to study the practice of professional marketing.

First, a part-time MBA (taken at Aston Business School) fired an interest in Marketing theory. Previously, I had very much been a "do-er". The notion that "an academic" with his or her "business school theories" might be useful to practice seemed ridiculous. However, the more I read, the more I found relevance. The work published by academics (or at least the ones I was interested in) was demonstrably rigorous and not based on "gut feel" or "dead reckoning", something I had heard a lot about in commerce.

Second, after doing the MBA, I became more reflective on my own practice and that of others. I began to see that organizations were largely full of **hugely** busy people who, like me, were focused on "doing" and not "thinking". Through no fault of their own, these dedicated and knowledgeable people did not have the time (or possibly the inclination) to reflect on their practices or on the strategic consequences of their day-to-day actions. They had questions, but no time to seek answers. Yes, they attended their yearly "blue skies" event (the buffet was usually excellent so it was a must do). **However**, the links between these "strategic" sessions and, crafting marketing strategy were tenuous to say the least. When strategy discussions did take place, issues of "marketing", even at the level of T-shirts and posters, rarely came into the agenda. Why this might have been the case is explored further in this chapter.

Shortly following the MBA, I very much wanted to build knowledge that informed marketing practice. In particular, I wanted to explore the ways in which organizations plan and create marketing strategy.

The central challenge that inspired this line of thinking is that …

Successful organizations place marketing in central and strategically important roles. For the best, marketers inform and shape the strategic change

{ Successful organizations place marketing in central and strategically important roles. }

agenda. By contrast, slow growth and indeed failure appears to flow from a lack of good marketing practice, much of which stems from unqualified practice. Consider this: how many organizations would employ an unqualified accountant? The answer is, of course, very few. Yet as a general rule, marketing practitioners, even those responsible for very large amounts of organizational spend, do not require a license to practice. Marketing is one of the few areas in business where it is common practice to employ those who may have significant practical experience, but no formal training (be that certification from the Chartered Institute of Marketing or a Masters from an educational institution).

There are of course some inspired and outstanding marketers with no formal qualifications. However, I make two points: first, if I employed someone to spend marketing money on behalf of my organization, I would want to know that they were qualified to do so. Second, the fact that someone has experience of "doing" marketing for X years may not reflect that their "doing" was effective or efficient.

So what does "good" look like? What is presented here is a brief combination of my passion, my research and the work of other influential marketing academics and practitioners – all tempered by insights from my own experience of ten years in senior marketing roles within commercial organizations. I leave it to you to take action. To lift a quote from *The Matrix*:

I can only show you the door. You're the one that has to walk through it.

Four practices of good marketers

Marketers as internal communicators of strategic value: using the language of the board room

For marketing to deliver strategic value, and in order to influence strategic discussions, marketers must use the language of the boardroom. Marketers must do this to clearly communicate the value that can and must be delivered by their activity.

Those who question the value of marketing activity and marketing expenditure must be answered with clear metrics that identify the outcomes of marketing activity. Only when marketing is seen as integral to the delivery of key organizational performance indices can marketing discussions take place in the strategic zone. Marketing can then relocate from the strategic margins and occupy more central and strategic ground.

In order to do this effectively, marketers must take responsibility and be accountable for the efficacy of their practice.

Marketers as contributors of measurable ROI: using not abusing the marketing budget

Accountability for marketers must start with the measurement of the outcomes of their expenditure. Few do so systematically. Some justifying such negligence with "well our business doesn't really ask for this so we tend not to bother". Let me ask you: *why should* organizations invest money in an activity that doesn't account for its expenditure?

The marketing budget is not a divine right; it is a resource that must be treated as such by those entrusted with it. Unless the benefits delivered by marketing activity are measured and reported, little argument can be made against budget reductions in times of austerity. During the economic turbulence of 2008–10, many marketers reported that their budgets were slashed as organizations sought to prop up balance sheets. The thinking behind this went as follows: "If we don't spend £1m on marketing this year, we'll have a hot £1m injection of cash straight into our bottom line." In a downturn this is precisely the opposite of what **should** happen; but it is for marketers to defend their budgets, not for the rest of the organizations to simply take it on faith and "get it" that marketing is important.

An illustration

Very recently I spoke to an audience of marketing practitioners on this very subject. There was appropriate nodding and "hummmmm yes"-ing in all of the right places. At the close I was buttonholed by a couple of bright young things who clearly disagreed with part of the presentation. The conversation went something like this:

Bright young thing #1 (BYT1):   "It's all well and good for you to say that you should justify all marketing expenditure." (mildly cheesed off)

Bright young thing #2 (BYT2):   "Yes." (nodding, and very much agreeing)

BYT1:   "But we've just had our marketing budget cut and there is nothing we can do about it." (the whole raised eyebrows bit, and an air of "well what have you got to say for yourself?")

BYT2:   "Yes." (still nodding).

Me: "I see your point. Clearly this is far from ideal. When the decision was made to reduce your budget what was your defense?" (trying not to be too smug as it was clear where this was going)

BYT1:   "We weren't at the meeting that decided this. We don't get asked to attend board meetings." (speaking slightly slower for my benefit, as in their eyes I was clearly a little slow, which was nice)

Me: "I see. So this decision was made without your input at all?"

BYT1:   "Yes." (firmer tone, but still patient with the presumed hard of learning – me)

Me:	"So presumably, after this decision was made you produced a report to highlight what the organization would lose as a result of these cuts?" (trying hard not to giggle)
BYT1:	"Well we didn't do that as we don't" (it was at about this point that the penny dropped) "measure our marketing spend."
Me:	"Right. So you don't measure and report the outcomes of your expenditure."
BYT1:	"Erm no."
Me:	"And you don't get invited to attend board meetings or have a say in what your budget should look like."
BYT1:	"No." (looking paler at this point)
BYT2:	"Mmmmmnnn. I think I see what you mean now."
BYT1:	"Yes."
Me:	"Well great! Thank you for coming."

This true anecdote illustrates the problems faced by marketers who cannot justify budgets and track marketing expenditure. At a very minimum, marketing spend should be matched to the objectives it aims to deliver, that is, to change in behavior within the target customers or markets.

Marketing: "the ideas department!

Ideas are a good thing. In fact they are the lifeblood of organizations and can be transformative in ways previously unimagined. Apart from the value of ideas per se, a steady stream of ideas is indicative of an engaged workforce – an asset of almost infinite value.

In order to generate ideas, many organizations implement "ideas schemes". Others have a culture where employees feel "empowered" to make suggestions on how the organization could do things differently. Either way, very often the marketing department becomes the repository of new ideas.

Two challenges therefore present themselves to marketers:

1. What do we do with these ideas? I ask this because my research in this area shows that CEOs overwhelmingly see themselves as presiding over innovative and well-informed organizations that regularly generate new ideas for new initiatives. By contrast, the same research highlights that CEOs perceived significant problems in their organization's ability to deliver on the initiatives. It appears that the ideas themselves are not the central issue. The challenge is the capacity of the organization to deliver

change. Additionally and in this context many organizations suffer from *initiative overload* whereby successive (and seemingly unrelated) ideas are farmed out to the organizational populace without any guidance on why it might be a good idea or how it fits into the overall strategic plan, or what resources are available to "make this happen".

2. How do we deal with the fact that all ideas *are not* good ideas? Just because someone says that they have had a good idea, and believe (with conviction if nothing else) that the organization should "definitely do this", doesn't *actually* make it a good idea. Calls for "free Bourbons for the third floor" may be inspired, and even inspiring, but that in itself is unlikely to be the driver for competitive success envisaged by the originator.

A strategic framework for evaluating ideas should be agreed upon that

$\Big\{$ … strategic framework for evaluating ideas $\Big\}$ at the very least serves to reference all new ideas against the following questions:

(a)   What are we already doing and how does this new idea fit into that "portfolio"?

(b)   How would this new idea change things for the better?

(c)   What will this new idea enable us to achieve, and why do we need to do that?

(d)   Do we have the resources and capabilities to deliver this new idea in the "right" way?

(e)   To what extent does this new idea yield benefit beyond the cost and disturbance that its implementation would create?

(f)   How does this idea contribute to our strategic intentions?

Ultimately, while each new idea should be assessed on their own merit, the critical reference point is how it contributes to achieving the organization's strategic agenda.

Marketers as builders of strategic brands, as creators of a strategic asset

Brands matter! There is a long and significant body of research that clearly supports the investments some organizations make to build their brands. Sadly, many organizations see "the Brand" as a visual thing, as the company logo, and no more.

Although this too is important, brands are so much more. Brands are prime communication devices. They provide a shortcut message that embodies a whole personality, ethos and culture for those internal and external to the organization. They present a disproportionate amount of information about the services and products that the organization represents.

By way of example, picture the brand logo for **Swatch** – the watch:

I do not own a Swatch and can't remember the last time I saw an advert for Swatch. Neither do you, possibly. But I am willing to bet that if we were talking about this now, we could make a pretty good guess about what kind of price we would have to pay to get one, why we might want one, where we might go to get one and maybe the kind of person who we might want to buy one for? All this from just a "picture"! Indeed. A brand such as this is a communicator and a differentiator. It represents a promise by the organization to its employees, customers, suppliers and stakeholders at large.

As such, a brand communicates the values and behaviors that those leading the organization would like all those associated with and working for the organization to adopt. This is *central* to service industries, but also highly relevant to those who have traditionally been seen as product-centric. In service-based organizations (especially large ones) it is unlikely that customers will ever meet the Marketing Director or the CEO – individuals who doubtlessly embody in their day-to-day actions the spirit of the organization's mission and vision, the spirit of the brand. For most customers, the frontline employee **is** the embodiment of the brand.

Clearly, and this takes us back to the first "good practice", Marketers must work internally across the organization to inspire people to embody the organization's brand(s) and values.

Consider two other "brands" to illustrate the significance of this:

In **Disney** World Florida, there is a themed retail park of sorts called Downtown Disney. I was lucky enough to visit it a few years ago in August. I make specific reference to the date as those familiar with the Floridian climate will know that the average temperature there at that time of the year is around 8 million degrees in the shade with 100 percent humidity. (I exaggerate, slightly, to make a point, but it was toasty!)

Picture the scene: my wife and I were leaving the park to return to our hotel when we overheard a conversation between a Disney employee who was picking up litter and another family of Disney visitors. The family remarked that it was very hot and that the Disney employee must be feeling it (he was perspiring profusely). They speculated that he probably couldn't wait to go on a break. To this the employee smiled and answered, "Well, I love my job and though it's hot, I know that the better I do my job, the cleaner the park will be and the better day you as our visitors will have. And that makes me happy!"

Usually, when I use this example to managers in organizations that do not have a customer-centric culture, I am met with a round of "yuk". I've never really got to the bottom of this reaction, but it seems to be grounded in a deep-seated disbelief that genuine enthusiasm for organizational values can actually exist.

That aside, this story illustrates the way in which a massively successful organization such as Disney instills its values on all levels of employees. It is highly likely that the gentleman playing the central role in this story was on a relatively low wage. It is also likely that he was probably not consulted on the strategic direction of the organization (though, as this is Disney we are talking about, he may have been). Notwithstanding, the custodians of the Disney brand had, at some level, briefed this employee and explained his role in delivering the Disney customer experience. He saw his role as much bigger than picking up litter. Indeed, it is on such practices that Disney's success is based.

By contrast to the aforesaid, a colleague and I recently returned from a conference in USA via **a significant international entry point to Europe**. We were, to say the least, a little jet lagged as we trundled through customs at that international point of entry and out into the arrivals area.

To get back to our hotel, we made our way to the taxi rank adjacent to the arrivals hall. The obligatory taxi rank marshal stood there, complete with high-visibility jacket and walkie-talkie. As we waited our turn, we noticed a woman exiting arrivals, looking rather confused. Seeing the high-visibility jacket and walkie-talkie (very impressive stuff to the untrained eye) she approached. In broken English she asked if the high-visibility jacket could be good enough to show her where she might catch a bus.

Now let me assure you that I am not an expert in the layout of this major international entry point. I have never been employed there and rarely use it. However, from my place in the queue, and I was pretty much standing right next to the high-visibility jacket, I could see the bus area opposite.

Returning to the situation. Once the question had been asked, and without actually looking directly at the woman, the high-visibility jacket stated with an air of authority and general indifference, "I don't do busses love," and walked off.

I turned to my travel companion, mindful that we had just returned from a country where customer service is king, and barely able to choke back my tears, I blubbed, "We're home!"

Marketing as a differentiator between high performance and poor performing organizations

In 2010, the Marketing Group at Aston Business School completed collecting one of the largest global databases of its kind. As part of a five-year study the database focuses on marketing practices and consists of information from 15 countries that span the globe and over 18,000 responses from organizations within that "zone". The research sought to identify best practices in marketing, by profiling the best corporate performers against the weakest corporate performers across a number of criteria. Our aim was to identify the organizational impact of effective marketing. Of the UK data, the most significant differences between high and low performing organizations are highlighted further. In summary, our findings consistently support the central role of effective marketing in creating competitive success.

Key findings

- Little significant difference in the market conditions faced the top performers compared with the weak performers. It was clear that both high- and low-performing companies see themselves as operating in increasingly turbulent trading environments. From this it is fair to infer that no one category of company profited from peculiar and favorable trading conditions. High and low corporate performance was not a function of being in a more or less conducive market. Differences found between the successful and ambivalent groups of companies related to their approach to the market and the marketing strategies adopted.

  > Differences found between the successful and ambivalent groups of companies related to their approach to the market and the marketing strategies adopted.

- Differences occur within both the marketing and the business approaches adopted by the two groups.

  - High performing companies are significantly more aggressive in their approach, taking a longer-term view of their markets and focusing on winning market share from their competitors. Differentiation in terms of both product or service offerings was also apparent. High performers actively seek to innovate and provide relative uniqueness.

  - The low performing companies, on the other hand, appear to be more focused on short-term defensive strategies. It is more important to the lower performers to defend what they already have rather than to aggressively target new areas. Low performers are also focused on improving efficiencies through cost reductions and product standardization, linking themselves to a less ambitious defensive type strategy.

■ High-performing companies identified clearly their key marketing assets and appeared to

{ ... identified clearly their key marketing assets and appeared to be exploiting these }

be exploiting these within their particular trading environment. They had significant advantages over their competitors with regard to three main areas: (1) Customer-based Assets, that is, company or brand name and reputation, credibility with customers, superior levels of customer support and relationships with key target customers; (2) Marketing Support Assets, that is, marketing information systems, copyrights and patents, cost-control systems, cost advantages in production and the extent or nature of the distribution network; (3) Assets Created through Strategic Alliances, that is, market access through partners, shared technology, managerial expertise and financial resources.

■ In addition to marketing assets, the best performers also had superior marketing capabilities for leveraging

{ ... superior marketing capabilities for leveraging and exploiting those assets }

and exploiting those assets. Advantages over competitors were found in terms of marketing abilities and skills such as: understanding customer needs and requirements; using information about markets, customers and competitors; creating, maintaining and enhancing relationships with customers or customer groups; launching successful new products and services; pricing. They were also better than their competitors at key management functions such as financial management, human resource management and marketing management.

■ The best performers, as already noted, were more likely than weaker performers to dif-

{ ... differentiate their products and services from competitors }

ferentiate their products and services from competitors. This differentiation could take a number of routes. Particularly significant is the way in which high performers differentiate themselves on the basis of technical product quality, the strength of relationships with customers (built through a superior level of service provided and speed of delivery to customers) and the degree of innovation built into the firm's offerings. Significantly, they were also likely to charge more than their competitors for their products and services, not to price at the lower end of the spectrum. This level of pricing is consistent with the premium product or service being provided. The high performers appear to offer a well-researched, customer-focused and well-delivered product or service and are therefore entitled to expect a premium above alternative suppliers who do not provide the innovative and customer-based benefits of the high performers. Interestingly, low-pricing strategies were more common among the weaker performers.

- Significant differences in implementation between the high performers and the low performers were observed in the extent to which they researched their markets and the emphasis they placed on creating strong and well-known brands.

> { ... extent to which they researched their markets and the emphasis placed on creating strong and well-known brands }

Rather than attempting to keep prices down through a strong focus on costs, the high performers take a proactive stance and attempt to develop new products for their markets. Emphasis is also placed by high-performing companies on building strong, long-term relationships with key customers. These relationships are regularly monitored and indeed nurtured through both an analysis of customer-satisfaction levels and regular communications with employees. Within the implementation of the marketing strategy, high performers appear prepared to invest more than low performers in media advertising (possibly supporting their brand, possibly on more promotional or tactical strategies). The Internet too was seen as being significantly more important for high-performing companies as a promotional tool.

This UK-based research evidence provides a number of interesting themes that distinguish high-performing companies from low-performing companies. Namely, high-performing companies appear to:

1. Focus on their markets and customers
2. Be more aggressive in pursuing their strategic goals, and do this through a blend of marketing-led approaches
3. Seek to maximize exploitable marketing assets and capabilities in a constant bid to achieve competitive advantage
4. Create distinct and differentiated product or service offerings that are preferred to those of their competitors
5. Price higher, to reflect the prestige nature of their offering
6. Be more innovative and, indeed, customer-led than the respective competitors

In an increasingly turbulent market, their key skills of innovating and of offering customer-focused products and services appear to have contributed significantly to their relative success.

Five pragmatic questions to re-energize your marketing efforts

So, why do customers buy from you?

An easy question to answer, you might think, but it is surprising how many senior managers of large organizations do not know. There are usually opinions and "gut-feeling" perceptions but few "know". In a boom period this is less problematic, as customers queue in droves to be separated from their money. So much latent demand exists that many markets can sustain a plethora of largely undifferentiated products and services. The scene changes, however, as economic downturns pose challenges for organizations distanced from their customer base. Those that have taken a laissez-faire approach to their market position, relative to competitors, lose sales and market share, and most of these have no idea why.

Do your customers buy from you because you offer greater value or because you charge the lowest price?

Organizations have to provide value to their targeted customer segments. If no value is provided, the age-old mantra of "it's all about price in our industry" is bound to make its way into strategic discussions. Beware of the salesperson who consistently suggests that their lack of performance is due to the fact that your products and services are too expensive! You do not need a salesperson to give things away.

If, however, you do have an undifferentiated product and you can find no reason why customers should buy from you as opposed to anyone else, then I'm afraid that it is all about price in your market. If this is the case, there should be only one reason for you to get up in the morning: to drive cost from your business. If you have the lowest cost base in an industry where price is king, in the event of a price war you will be the last one standing. Interestingly, if this is the case, your organization is clearly competing in a commodity market. You might want to consider getting rid of your direct sales force, as this is a significant cost and they are more than likely just presenting prices and taking orders. Consider moving the sales process toward an online order-placement environment. This is great for commodity markets where selling isn't really important – where the only thing that matters is being the cheapest.

What do your customers think about your organization, your products and services and your Brand?

The answers to these questions are central to the strategic decisions of organizations, and should be driven by rigorous research.

When strategic discussions degenerate into "this is what I think" versus "no you're wrong, this is what I think", the side with the best information wins – unless, of course, there are other agendas like "hey it's my company and we're doing it".

To get a better handle on what customers think, many organizations turn to satisfaction measures. This is good, as at the very least, these organizations have some interest in customers. However, there are three main problems with satisfaction scores:

(a) Every organization I have ever worked with that collects satisfaction scores has "high satisfaction". This can be a result of the administrators of the system "gaming" the process of data collection. The focus of the process becomes "getting high satisfaction scores", as opposed to "gaining insight into customers' feelings and perceptions". The latter actually has the potential to contribute to strategy.

(b) The process of reporting satisfaction scores becomes routine. Satisfaction scores are wheeled out at the relevant monthly meeting. The person tasked with reporting them highlights that they are up or down by 0.3 percent. No discussion takes place and there is no analysis of overall trends. No interrogation is made of this important data to identify the cause(s) of the upturn or downturn.

(c) Measures and questionnaires are often poorly constructed. This relates to the earlier discussion regarding unqualified practice. A well-designed questionnaire requires some expertise. This is not about blame per se, as many customer-satisfaction survey designers indeed give the survey their "best shot". However, as this is often the *only* instrument that gives organizations any customer feedback regarding service and product delivery, a more scientific approach is required.

While I applaud the principle of measuring customer satisfaction, if organizations spend time and money gathering this information, they should be thoughtful in the creation of the instrument and analytical and open in its interpretation. Fundamentally, and at a minimum, the survey instrument should be a valid tool to provide reliable data.

Of note, a complementary and often neglected qualitative approach is also useful. *Talking* to existing, lapsed and potential customers gives organizations incredible insight into the positives and negatives of what it's like to do business with them. Again, if this approach is adopted, the organization has to be prepared to listen and, more importantly, to react.

What do your customers think about your competitors?

Customers' perceptions of competitors are also of great importance. Organizations do not sit alone in their competitive landscape. Customers (both existing and potential) will compare competitors in any given market. Indeed the ease of doing so has never been greater, with the advent of discussion forums and web-based comparison tools.

Sadly, competitors are often ignored or their competitive actions rationalized away as something "we wouldn't want to do". Certainly, when a competitor launches a new product or service into a market in which you compete, it is important to know this quickly. An assessment can then be made of the perceived value that this new product or service provides for customers, and of the potential impact on your products and services. Strategic decisions of whether to react or not can thus be made in a structured, reasoned and orderly fashion.

How can and why would you segment your market?

A market segment represents a cluster of customers who are likely to behave (or choose products and services) in a similar way. A very efficient way of selling products and services is to target segments within markets. This repositions an organization away from a one-size-fits-all approach and allows for a more thoughtful, efficient deployment of resources.

For those attempting to segment their market for the first time, several approaches exist. Many organizations first segment by geographic and industry classifications. Arguably, segmentation by customer "need" is much more effective to address seemingly undifferentiated markets.

An unsegmented approach to sales and marketing is very much like using a shotgun. The logic of this approach is that when you pull the trigger, you are bound to hit **something** and the effect on that something is likely to be quite significant. However, you will also miss quite a lot! A segmented approach is more akin to using a sniper rifle. Each cartridge may cost more, but you are more likely to hit what you aim at – with much less waste.

Segmentation also allows you to define which customers add value to *your* organization. It is easy to slip into a mindset that all customers are "good", and this has intuitive appeal. **But** as time passes, some customers may become exceedingly demanding. This should be factored into a "cost to serve" that could form part of contract renegotiations. If "awkward" customers don't wish to meet your terms, then an amicable parting may be a good idea. In fact, it would be great if they went to your nearest competitor. Help them pack! You can then dedicate the resources released to customers who represent mutual potential value: where you can add to their value at the same time as they add value to your organization.

What is "the plan"? How do you *inform it?*

There should be a marketing plan. The plan should address these fundamental questions: What is the organization trying to achieve and how does marketing expenditure contribute to this? How will everyone in the organization know the envisaged outcomes of the plan, and how will they know what *individually* they have to do to make it happen?

The marketing plan should be driven by market-based information. Once organizations are aware of the position they occupy in the markets they serve, and of what value their products and services create, informed strategic decisions can be made about the future. In this way, organizations spend less time reacting to competitors' moves, more time innovating and leading their markets.

Summary

There are five questions for conducting marketing as a profession that ushers in strategic change:

1. Why do customers buy from you?
2. What do your customers think about your organization, your products and services and your Brand?
3. What do your customers think about your competitors?
4. How can and why would you segment your market?
5. What is "the plan"? How do you inform it?

Action points

Evidence supports the fact that marketing is central to organizational success. More than ever, those making marketing decisions in organizations need to:

- Effectively communicate the value of their activity internally
- Measure return on marketing spend, mindful of their organization's strategy and "bottom line"
- Capture and develop the creative and innovative capacity of their organization to drive value creation
- Identify and develop brands as strategic assets, enacted through the behavior of their employees
- Position marketing as an activity to drive differentiation from competitors and to lead their organizations to higher performance
- Consider how answers to the aforementioned five questions might reenergize their marketing activity

Self-assessment tool

Tables 10.1 and 10.2 present an assessment framework for those considering the effectiveness (or otherwise) of marketing practice in their organization. It draws on, and is informed by, the previous discussions but is not designed to be a "how you should do marketing in your organization" template.

The best marketing strategies flow from informed discussions. The following framework is designed to highlight some interesting "first touch" areas. As a minimum, you, or those responsible for marketing in your organization, should be able to answer these questions *and* point to data that is systematically collected and reviewed to support those answers.

To what extent are you asking the right questions to inform your marketing activity?

Table 10.1 How good is my organization at deploying change-ushering marketing?

Attribute	Never	Sometimes	Mostly	Always	Cumulative Score
By establishing why our customers buy from us	0	1	2	3	
By ascertaining what our customers think about our company/ our products and services/our Brand	0	1	2	3	
By clarifying what our customers think about our competitors	0	1	2	3	
By defining how our market is or could be segmented	0	1	2	3	
By scoping our marketing "plan" and how we make it happen	0	1	2	3	

Table 10.2 Benchmark scores

0–3	4–8	9–12	13–15
In the danger zone!	Some foundations that need development	Good, but room for improvement	Moving toward consistent high performance

Further reading

Lee, N. and Lings, I. (2008) *Doing Business Research*, London: Sage.

MacDonald, M. and Wilson, H. (2011) *Marketing Plans: How to Prepare Them, How to Use Them – Seventh Edition*, London: Wiley.

Mooi, E., Sarstedt, E. and Sarstedt, M. (2011) *A Concise Guide to Market Research. The Process, Data, and Methods Using IBM SPSS Statistics*, London: Springer.

CHAPTER 11

Securing the Benefits of Inward Investment

Nigel Driffield and Jim Love

Two rationales for attracting inward investment that affects structured regional change

Introduction

The analysis presented here is based on some 20 years of studying the impacts of international capital flows, on both host and home economies. My Ph.D. is in economics, and so my academic journey has meandered through labor economics, regional science, industrial economics, finance, statistical methodology and international business and management. This in part reflects the change in emphasis that policymakers have attached to inward investment. When my

{ *… the change in emphasis that policymakers have attached to inward investment* }

work started, the Thatcher government had recognized the importance of inward investment for the UK economy, introducing new working practices and new technology; but the emphasis at the time was on tackling a growing problem of payment imbalance. As UK manufacturing shrank rapidly, imports rose sharply. In the UK, by encouraging Japanese electronics and automotive firms to manufacture, UK imports declined and a key solution to the challenge of a rising trade deficit was attained.

Incoming firms sought to locate in areas of the UK that had undergone severe industrialization. Concurrently, competition for both UK and EU regional funds (designed to reverse disparities between regions in terms of employment) began to erupt between regions, and focus intensified onto new technology and productivity growth.

While "industrial policy" in some form seems to have returned to the agenda of politicians at the national and European levels, one dimension of industrial policy never went away: the attraction of FDI to stimulate economic development. Indeed, for much of the period between 1985 and 2010, this could be seen as the dominant aspect of British industrial policy. It remains highly significant today. The consensus view among policymakers and international organizations is that FDI brings a "package" of benefits that includes new technologies, the upgrading of skills, the generation of jobs and growth of exports (i.e. European Bank for Reconstruction and Development (EBRD), 1998). Not surprisingly, in the British case, this has over many years involved the use of substantial subsidies to attract FDI.

As noted in the introduction, the British government has welcomed incoming FDI, and has backed this with substantial subsidies. It credits FDI with bringing new jobs, new management techniques, innovation, dynamism and competition to the economy. For many years, at the regional level, the emphasis has been on alleviating structural unemployment via inward investment inflows. Decentralization of industrial policy to Regional Development Agencies intensified competition between agencies through subsidy packages to inward investors.

Large subsidies were justified on the basis that inward investment brought a range of attributes and were likely to benefit regional host economies. These include a wider range of local decision-making authority, more extensive and superior local linkages and a more strategic position within the UK. For the British regions the emphasis has been on using inward investment to

(i) reduce structural unemployment and (ii) to reduce inequalities. Both of these benefits manifested themselves intra-regionally by raising productivity through technology transfer and spillover effects.

Identifying and measuring beneficial effects of inward FDI

The relative size of the subsidies that were offered grew exponentially through the 1980s, with certain examples attracting a good deal of attention. For example, the Mercedes plant in Alabama, USA, was subsidized to the tune of nearly $170,000 per new job created. This led policymakers to three conclusions:

1. This level of subsidy was not sustainable, especially with countries like Malaysia and Taiwan, as well as regions like Central and Eastern Europe, seeking to compete for this investment.
2. The main challenge had changed – from simply attracting inward investment, to finding ways to maximize the benefits of that investment.
3. Better targeting of public spending was required.

Theoretically, one can build on the existing analysis of the multinational enterprise. Arguably, the most important outcome of attracting internationally mobile capital to a region is that it reallocates resources to more productive units. The key questions therefore for both policymakers and firms looking to justify the need for public investment are:

1. What is the size of this beneficial effect?
2. What are the secondary effects in terms of, for example, the impacts on productivity in neighboring firms or related sectors (through the supply chain), and more generally on skills, investment, competition and competitiveness?

The FDI Situation

The fundamental objective of attracting internationally mobile capital to a region is to stimulate employment. Firstly, in direct terms, this manifests through

> The fundamental objective of attracting internationally mobile capital to a region is to stimulate employment.

the jobs created by the firm concerned. Secondly however, and potentially larger, are the secondary employment gains coming from multiplier effects such as increased activity in the supply chain or in related industries that the incoming capital enables.

Typically, however, it emerged on inspection that, for two reasons, the size of subsidies required to attract internationally mobile capital was not justified by the jobs created. Firstly, when

> { … size of subsidies required to attract internationally mobile capital was not justified by the jobs created }

a new investment arrived in a given location, many of the people employed in the new facility had already been in employment elsewhere. They were attracted to the new employer not just by higher earnings (generated through the higher productivity of the new facility) but also by potentially long-term career prospects associated with a large multinational. This generates greater competition for skilled workers. Firms in the locality and surrounding area experience increased competition for skilled workers. This drives up wages, and reduces employment in indigenous firms. To give a real example, several years ago after publishing a paper suggesting that for some sectors of the UK economy this "employment substitution" (the number of jobs lost in the UK-owned sector as a result of inward investment) was up to one-third of the direct employment created, I was contacted by the Royal Mail. I was genuinely puzzled about how the Royal Mail could make use of an econometric analysis of inward investment in UK manufacturing. They explained that they witness the effect of "employment substitution" all the time. For many people the Royal Mail serves as an entry into the UK job market. With deregulation and casualization, many workers do not see it as a long-term career plan. Working on the basis that it is always easier to get a job when you have one, people enter this sector as a starting point. As such, when new opportunities arise, workers move on, and the Post Office has to start recruiting again. This is not necessarily a bad thing. It may be that the inward investment is part of the upgrading of the local economy, and that the new postal workers are drawn from the pool of hitherto unemployed. It does nevertheless illustrate the problems of linking subsidies to employment creation.

Having discussed the links between inward investment policy and employment creation, attention then turns to the more indirect effect. From a national, if not local policy perspective, these are potentially more important. Arguably a fundamental question arises: does the attraction of internationally mobile capital lead to an increase in competitiveness?

This question encompasses a dichotomy: trade flow versus the flows and creation of new technology, competition and skills. In the past 15 years or so I have examined most of

> ... dichotomy: trade flow versus the flows and creation of new technology, competition and skills

these issues, and come to the following conclusions:

1. FDI flows are an important part of the competitive process. FDI is attractive for industries where dominant indigenous firms have high market shares, and where new entrants can increase competition. *Intra-industry FDI* (e.g. the German car industry investing in the US while the US car industry invests in Germany) is also an important part of this.

2. FDI flows are strongly associated with both trade and technology flows. The traditional literature sees trade and FDI as being substitutional. This is far from the case. Large firms use FDI to both increase trade and to bring new technology into a given geographic area.

3. The more skills an individual has, the better placed that person is to gain from FDI, which contributes strongly to augmenting the capability and capacity of skilled labor. Demand for skilled labor always rises in the presence of FDI. This sometimes leads to increased wage inequality as unskilled workers find they are competing with suppliers in China, while skilled workers find themselves in greater demand.

4. Inward investment increases productivity in the host country. A big part of this is the simple "batting average effect". When a new firm enters it typically has higher than average productivity. Thus, in the absence of any other effects, average productivity rises. Of more interest, however, are the effects that may lead to productivity increasing elsewhere.

Analysis provides several reasons why productivity in other firms may increase as a result of inward investment. Typically foreign firms are more productive

> ... productivity in other firms may increase as a result of inward investment

than domestic firms. One possibility is that "catching up" occurs as a result of FDI. This process encompasses a number of related issues. Notwithstanding, it is essentially linked to the idea that inward investment stimulates domestic productivity growth as efficiency improvements are generated through increased competition.

Most of the studies to date focus on the transfer – of ideas, technology or knowledge – that occurs between inward investors and domestic firms. This happens largely through informal mechanisms. It can occur (i) directly, through the licensing of a particular technology, (ii) through supplier networks or subcontracting arrangements, or (iii) indirectly as knowledge becomes public and spillovers are assimilated by the domestic sector. Additionally, the "ripple through" effects of changes in production and working practices triggered by the presence of new inward investors have been particularly important.

An important concept in the study of such spillovers described earlier is the extent to which "agglomeration economies" occur through FDI. Such economies arise from the geographic proximity of similar, technologically advanced enterprises. The presence of MNEs (multinational enterprises), given that they are leaders (in both technological and capital accumulation), serves to further stimulate the possibility for agglomeration in such locations (Cantwell, 1989). This leads to increased potential for technology transfer, and to improvements in the technological capabilities of domestic firms.

The third contributor to increased domestic productivity emanates from the types of nontechnological advantages that MNEs may possess and thus bring. Included are managerial abilities, the capability to exploit scale economies and the well-honed ability to coordinate disparate resources. If these capabilities are learned by host-country industries, performance may improve exponentially. This is often referred to as the "demonstration effect". The so-called Japanization of UK industry of the 1980s and 1990s is a case in point. FDI is also an important source of "knowledge capital", potentially more important for productivity growth than physical capital. This is also easier to transfer between countries than physical capital.

We must also draw attention to the more indirect benefits of FDI: namely, the wider introduction of new technology.

{ ... more indirect benefits of FDI: wider introduction of new technology }

For example, there has been much debate in recent years over the scale and scope of productivity spillovers generated by foreign manufacturing investment. One cause of such spillovers is expected to be the strength of extended buyer-supplier relationships between foreign manufacturers and their domestically owned counterparts. This is potentially the most beneficial effect that FDI has on industrial and regional development within the host country. Extensive policy resources have been expended in the UK and elsewhere on seeking to foster linkages between foreign manufacturers and local (within-region) supply and services bases. Such linkages are seen as (a) vital for generating the indirect multiplier impacts expected from foreign firms in their host regions and (b) as the most likely vehicle for technology transfer.

The previous discussion provides succor to policymakers seeking to justify incentives offered to inward investors. It does, however, suggest that much of the perceived benefit of inward investment to host countries or regions is dependent on the existence of *informal* productivity spillovers occurring between the foreign and domestic sector. The beneficial effects of inward investment (and in turn the justification for seeking to attract it) need to be quantified by detailed analysis. While there is evidence that spillovers do occur between foreign and domestic firms, an important determinant of productivity externalities from FDI is the size of the technological advantage that the foreign firms possess. Moreover, while these spillovers do lead to increased demand for skilled labor in the domestic sector, the extent of the spillover effect is dependent on the size of the foreign productivity differential. If the technology gap between the foreign and domestic sectors is very large, it is doubtful that domestic firms can assimilate the imported technology. In such a case, wages will still increase, as will the skill differentials, but without the desired accompanying gain in regional productivity. While the technology gain to the host country still occurs overall, employment gain is likely to be limited.

Despite evidence that FDI delivers beneficial spillover effects in terms of productivity and wages, it can disadvantage the lower-skilled work force. We must have an understanding of (a) the possible negative impacts of FDI

{ ... FDI delivers beneficial spillover effects in terms of productivity and wages }

{ ... but it can disadvantage the lower-skilled work force }

upon the labor market as well as (b) the potential benefits that include wider technological and nontechnological transfers, even if decision-making to date has been largely based on the latter.

The FDI Problem

Inward investment policy has largely been used to generate employment. That being the case, the policy lessons from the previous analysis are relatively clear. Attract firms that are seeking low-cost locations to locate relatively large numbers of low-skill workers. This, however, does not represent a long-term strategy. As various regions of the UK have found, there will always be somewhere cheaper (Eastern Europe). Indeed Malaysia has had a similar experience with China.

Put simply, governments intervene when markets fail. Market failure can be specified in many different forms. In the context of this evaluation, the most important elements are: incomplete markets, externalities and information asymmetries.

{ ... incomplete markets, externalities and information asymmetries }

metries. These principles should be weighed up and expressed in every investment subsidy scheme.[1]

- Incomplete markets are interpreted as the existence of a gap in the availability of private sector external finance (e.g. formal or informal equity capital) to firms for start-up and expansion activity in particular regions. This can be related to the unwillingness of the private sector to become involved in projects that they deem to be "high risk".

- Externalities are viewed as the positive indirect effects that result from firms being located together. Positive externalities include: collaboration and networking opportunities (technological externalities such as spillovers, linkages), information transfer, the freeing up of internal human and financial capital (that can be utilized in other innovative actions within the firm), the leverage of additional private sector financial support, the range of perceived or actual benefits associated with large urban labor markets (e.g., skill sets).

- Information asymmetry arises when firms are unaware of sources and mechanisms to access the necessary amounts of external finance required for new plants and/or the in situ expansion of existing operations.

Implications for FDI

The analysis presented previously suggests that there is a high degree of bi-modality, not only in terms of the motivation for FDI to occur (i.e. technology exploiting versus efficiency seeking), but also in the likely outcomes of these investments.

Domestic productivity in the host country rises substantially only when FDI funds the arrival of a strong technology-based firm.

FDI that introduces new technology to the source country generates an increase in productivity over and above the simple "batting average" effect. In contrast to the impacts of FDI associated with technological advantages, FDI motivated by technology sourcing or efficiency seeking generates little in the way of technology transfer. In the short-term this can even cause domestic productivity to decline.

Many attempts have been made to measure spillover effects from FDI in the host country, based on developing, developed and transition economies. This large body of literature reports a wide range of differing results, ranging from large positive effects, to significant negative effects, with a large range of studies reporting very small effects. More recently, the literature has begun to highlight other important considerations, such as linkages between foreign and domestic sectors and the relationship between inward investors, preexisting clusters and technological differences between countries.

Need

Our results have policy implications – pointing to key criteria for evaluating the effectiveness of FDI. National and regional governments spend substantial resources attracting inward investors, at least partly in the expectation (or hope) of capturing productivity spillovers from more productive foreign firms. Our results demonstrate that this should not be taken as a given. Public gains should not be assumed to justify FDI expenditure. Much more attention should be paid to the characteristics of the inward investor and the motivation for investing before deciding whether public support is worthwhile.

Inward investment into the UK comes overwhelmingly from sectors and countries that have a technological advantage over the corresponding UK sector. Thus policy initiatives designed to boost technological development through inward investment may be valid. Technology differences matter much more than labor cost differences in terms of the positive effects of inward FDI: acquiring technology through inward investment increases the demand for skilled labor, decreases demand for unskilled labor and produces positive spillovers on domestic productivity. However, this is far from the complete picture. The fact that the bulk of inward FDI also comes from sectors that have lower unit labor costs than the UK equivalent, coupled with some evidence of a trend toward technology-sourcing FDI into the UK, suggests that the policy preoccupation with a flexible labor market as a major attractor of inward investment may be overstated.

Policymakers are now putting the onus on firms to justify the need for subsidy, not merely in terms of employment generation, but also in terms of the wider economic benefits discussed. On at least one level, this places firms in a relatively difficult position, of having to examine what spillovers may come from their investment. At the same time policymakers seek to minimize any informal technology transfer away from the firm.

To help firms undertake the new type of analysis required to justify the need for subsidy, we have created a simple taxonomy (see **Table 11.1**). Based on technology differences and factor cost differences, our taxonomy links

Table 11.1 Typology of motivations for FDI

	Cost to host $<$ Cost to source	Cost to host $>$ Cost to source
technology of host $>$ technology of source	Type 1 technology sourcing/ location advantage	Type 2 technology sourcing
technology of host $<$ technology of source	Type 3 ownership advantage/efficiency seeking	Type 4 ownership advantage

firms' motivation to seek inward investment with their likely overall effects. The economics literature consistently shows empirically that factor cost differentials, and in particular unit labor cost differentials, are an important determinant of FDI flows. The possibility that FDI into high- and low-cost locations (relative to the source country) generates differential productivity, and labor demand effects has largely been ignored by both the academic literature, and by policymakers.

Type 1 is where the host economy is more technologically advanced and has lower production costs than the source investor. This implies inward investment that may be motivated by technology sourcing and has the additional advantage of exploiting the host's locational advantage (lower costs). Type 2 is "pure" technology-sourcing investment, attracted by the host's technological intensity despite its higher costs.

Types 3 and 4 both have at the center the idea that firms engage in FDI in order to exploit home-based technology in overseas markets. This is typically seen as the most common form of firm-specific advantage that leads to firms becoming multinational, and is usually referred to as a key "ownership advantage". Type 3 has the additional element of "efficiency seeking", that is seeking to locate activities in lower cost locations, this cost difference being seen as a key location advantage for the firm. Type 4 is the "pure" ownership-advantage motivation, where source-country technological intensity is greater than that of the corresponding host sector and FDI occurs despite the host sector having higher unit labor costs. If the motivations of these types of FDI are different, their requirements from the host country are also likely to differ, and the policy offerings should reflect this.

This suggests there- { ... there needs to be more discrimination }
fore that there needs to   in policies designed to attract FDI
be more discrimination
in policies designed to
attract FDI. There is clearly a place for seeking investment that will create employment for lower-skill workers. There are also clear benefits to the UK economy for attracting frontier technology and the world's leading firms, in both high-tech manufacturing and knowledge-intensive services. It is important, however, to recognize that these are essentially mutually exclusive. The first may be attracted by some form of employment subsidy, the second almost certainly not. The latter is more likely to be attracted by high quality facilities and infrastructure, a well-educated workforce, and, last but not least, strong protection of intellectual property rights at the country level. There may well be technology transfer or spillovers from this type of investment, but it is also important to understand that the firm will do all it can to prevent this.

Good FDI practice

The fundamental principle here is that markets work. Firms are very good at spotting locations. Intervention should therefore be focused around raising awareness of benefits of different locations, that is, large populations of factory workers versus proximity to other technical organizations.

In that context, to be a good investor:

1. Know what you want to achieve, and be able to demonstrate the likely benefits to the host country. This requires both policymakers and firms to make objectives clear and specific.

2. Establish the sustainability of those new jobs or that new technology. While it is still possible for firms to obtain strategic financing for investment on the basis of either protecting jobs or updating existing plant, the political will to do this for inward investors is dwindling.

3. Recognize the link between location and technology, and also recognize that labor costs are a tiny part of a location decision. This has been recognized recently by foreign-owned car manufacturers in the UK bemoaning a lack of suppliers.

Bad FDI practice

Avoid being an investor who:

■ Does not think through the specific benefits

- Does not match the cost to the actual benefits being created
- Exaggerates (or guesses) indirect benefits to justify higher investment figures
- Follows targets that are not holistic: that is, a target of raising regional jobs without capping the investment per head or the total investment that could be justified by the benefit

Frame to our analysis

Given that indiscriminate FDI is not sustainable, one needs to know more about the likely beneficial effects, their scale and scope, of the impacts of FDI. The

$\Big\{$ ... indiscriminate FDI is not sustainable $\Big\}$

lack of consensus in the findings concerning the impact of inward investment has rather unfortunately led to the assertion in some quarters that one cannot glean anything from large-scale work. Rather, one can only learn from a case-by-case analysis. This line of argument suggests that because all inward investment projects are different, there is very little to be gained by examining them in the aggregate analysis. This is erroneous. Analysis of the impacts of inward investment on host countries, over 20 years tells a number of things that can inform policymakers and firms. Internationally mobile capital, by definition, seeks the best combination of resources, infrastructure, technology and market conditions. Incentives can only do so much to overcome any location disadvantage. Typically, incentives can sway the balance when a firm is, say, deliberating between the West Midlands or the Ruhr valley, but it will not attract a firm to France if China is simply a cheaper location. Largely, inward investment agencies recognize this, and seek to target their efforts more effectively. The essential problem therefore is how to attract beneficial FDI. Do you target particular types of investment (by sector, for example) or investments from certain countries?

Core issues

Our argument starts from the fact that there often exists a disconnection between policies designed to attract inward investment, and the needs of the local community. Typically, firms have seen this as having outside of their remit. They are merely happy to take whatever capital incentive is on offer and get on with business. Where firms do place excessive emphasis on the need for subsidies – and this still happens more than the informed reader would imagine – this leads to bad location decisions and higher input costs in the medium term. Simplifying slightly and ignoring FDI designed to access natural resources (typically these days flowing to developing countries), FDI occurs for one of the following two reasons:

1. Either it is motivated by the desire to exploit intellectual property or new technology in new markets, in conditions where (i) either exporting is too expensive or won't guarantee market access, or (ii) where licensing the product is not a viable alternative

   { ... motivated by the desire to exploit intellectual property or new technology in new markets }

2. Or it is motivated by the desire to relocate to lower-cost locations, often independent of IPR or new technology

   { ... motivated by the desire to relocate to lower-cost locations }

The main problem is that policy instruments, and firms responses to them, ignore this key distinction. Further, with the global reduction in public spending, inward investment agencies around the world are seeking to better target their spending. The onus on firms is to justify incentives. Historically, this has been based merely on the employment created, but firms are finding themselves being asked more fundamental (and challenging) questions to justify intervention from government.

Initial conclusions and main findings

Many studies from around the world have argued that based on the standard "cost per job" methodology the size of investment subsidies cannot be justified in terms of direct employment alone. This has lead both national and local policymakers to shift their focus to the size and scope of indirect effects, such as technology transfer, productivity spillovers or gains in employment up or down the supply chain.

This presents a number of challenges for researchers including:

- How do we measure productivity?
- How do we address the counterfactual (how worse things might have been without the inward investor)?

■ How do we ascribe the observed productivity (employment) growth to the observed investment rather than a series of other (unobserved?) events?

■ How do we distinguish between local and national effects?

The challenge for the academic is to bring a series of rather imperfect models and methods to a problem where small differences between numbers matter. In addition, to "net out" the "crowding out effect" – new firms competing away the less competitive incumbents – this phenomenon increases competitiveness nationally, but may increase regional disparity.

There are sources of spillovers but you have to know where to look for them, especially in terms of the stimuli for productivity growth in the inward investors.

1. Inward investors who engage with suppliers or customers up or down the supply chain do generate technology transfer effects.

2. Much of the worlds FDI is still transatlantic, motivated by the desire to exploit technology generated at home. This model explains Ford's, Singer's and Hoover's activity in the 1950s – and it still works well today. These firms generate aggregate productivity growth (they are much more productive than average) but want to keep their technology to themselves. Spillovers are therefore small but positive.

3. Other firms are attracted by subsidy and the availability of low labor costs in the regions. They generate big employment gains – but typically in unskilled jobs, with a high proportion of skilled jobs going to expats. Of course, if your region has lots of unemployed unskilled workers this may be no bad thing.

4. A third stream of firms come to access indigenous technology – no spillovers (nothing to spill over), no productivity effect but increased demand for key workers.

5. Inward investment associated with increased wage disparity increases wage effects nationally for skilled workers but only locally for unskilled workers.

6. Justifying high-cost-per-job subsidies on the basis of spillovers, technology transfer or increased competition is probably erroneous.

Summary

There are two rationales for attracting inward investment that affects structured regional change:

1. To generate employment
2. To stimulate the wider introduction of new technology

Action points

■ Consider the likely impacts of not just inward investment but also outward investment on the region.

■ Recognize that FDI involves a large range of extremely heterogeneous factors that must be considered to ensure a good return on investment.

■ Distinguish between investments that attract a subsidy (e.g. matched funding from host region) from those that do not.

■ Distinguish between local, regional and national effects of FDI.

■ Look at the wider impact on different types of employment – services/manufacturing, skilled/unskilled etc. – that FDI has on a region.

Self-assessment tool

To what extent is your organization creating high quality inward investment propositions? (**Tables 11.2, 11.3**)

Table 11.2 How good is my organization at pursuing change-empowering inward investment by ensuring?

Attribute	Never	Sometimes	Mostly	Always	Cumulative Score
The specific benefits of FDI are thought through in detail	0	1	2	3	
The likely benefits can be demonstrated to the host country	0	1	2	3	
The sustainability of those benefits is well established	0	1	2	3	
The significant factors that influence location decisions are identified	0	1	2	3	

Table 11.3 Benchmark scores

0–3	4–6	7–9	10–12
In the danger zone!	Some foundations that need development	Good, but room for improvement	Moving toward consistent high performance

Notes

1. An example of this is the recently revised business case for the selective finance investment in England (SFIE) Scheme.

Further reading

Barrell, R. and Pain, N. (1999) (eds) *Innovation, Investment and the Diffusion of Technology in Europe: German Direct Investment and Economic Growth in Postwar Europe*, Cambridge: Cambridge University Press.

Cantwell, J. (1989) *Technological Innovation and Multinational Corporations*, Oxford: Prentice Hall.

Caves, R. E. and Barton, D. R. (1990) *Efficiency in U.S. Manufacturing Industries*, Cambridge, MA: MIT Press.

Driffield, N. and Love, J. (2007) "Linking FDI Motivation and Host Economy Productivity Effects: Conceptual and Empirical Analysis", *Journal of International Business Studies*, 38(2), 460–73.

Driffield, N., Love, J. H. and Menghinello, S. (2010) "The Multinational Enterprise as a Source of International Knowledge Flows: Direct Evidence from Italy", *Journal of International Business Studies*, 41(2), pp. 350–9.

Driffield, N. L. (1996) *Global Competition and the UK Labour Market*, Reading: Harwood.

Driffield, N. L. (2004) "Regional Policy and Spillovers from FDI in the UK", *Annals of Regional Science*, 38(4), pp. 579–94.

Dunning, J. H. (1993) *Multinational Enterprises and the Global Economy*, Reading: Addison-Wesley.

Dunning, J. H. (1998) "Location and the Multinational Enterprise: A Neglected Factor?" *Journal of International Business Studies*, 29(1), pp. 45–66.

Harris, R. I. D. and Robinson, C. (2005) "The Impact of Regional Selective Assistance on Sources of Productivity Growth: Plant Level Evidence from UK Manufacturing 1990–1998", *Regional Studies*, 39(6), August, pp. 751–65.

Menghinello, S., DePropris, L. and Driffield, N. (2010) "Localised Competitive Advantages: Local Industrial Systems in Italy as Engines of International Trade and Economic Development", *Journal of Economic Geography*, 10(4), pp. 539–58.

Temouri, Y., Driffield, N. and Anon Higon, D. (2010) "Offshoring: A Multi-country Study of FDI in High-technology Sectors", *Futures*, 42(9), pp. 960–70.

CHAPTER 12

Measurement of Project Management Performance: A Case Study in the Indian Oil Industry

Prasanta Dey

Eight steps for projectizing continuous improvement to deliver desired change

Introduction

I was driven to research the subject of project management, and in particular the management of project management performance, as a result of my experience as a senior project manager working on large-scale construction projects in India's oil industry. Such projects were, and continue to be, inevitably characterized by technical complexity, environmental and social sensitivity, capital intensiveness and the involvement of many stakeholders (i.e. client, consultants, contractors, suppliers at its most basic). Delivery to schedule, to cost, to scope and to quality is never assured. In fact, there are many instances of project failure.

Projects are complex to implement for many reasons: uncertainty over exact design conditions that will be expected upon completion; the influence

{ Projects are complex to implement, uncertain and subject to external factors }

of external factors, including environmental events beyond human control; external causes that limit availability of necessary resources (i.e. techniques and technology); changes in governments, legislation and regulations; and changes in the economic and political environment.

Additionally, although there are instances of both success and failure of projects in Indian oil industry, projects in that context often suffer from an inaccurate prediction of demand such that calls for augmentation of faci-

{ ... availability of necessary resources, changes, inaccurate prediction of demand }

lities start soon after completion of most projects. Fundamentally these projects suffer from insufficient forethought and attention to supply chain integration, relationship management, project planning and evolving social needs.

To be clear, initial forethought is insufficient to guarantee performance. Thus the focus of this chapter is on performance management and measurement per se, on the practice of project management, which is greatly enhanced by understanding and applying a definitive project management performance measurement methodology. The framework on which my work expands, and for which there is a unique tool that measures an organization's "project management maturity", identifies nine skill sets required for effective project management.

{ ... nine skill sets required for effective project management }

These nine disciplines, briefly described in the body of this chapter as critical success factors (CSFs), collectively provide a framework for holistic project planning and control (Please refer to Figures 12.1 and 12.2).

Clearly, organizations not only need to adopt effective project management methodologies but also to constantly analyze the project plan's effectiveness and improve its relevance. The good news is that project management maturity analysis and performance measurement methods exist. The bad news is that most, and especially performance measurement methods, are neither holistic nor practical. More significantly, most are not easy to adapt or apply.

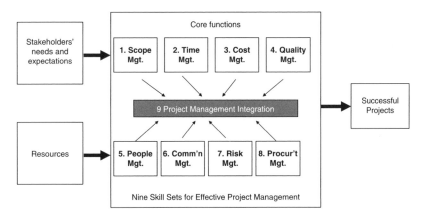

Figure 12.1 Project management framework

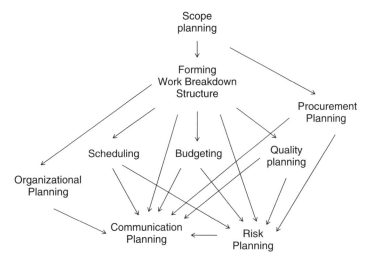

Figure 12.2 Project planning processes

Consequently, few organizations have implemented systematic processes to ensure that their project performance measurement systems are appropriate for their environment and strategic needs. Studies have concentrated on identifying how performance measurement can be structured and how performance can be improved but have not addressed how such improvements should be prioritized. Neither have they provided an approach with which to plan for and implement project improvements.

This chapter attempts to address the aforementioned challenges by presenting a holistic project management performance measurement (PMPM) framework that, while born from research in a gritty operational environment, is nevertheless practical and relatively simple to apply. To demonstrate its efficacy, this chapter contains a case study of how the PMPM methodology was applied to a Fortune 500 organization operating in Indian oil industry.

Proposed project management performance measurement framework

Figure 12.3 shows the proposed *performance measurement framework* with its **eight steps** that are as follows:

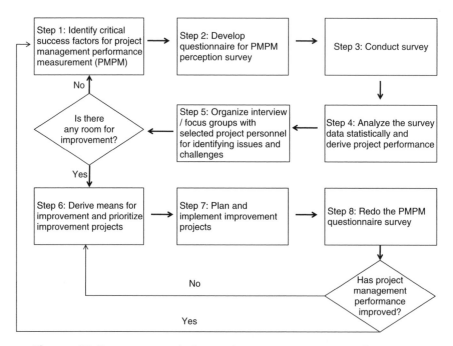

Figure 12.3 Framework for project management performance measurement

Step 1: *Identify critical success factors for project management performance measurement (PMPM)*: **Critical success factors** (CSF) are the characteristics, conditions or variables that individually and collectively have a major impact on the project's success. While CSFs will vary across industries and organizations in line with business needs and management perceptions, we place emphasis on effective project management processes and accordingly consider our generic CSF to be: delivery to (1) **scope**, (2) **time**, (3) **cost**, and

(4) **quality**, through (5) **designated human resource**, (6) **effective communication**, (7) **efficient procurement** and (8) **responsible risk management**. All eight are critical for project success. A **ninth CSF**, which binds all together, is what we term "**project integration**". This ninth CSF practically manifests as the following "work breakdown structure" and in reality provides the handle on "project leadership".

Step 2: *Develop questionnaire for PMPM perception survey*: The next step is to design a questionnaire using the identified CSFs to capture perceptions of the project team members on their project management practices. Such a questionnaire is likely to have various sections.

Step 3: *Conduct survey*: A sample survey should be carried out in order to understand the perceptions of members of the project team on their project management practices and performance. Ideally those completing the questionnaire/survey will have more than five years of experience in managing projects and should be chosen from across the hierarchies of the organization to be representative of the organization as a whole.

Step 4: *Analyze the survey data statistically and derive project performance*: For accuracy and impartiality, responses could be analyzed using statistical computation tool (e.g. SPSS, MS Excel).

Step 5: *Organize interview/focus groups with selected project personnel to identify issues and challenges*: Interview a few senior project executives in order to capture their perceptions on project management maturity and to validate the outcomes of the questionnaire survey. The aim is to identify issues and challenges in order to achieve superior performance against each CSF.

Step 6: *Derive means for improvement and prioritize improvement projects*: Analyze the issues and challenges to determine improvement projects. Prioritize improvement projects using criteria brainstormed for this purpose by the senior executives.

Step 7: *Plan and implement improvement projects*: Put the selected improvement projects into practice in a planned manner, involving and consulting all relevant stakeholders as necessary.

Step 8: *Redo the PMPM questionnaire survey*: The project management perception survey should then be repeated in order to determine whether substantial improvement has been achieved.

By pursuing this process, the management of a project's performance becomes, in its own right, a dynamic capability.

Application of the proposed project management maturity framework

Of course, the aim of conducting project management reviews is to achieve "World Class Capital Project Delivery", consistently, for every project. The following paragraphs demonstrate the application of the proposed framework in a real-life project using the step-by-step approach described previously.

Step 1:   *Identify critical success factors for project management perfor-mance measurement (PMPM)*: Six project executives (an executive project director, two chief project managers and three project man-agers) were chosen to identify the most critical success factors in the context of their project. They brainstormed to specify the prin-cipal project management performance measurements that were particularly relevant to their organization/project. They decided to measure project process performance across all nine project knowl-edge areas (integration, scope, time, cost, quality, human resource, communication, procurement and risk) relative to a specific project. These are in fact the nine generic CSFs of any project and, signifi-cantly, an assessment of these at an organizational level provides an indication of the organization's project management maturity.

Step 2:   *Develop questionnaire for PMPM perception survey*: The struc-ture of the self-assessment questionnaire scoped as a consequence of step 1 should contain nine project management knowledge areas and an "overview", with each subject area assessed against mul-tiple, sometimes apparently repeating questions. Each question is rated from Level 1 (lowest rating) through to Level 5 (highest rat-ing). The original six project executives from "step 1" were invited to participate in the self-assessment questionnaire survey. They each had more than 15 years of experience in delivering capital projects. (This questionnaire has been refined and is now available for application within other organizations.)

Step 3:   *Conduct survey*: The questionnaire was mailed to each of the six individuals. They had each been briefed on how to respond to the survey questionnaire and been instructed not to interact with each other while completing the survey. Hence, responses were com-pletely reflective of individual perceptions.

Step 4:   *Analyze the survey data statistically and derive project perfor-mance*: The responses were analyzed using MS Excel. **Table 12.1**

Table 12.1 Project management performance level of the organization under study

Project management knowledge areas	Average maturity level	Prioritized problem areas
Project Integration Management	2.13	Absence of customized project management processes, change control
Project Scope Management	2.06	Change control
Project Time Management	1.97	Schedule control
Project Cost Management	1.53	Cost control
Project Quality Management	2.50	Suppliers' and contractors' quality improvement
Project Human Resource Management	2.00	Organization planning and team development
Project Communications Management	1.88	Performance reporting and issues Tracking and Management
Project Risk Management	1.63	All sub-areas need attention
Project Procurement Management	2.29	Stakeholders' selection on the basis of quality

shows the average project management performance of the concerned organization against each knowledge area. Additionally, as participants were asked to provide their rationale for their responses, those comments were analyzed, consolidated and depicted in column three of the table.

Interpretation: Table 12.1 reveals that the organization had gross average maturity close to 2 (relatively low). While quality management and procurement were relatively strong, cost management and risk management were the weakest areas. Overall and in particular the organization was lacking strength in the management of project risks, communications, time and costs. Looking at the more qualitative information, they also lacked strength in the management of integration and team development (organizational planning and human resource management). Clearly, there was a lot of room for improvement.

Step 5: *Organize interview/focus groups with selected project personnel for identifying issues and challenges*: Three senior project executives (different from earlier group but also individuals with more than 15 years of experience) were identified for semi-structured interviews in order to validate the findings from the questionnaire/survey. The discussion was across the nine knowledge areas as the earlier participants had agreed to consider all project management knowledge areas as CSFs. Additionally, various project management documents such as contracts, purchase orders, design specifications, minutes of the meetings, etc. were reviewed. There was no major disagreement on the organization's project management performance from that revealed in the questionnaire/survey. The following paragraphs demonstrate the organization's project management maturity in each knowledge area.

Integration management

Although the organization under study had ISO 9000 and ISO 14000 certifications, project management practices were experience-based and depended totally on human skill. While there were project plans (business cases, activity networks, budgets, specifications, design and drawings, etc.), there were no **customized documented project management processes for each strategic project**. Project planning and implementation were managed through individuals with their different project management skills largely using various communication meetings and other means of communication such as standard reports, minutes of the meetings and e-mails.

Project changes were not formally documented if these did not have time and cost implications. Project changes that had time and cost implications were formally approved through the organization's hierarchical governance.

There was a project management office (PMO) manned by experienced persons with functional (mechanical, electrical, civil, telecommunication, human resource management, finance and information) expertise. Projects were managed as unique activities as well as through the matrix organization depending on the importance of the project.

Formal contract closings were done for all projects. However, there was no formal project evaluation report on the lessons learned.

Scope management

Project scope was developed from the business case with the involvement of the concerned stakeholders. However, there was no protocol for project scope change control. Project review meetings addressed the issues of scope management. Anything beyond the control of the project manager went through the organizational formal hierarchy for sanction. Beyond this there was no formal procedure. Scope change control often created major problem among the stakeholders.

Time management

Project activities evolved from the project scope (work breakdown structure). Estimates of activity duration were deterministic and mainly based on the planners' past experience. Suppliers and contractors were also involved in many cases providing valued information on activity durations. Therefore, development of accurate project schedules was an issue. Project scheduling was done using single point time estimation method. Probabilistic scheduling was never done though activity networks were developed using project management software (e.g. MS Project, PRIMAVERA). This shortcoming presented a major challenge as, in the context of time management, schedule control is essential.

Cost management

The business case/feasibility report for any specific project indicates the resource requirements and forms the basis for cost estimate. Both past data and supplier budgetary quotations help develop project cost estimate. Within the organization in question, there was no cost database. The cost estimates were not linked with activity schedule network. Project budget was controlled by the finance department, which produced reports on a regular basis. There was no earned value management practice in the organization for project cost control. Cost control was for this organization the major issue, the lowest ranked CSF, in the organization's project management.

Both time and cost management are directly related to scope management. The fact that an integrated approach to project change management was absent in the organization's project management practices exacerbated the particular underperformance of these three individual CSFs.

Quality management

In the organization under study, specification for every project was incorporated in the business case/feasibility report, which also comprised the system design. Depending on the type of project, detailed specifications and bill of materials were developed by the concerned stakeholders (e.g. suppliers, designers, contractors, etc.) and subsequently detailed by the project engineering group. These were approved by the project manager or appropriate competent authority in the organizational hierarchy. Inspections were carried out as planned, either on-site or supplier premises. However, there was no standardized process for managing project quality. Moreover, the quality standards of suppliers and contractors was in question and became the major issue as the contemporary approach to supplier and contractor selection was governed by "lowest cost" criteria.

Human resource management

There was no formal process for project organizational planning, or for the forming of a responsibility matrix or for the delineation of team development activities. However, a project-specific organization breakdown structure was developed. There was no formal project personnel selection and no work package authorization process existed. Although the project personnel were technically and functionally qualified and experienced, on many occasions they did not have project management expertise. In many projects, basic project management skill gaps were quite visible.

Communication management

Although there were a few report formats mainly to monitor and control project progress at the operational level, communication across project stakeholders was mostly informal (mainly through minutes of the meetings). Although information technology-based communication systems (MS Project, MS Office, e-mail, etc.) existed, there was no formal protocol for inter- and intra-organization communication. The minutes of project review meeting worked as authentic documents for project control.

Risk management

A risk management culture existed within the organization. In fact, many projects were initiated to mitigate business and technical risks. However, there was no formal risk management practice (e.g. logging risks through the use of a risk register; planning, monitoring and controlling of risks) in managing projects. However, informal risk identification and analysis were carried out and suitable mitigating measures were suggested mainly using past experience. The approach to risk management was more reactive than proactive.

Procurement management

Project procurement planning was undertaken in the early stage of each project along with activity planning. Normal tendering processes were consistently adopted to engage suppliers and contractors. Major suppliers and contractors were selected on the basis of their technical attributes along with their pricing offer. There was no long-term relationship among the project stakeholders (consultants, suppliers and contractors).

In summary

Taking all these factors into account, we concluded from the stakeholder interviews that the overall project management maturity of the organization under study was medium to low. Although projects were planned and scheduled using leading project management software, and monitored and controlled through a number of project review meetings throughout the project's phases, the organization lacked effective project management approaches. The interviewees agreed that standardized project management processes that could be customized specifically to each project would improve the practice of project management throughout the organization.

Step 6: *Derive means for improvement and prioritize improvement projects*: The nine project executives, those who had taken part earlier in both the questionnaire survey and interviews were chosen to participate in a focus group. They first reviewed the entire analysis and performance. Through brainstorming, they came out with a few recommendations against each knowledge area as depicted in **Table 12.2**. Their recommendations were supported by contemporary literature (column four of Table 12.2). They identified a few improvement projects from the list of recommendations, implementation of which would ensure superior project management:

- Organizing project management training
- Developing processes for managing external supplier relationships
- Improving communication across the stakeholders
- Developing risk management practices within project management

Table 12.2 Recommended actions for improving project management practices of the organization under study

Knowledge areas	Problem areas	Recommendations	Relevant best practices models/frameworks
Project Integration Management	Absence of customized project management processes, absence of change control processes	Fostering project management culture across the organization, developing project governance structure for each project, continuous improvement of standard project management processes, customizing project management processes for each strategic project, organizing relevant project management training, managing project portfolio across the organization	Dai and Wells (2004); Ibbs, Wong and Kwak (2001); Dey and Ramcharan (2008)
Project Scope Management	Change control	Practicing customized project management through appropriate training	Ibbs, Wong and Kwak (2001); Dey (2006)
Project Time Management	Schedule control	Practicing customized project management through appropriate training	Ibbs, Wong and Kwak (2001); Iyer and Jha (2006)
Project Cost Management	Cost control	Practicing customized project management through appropriate training	Ibbs, Wong and Kwak, (2001); Iyer and Jha (2005)

Project Quality Management	Standardized processes for project quality management is absent	Developing a robust quality management plan for each project by linking material specifications to activity specifications	Arditi and Gunaydin (1997); Winch, Usmani and Edkins (1998)
Project Human Resource Management	Organizational planning and team development	Developing project governance structure for each project with clear roles and responsibility of each stakeholder. Objective selection of project people and assigning of responsibilities	Belout and Gauvreau (2004); Bubshail and Farooq (1999); Loo (2000)
Project Communications Management	Performance reporting and issues Tracking and Management	Developing an integrated planning, monitoring and controlling framework with clear links to the concerned stakeholders	Charoenngam et al. (2004); Jha and Misra (2007); Ahuja, Yang and Shankar (2009)
Project Risk Management	All subareas need attention	Developing an integrated project risk management framework and training the project personnel to practice it	Raz and Michael (2001) Thomas, Kalidindi and Ananthanarayanan (2003); Wang, Dulaim and Aguria (2004); Dey (2010); Dey, Clegg and Bennett (2010)
Project Procurement Management	Strategic supplier and contractor selection and relationship management	Developing procurement portfolio for each project, selection of strategic suppliers and contractors, and establishing desired relationship with all the stakeholders	Vrijhoef and Koskela (2000); Ho, Xu and Dey (2009); Ho, Dey and Lockström (2011)

These four improvement projects are quite different. Brief descriptions of the projects are as follows.

- "Organizing project management training" – to expose all project personnel to formal project management training before entrusting them with any project management activity. The training was to cover the nine project management knowledge areas. Participants were exposed to both technical and human aspects of project management. Phases include: identifying project management training needs across the organization, designing curriculum and modules, identifying training facilitators (external/internal) and venues, and defining training evaluation framework. This project is neither technically complex nor risky in terms of planning and implementation but its evaluation is challenging, it is cost intensive and time consuming, as many executives need to be trained.

- "Developing processes for managing external supplier relationship" – to ensure selection of quality suppliers/contractors, integration of suppliers/contractors and establishment of effective purchasing process. This was relatively complex, risky, time consuming and cost intensive, as it included implementation of sophisticated information technology (e.g. for Enterprise Resource Planning).

- "Improving communications across stakeholders" – required analysis of existing communications, evaluation and selection of communication technology, development of a communication framework, and the training project personnel for effective communication. This project was relative easy to implement and the least cost intensive. If implemented successfully, it was envisaged that this would have a positive impact on the overall project management performance of the organization concerned.

- "Developing risk management practices" – one of the weakest areas in this case study, this demanded the development of a risk management framework, the procurement of appropriate software and hardware and the training of project personnel who needed to adopt the new framework. This project was complex and required both considerable time and cost. If successfully implemented, this would have improved overall project performance.

Based on this analysis, the improvement projects were prioritized using the criteria such as technical complexity, risk, duration, capital and operating cost, user-friendliness and impact on overall project performance. **Figure 12.4** shows the matrix for project prioritization. Participants prioritized the projects

Criteria	Improvement Projects	Project Management training	Implementing Supplier relationship management	Project communication improvement	Implementing project risk management practices
Complexity		Medium	High	Medium	High
Risk		Low	High	Low	High
Implementation Cost		High	Medium	Medium	Medium
Operating cost		High	High	Low	Low
Project duration		Long	Long	Medium	Medium
User-friendliness after implementation		Not applicable	Low	Medium	Medium
Impact on overall project performance		Medium	Medium	High	Medium

Figure 12.4 Project comparison matrix with respect to a few criteria

using the information as depicted in Figure 12.4, and "improving communication across stakeholders" received highest priority followed sequentially by "developing risk management practices", "organizing project management training" and "developing processes for managing external supplier".

As an aside and interestingly, a root-cause analysis revealed that poor communication among the project stakeholders (both internal and external) was due to the absence of an appropriate communication system, the lack of appropriate communication processes and little training for the system that was actually used. Clearly, as is often the case, improvement projects impacted on each other systemically.

Step 7: *Plan and implement improvement projects*: A team of five people was formed to develop scope for the "Project communication improvement" project. The work breakdown structure of the project is shown in **Figure 12.5**. The aforesaid had been formed through root-cause analysis using cause and effect diagram. The first level is the project, the second level represents the work packages and the third level is the activities. Project duration was 18 months. Budget and specifications information are withheld for confidentiality; but we can confirm that the project was delivered on time and within budget.

Step 8: *Measure project management performance again*: Using the PMPM questionnaire, project management performance was remeasured six months after completion of the "communication improvement project". The outcome has been depicted in **Table 12.3**. Gratifyingly, all-round improvement was observed across all nine knowledge areas.

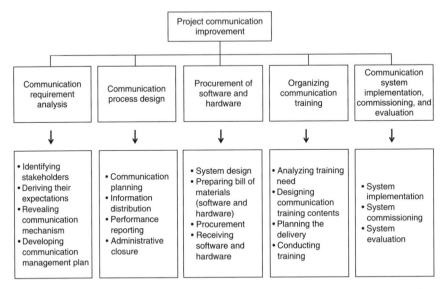

Figure 12.5 Work breakdown structure of the project communication improvement project

Table 12.3 Project management performance level of the organization under study after commissioning the communication improvement project

Project management knowledge areas	Average maturity level
Project Integration Management	3.02
Project Scope Management	2.95
Project Time Management	3.25
Project Cost Management	3.32
Project Quality Management	2.92
Project Human Resource Management	3.55
Project Communications Management	3.67
Project Risk Management	2.8
Project Procurement Management	3.1

Discussion

This study develops a framework for analyzing project management performance using critical success factors, extending previous research conducted on construction projects in India. The proposed method can be applied to measure the absolute project management performance of any organization – qualitatively and quantitatively. Although the representatives of the case study organization chose to measure performance across each project management knowledge area, the proposed PMPM framework is flexible enough to consider any single critical success factor on its own. This is a holistic framework that helps project managers identify improvement projects, prioritizes those projects using criteria and develop an implementation plan.

The results of PMPM after the commissioning of "communication improvement project" reveals that communication has strong impact on overall project management performance. This is mainly because communication across the project stakeholders improves coordination and relationships, decision-making and resolution of issues related to technical complexity, project-specific change management and specification. Organizations planning major projects, especially if those are to unfold in the Indian oil industry should seriously consider analyzing their PMPM using our proposed methodology. Dynamic evaluation of projects is absolutely necessary to track progress and accelerate decisions in order to remain on time, to scope, to quality and within budget in order to deliver a successful project.

{ ... communication has strong impact on overall project management performance }

Conclusion

The purpose of this project management performance measurement framework is to foster a culture of continuous quality improvement that should add value and lubricate continuous change of a continuous improvement nature within any organization. The step-by-step approach is user-friendly and sufficiently flexible to be applied to any project. As demonstrated by the case study on an organization within the Indian oil industry, the study shows the pragmatism and effectiveness of the proposed framework. Additionally, as the PMPM effectively involves project executives in the analysis of performance, it locks in their commitment to review projects systemically and to implement identified improvements.

Summary

There are eight steps for projectizing continuous improvement to deliver desired change:

1. Identify critical success factors for project management performance management
2. Develop a questionnaire for PMPM survey
3. Conduct the survey
4. Analyze the survey data statistically and summarize project performance
5. Organize interview/focus groups with selected project team members to consolidate issues and challenges
6. Propose means for improvement and prioritize improvement projects
7. Plan and implement improvement projects
8. Measure project management performance again

Action points

Organizations should emphasize the following actions in order to be successful in implementing and operating major projects:

■ Conduct a detailed project feasibility analysis covering market, technical, financial, environmental and social needs before making an investment decision. Use multiple evaluation criteria such as complexity, flexibility, adaptability, return on investment, cost, environment friendliness and employability.

■ Analyze risk as part of the project-planning phase. This includes identification of risk factors, analysis of their effects (by probability and impact) and development of appropriate responses in order to safeguard the investment.

■ Detail your project plan covering scope, schedule, budget, quality, human resources, procurement, communication and risk before commencing implementation. Appropriate leadership and project governance across the project stakeholders needs proper attention.

■ Keep your project plan flexible to adopt the necessary changes as they arrive. Have a scope management plan in place to deal with any contingency.

■ Integrate decisions at the strategic, tactical and operational levels to achieve desired project goals.

Self-assessment tool

To what extent has your organization adopted sound project management principles? (**Tables 12.4**, **12.5**)

Table 12.4 How good is my organization at projectizing desired change?

Attribute	Never	Sometimes	Mostly	Always	Cumulative Score
By organizing project management training	0	1	2	3	
By developing processes for managing external supplier relationships	0	1	2	3	
By improving communication across the stakeholders	0	1	2	3	
By developing risk management practices within project management	0	1	2	3	

Table 12.5 Benchmark scores

0–3	4–6	7–9	10–12
In the danger zone!	Some foundations that need development	Good, but room for improvement	Moving toward consistent high performance

Further reading

Pinto, J. K. (2007) *Project Management: Achieving Competitive Advantage and MS Project*, New Jersey: Prentice Hall.

Turner, R. J. (2008) *The Handbook of Project-based Management: Leading Strategic Change in Organizations*, New York: McGraw Hill.

Morris, P. W. G, and Pinto, J. K. (2007) *Guide to Project, Program, and Portfolio Management*, Chichester: John Wiley and Sons.

Further references

Ahuja, V., Yang, J. and Shankar, R. (2009) "Study of ICT Adoption for Building Project Management in the Indian Construction Industry", *Automat Construct*, 18(4), pp. 415–23.

Arditi, D. and Gunaydin, H. M. (1997) "Total Quality Management in the Construction Process", *International Journal of Project Management*, 15(4), pp. 235–43.

Belout, A. and Gauvreau, C. (2004) "Factors Influencing Project Success: The Impact of Human Resource Management", *International Journal of Project Management*, 22(1), pp. 1–11.

Bubshail, A. A. and Farooq, G. (1999) "Team Building and Project Success", *Cost Engineering*, 41(7), pp. 34–8.

Charoenngam, C., Ogunlana, S., Ning-Fu, K. and Dey, P. (2004) "Reengineering Construction Communication in Distance Management Framework", *Business Process Management Journal*, 10(6), pp. 645–67.

Dai, C. X. and Wells, W. G. (2004) "An Exploration of Project Management Office Features and their Relationship to Project Performance", *International Journal of Project Management*, 22(7), pp. 523–32.

Dey, P. K. (2006) "Integrated Approach to Project Selection Using Multiple Attribute Decision-making Technique", *International Journal of Production Economics*, 103, pp. 90–103.

Dey, P. K. (2010) "Managing Project Risk Using Combined Analytic Hierarchy Process and Risk Map", *Applied Soft Computing*, 10(4), pp. 990–1000.

Dey, P. K., Clegg, B. T. and Bennett, D. J. (2010) "Managing Enterprise Resource Planning Projects", *Business Process Management Journal*, 16(2), pp. 282–94.

Dey, P. K. and Ramcharan, E. (2008) "Analytic Hierarchy Process Helps Select Site for Limestone Quarry Expansion in Barbados", *Journal of Environmental Management*, 88(4), pp. 1384–95.

Ho, W., Dey, P. K. and Lockström, M. (2011) "Strategic Sourcing: A Combined QFD and AHP Approach in Manufacturing", *Supply Chain Management: An International Journal*, 16(6), pp. 446–61.

Ho, W., Xu, X. and Dey, P. K. (2010) "Multi-criteria Decision Making Approaches for Supplier Evaluation and Selection: A Literature Review", *European Journal of Operational Research*, 202(1), pp. 16–24.

Ibbs, C. W., Wong, C. K. and Kwak, Y. H. (2001) "Project Change Management System", *Journal of Management in Engineering*, 17(3), pp. 159–65.

Iyer, K. C. and Jha, K. N. (2006) "Critical Factor Affecting Schedule Performance: Evidence from Indian Construction Projects", *Journal of Construction Engineering and Management*, 132(8), pp. 871–81.

Jha, K. N. and Misra, S. (2007) "Ranking and Classification of Construction Coordination Activities in Indian Projects", *Construction Management and Economics*, 25(4), pp. 409–21.

Loo, R. (2000) "Journaling: A Learning Tool for Project Management Training and Team Building", *Project Management Journal*, 33(4), pp. 61–6.

Raz, T. and Michael, E. (2001) "Use and Benefits of Tools for Project Risk Management", *International Journal of Project Management*, 19(1), pp. 9–17.

Thomas, A. V., Kalidindi, S. N. and Ananthanarayanan, K. (2003) "Risk Perception Analysis of BOT Road Project Participants in India", *Construction Management and Economics*, 21(4), pp. 393–407.

Vrijhoef, R. and Koskela, L. (2000) "The Four Roles of Supply Chain Management in Construction", *European Journal of Purchasing Supply Management*, 6(3–4), pp. 169–78.

Wang, S. Q., Dulaim, M. F. and Aguria, M. Y. (2004) "Risk Management Framework for Construction Projects in Developing Countries", *Construction Management and Economics*, 22(3), pp. 237–52.

Winch G., Usmani, A. and Edkins, A. (1998) "Towards Total Project Quality: A Gap Analysis Approach", *Construction Management and Economics*, 16(2), pp. 193–207.

Epilogue: Five Real-Life Stories of Corporate Change

Cora Lynn Heimer Rathbone

As individuals and even more as organizations, the prior 12 chapters show how we can develop to be more responsive to change. Let me offer you some stories that exemplify the chapters and synthesize their key points using as lenses five of the corporate clients that I have had the honor of serving over the last 25 years.

Section 1: having a heart that welcomes change

When thinking about our willingness to change, I anecdotally cast back to a senior executive within a professional firm (first real-life story) who, with deep and widely recognized expertise as his strength, whispered to me: "Change doesn't galvanize me, it petrifies me." Though somewhat shocked at the time, the years that have followed assure me that he was not alone.

How can we develop a hearty approach to change? How can we build a people who however good they are at "thinking" can also "feel" their way through change, a people who start the waves others have to surf and surf the waves others create? Follow me through a study of this earnest executive via the principal points of the following three chapters.

Apropos **matters of the heart**, fostering a desire for change:

1. *Two HRM capabilities that drive change from the inside out*
   The aforementioned executive would have benefited greatly if his highly honed skills, which he gladly (1) "exploited" in the service of his clients and his organization, had been subjected earlier in his career to (2) "exploratory" development. Through cross-organizational projects or best practice exchanges with competitor organizations, his skill set could have been broadened. Effectively, his comfort with a few key and high-spending clients and his loyalty to his long-term employer buffered him from change to an extent that became counterproductive for his ability to adapt.

2. *Five factors for responding to change from the outside in*
   While this loyal executive shared the strong (1) ideological vision of his firm, understood and worked through the (2) institutional politics by which decisions were made and at the same time endorsed, as long as they did not interfere within his sphere of control, the (3) leaders of change peppered around the organization, he did not see himself as part of the (4) change implementation machinery and did not allow anyone the (5) possibility space to try new things that impinged on his area of responsibility. Thus he protected his operation and himself within it, from significant change.

3. *Two forces that fuel entrepreneurial growth and sustainable change*
   Though the CEO of this enterprise instigated the (1) external facilitation of a group strategy, a process that strongly supported both the crafting of the strategy and its implementation, a process that included every major player among whom was our erstwhile senior executive, this one individual's lack of (2) entrepreneurial spirit, his fear that he would be stretched beyond his technical competence and his lack of self-confidence in the new ways of operating, impaired the success of the strategy and constrained the anticipated growth of the firm.

Section 2: having a head for thinking through change

When thinking of the logic for embracing change, my mind hooks onto a more recent executive team that faced radical change to their industry. The team recognized their almost inevitable institutional demise if they did not transform organizationally. They were concurrently deeply wedded to the logic underpinning their business and operations. For any change to succeed and be led by this team, those changes needed to be rooted deeply in the soil of historic success. Fortunately, this organization knew what it needed to transform into. That is not always the case. Notwithstanding, given the culture of the organization, the process of analysis and collective decision-making were crucial to success. Follow me through this second real-life story as we apply to it the principal points of the next two chapters:

Apropos **matters of the head**, framing the thinking around change:

4. *Six actions for collating collective intelligence to inform and accelerate change*

The organization in question (1) recognized the importance of effectively communicating knowledge across a wide spectrum of internal and external stakeholders, (2) used a standard vocabulary (semantic technology – that to an extent became a language of its own), (3) made great effort to increase the flow of knowledge, (4) linked that data with other relevant data in related and relevant organizations and (5) published the data in a timely and expected manner. However, the fact that it used its standard language (its own semantic technology) created a sense of those "in the know" and those who were not. Additionally, the fact that they (6) did not organize their knowledge systematically from an early stage in their organizational existence meant there was a lot of catching up to do to instill the trust that history had eroded. As a consequence, the phenomenal internal change that they underwent as an organization over a three-year period was not sufficiently visible to significant external partners, undermining greater collaboration, and decelerating – to some extent truncating – the very change such strong management of information afforded.

5. *Seven steps to collaborative decision-making for robust, innovative, broadly owned change*
   Decisions were made rigorously – but by only a few at the very top of the organization. Such decisions by their very nature took time, produced inertia and inhibited decision-making and accountability further down and through the ranks. No real attempt was made to reach decisions collaboratively through a transparent decision-making process that would bring to the open opinions and knowledge, to innovate through the exploration of fresh ideas and new connections. Thus change was constrained, conservative and not broadly welcomed partly because it was seen as only drawing on the wisdom of a few.

Section 3: having a capability to effect change

With reference to equipping organizations for agility, I think first of two major corporates (third and fourth real-life stories) where the process and cornerstones of managing change were key to unlocking the logic and the volition to see change through. Let me use both organizations interchangeably, starting with the one whose core capability lay in the development of lifestyle services, to elaborate the key points of Chapters 6 to 11. For the final chapter, I reserve my last and fifth real-life story, that of a mission-critical organization.

Apropos **matters of the body** – enabling action toward change:

6. *Eight characteristics that drive high performance and team-delivered change*
   Innovation was and continues to be at the heart of our lifestyle organization. To this end, diverse groups of individuals from different disciplines had to learn to quickly come together and to then disband, to work as temporal teams whose remit it was to drive invention into commercial opportunities. These teams had to quickly (1) develop clear purpose (what invention? within what commercial context?), (2) share meaning around that purpose, (3) establish clear objectives that evidenced achievement of that purpose and (4) define clear roles for each individual team member. Because individual team members were going to act more often than not in virtual mode and remotely, they needed to ensure (5) clear communication by agreeing and implementing a communication strategy that included specified time for (6) reflection and timely challenge. In this manner the team created a (7) strong sense of belonging and ensured that team members considered the team to be a (8) "home team" even if that was for the temporal purposes of bringing a new idea into intrapreneurial reality. The fact that all eight factors could be brought into play to create focused teams augured well for organizational change and sustained innovation!

7. *Seven enablers of leader-follower relationships that sustain impetus for change*
   Within my second corporate, a quasi-industrial, well-established, significantly hierarchical and high power-distance global organization, relationships as well as professional excellence matter greatly. Subterfuge, however, was often used to reinforce positions of power. (1) Issues were often purposely not openly tabled and (2) differences in relationships were allowed, some would say encouraged. Such differences in relationships were (3) analyzed, though not to remove the differences per se, with (4) natural biases managed to ensure logic dominated at all times. (5) Performance was objectively evaluated through formal though not transparent processes. Seldom was the (6) opinion of other members of the team sought. (7) Notwithstanding, all of the aforesaid was done with decorum to ensure that at the very least on the surface of things a positive note was maintained at all times. This created a highly change-averse environment where power lay in the hands of a few whose favor was sought by those who had little to gain from trying new things at the expense of delivering reliable performance.

8. *Five principles for accommodating cultural nuances to accelerate envisaged change*

   Returning to my lifestyle services client organization, the pace of change in their industry and their response to it ensured a (1) raised sense of urgency. Doing nothing differently was not an option for survival, never mind success. Because of the complexity of change, they made great efforts to (2) involve their people at relevant junctions in decision-making. (3) In the same vein, the organization carried out regular training needs analysis, delivered relevant programs that addressed those needs and (4) institutionalized talent management. In short, the organization provided carefully for the development of its future leaders. However, the constant pressure of long hours, together with the expectation that people would regularly go beyond the call of duty, meant that the (2) care afforded to employees as human beings was questioned by many. This made it difficult to establish a climate of personal trust. While the organization was built for driving the change that others would have to follow, it was in danger of being unable to sustain this momentum given their lack of attention to the human factors.

9. *Four strategies toward key external relationships to effectively implement strategic change*

   Flipping to my quasi-industrial real-life story, when dealing with its B2B clients, this organization built an internal, highly professional team to look after its "key accounts". They knew which organizations required nothing more than a (1) watching relationship from them, whose development might be important for the future but were unlikely to ever amount to much. They also knew with whom they needed to nurture (2) a holding relationship, principally small-scale clients who operated in relatively stable institutional contexts. There were a small but important number of organizations with whom they fostered (3) a probing relationship, to develop sufficient confidence to work with them on a larger scale, to share more risk given their potential as future valuable clients. Then there were a handful of special clients with whom they had (4) a grooming relationship, sharing high-quality information and for high-value and long-term contracts that were mutually advantageous. As such, even as a giant whose DNA was driven by predictability and consistency, this organization partnered relevant B2B client organizations to build a capacity for purposeful client-centric change.

10. *Five questions for conducting marketing as a profession that ushers in strategic change*

Returning to our lifestyle services organization, the entrepreneurial project teams had to consider as an integral part of their deliberations (1) why customers traditionally bought from them, and (2) what their customers thought about their organization, products, services and their Brand in order to understand the extent to which they could leverage their strong reputation to launch a new product or service. They also needed to understand (3) what their customers thought about their competitors in order to better use the intrapreneurial concept not only for success in its own right but to further differentiate themselves from the competition. To position their innovation for optimal commercial success, they needed to (4) understand to which segment of their market it would most appeal. All of this contributed to an understanding of what their (5) marketing plan had to be and (6) how best they could as a project team inform that, working collaboratively with their formidable corporate marketing team to that end.

11. *Two rationales for attracting inward investment that affects structured regional change*

    A final swing back to our industrial client allows us to apply the main points of this penultimate chapter from the perspective of an organization entering a region that pays it, the incoming organization, for the privilege. Now, few entities decline a free handout. However, as "there is no such thing as a free lunch", smart organizations only install themselves into a new region or location – all other things (such as proximity to strategic client markets or to sources of rare raw materials) being equal – if such locations fulfill two main criteria: they provide access to sufficient best qualified and most competent people (potential employees) for long-term operational viability and are "home" to other necessary expert organizations and potential partners for the incoming organization to optimize strategic gain. (Think Silicon Valley!) Because a given region ceased to fulfill the second criteria, my client sold their manufacturing capability in that "regional development" location, consolidating operations as they retrenched to an original site.

12. *Eight steps for projectizing continuous improvement to deliver desired change*

    Let me turn to my final and fifth real-life story, that of a mission-critical organization for which projectization and continuous improvement is the key to innovation and sustainable change. Though this organization did not, to my knowledge, systematically apply this eight-step process, it would benefit from doing so to almost every corner of its operations on a six-monthly or annual basis. By (1) identifying key success factors for individual critical projects and (2) developing a questionnaire to measure their project management performance against those criteria, the organization could (3) conduct the survey among those responsible and those impacted by those critical projects to objectively (4) analyze and statistically summarize performance. To ensure their conclusions were correct they could (5) organize interviews and focus groups with selected project team members before consolidating issues and challenges. With such validation they would have the mandate to (6) propose improvements and prioritize the same before proceeding to (7) plan and implement such enhancements. The process lends itself to regular repetition in order to (8) iteratively measure project management performance and deliver continuous improvement, which over the course of time is sure to produce significant change.

So, retrofitted to five real-life cases, our chapters inform and provide fresh insight to how five very different organizations were ideally places for or could have been better able to embrace change. Armed with these concepts from the start, I have no doubt that any organization – be it public, private or third sector – can be better equipped to create, respond to and manage change to their advantage and that of their wider stakeholders.

So, I repeat, are you personally and organizationally ready for change? Are you ready to develop an organizational capacity for change? We are!

Index

Page numbers followed by 'n' denotes notes.